ISBN 978-1-331-91950-6
PIBN 10253975

1 MONTH OF
FREE
READING

at
www.ForgottenBooks.com

By purchasing this book you are
eligible for one month membership to
ForgottenBooks.com, giving you
unlimited access to our entire
collection of over 700,000 titles via
our web site and mobile apps.

To claim your free month visit:
www.forgottenbooks.com/free253975

Similar Books Are Available from
www.forgottenbooks.com

SARAWAK;

ITS INHABITANTS AND PRODUCTIONS:

BEING

NOTES DURING A RESIDENCE

IN THAT COUNTRY WITH

HIS EXCELLENCY MR. BROOKE.

(Sir).

BY HUGH LOW

COLONIAL SECRETARY AT LABUH-AN.

LONDON:

RICHARD BENTLEY, NEW BURLINGTON STREET,

Publisher in Ordinary to Her Majesty.

1848.

LONDON :
R. CLAY, PRINTER, BREAD STREET HILL.

You know the circumstances of haste under which it has been written, and I trust, in consequence, much to your kind indulgence for its many imperfections; but should the Volume be found to contain any new or interesting particulars, I shall have the greatest satisfaction in acknowledging that your great kindness, and the facilities and protection you afforded me, alone enabled me to collect and supply them.

With sentiments of the deepest respect and gratitude,

I am,

MY DEAR MR. BROOKE,

Your most obedient and humble Servant,

HUGH LOW

LEYDEN,
   Dec. 13, 1847.

PREFACE.

THE remarks contained in the following pages have been prepared from notes collected during a residence of about thirty months in Sarawak, and the west coast of Borneo. My object, (the collection of plants and seeds,) led me more into the country, and amongst the tribes of aborigines, than any other Englishman who has yet visited the shores of this Island; and I trust that, though very incomplete, this Work may, in the absence of others on the subject, be found to contain some interesting information respecting the domestic economy of the people.

On my arrival in England, in October last, I had no intention of publishing any account of the Island; and, in consequence, many of my notes, particularly those on the subject of the languages and superstitions of the various tribes, were left in Borneo, my purpose being to present them to the public, when a longer residence and further inquiries in the country should have rendered them less unworthy of attention.

Though thirty months may seem to promise a less meagre and unsatisfactory account than that contained in the pages which follow, it must be recollected, that a great part of that time was spent before I had sufficiently acquired the native languages to trust my remarks on paper, so that these may be considered as but the result of one year's inquiry.

A further cause of their present imperfection is the want of time under which I laboured in their preparation for the press, consequent on the necessary arrangements for an early departure for the East. It is with the greatest diffidence I now offer them for the public approval, and crave for them that indulgence which, under other circumstances, could not be expected or allowed.

I wish in this place to acknowledge my obligations to the numerous friends, both here and in the East, who were kind enough to interest themselves in my proceedings. To the Earl of Auckland I am under the greatest obligations for letters to the Official Residents in the Straits Settlements, particularly for one to the Honourable the Governor, Lieutenant-Colonel Butterworth, C.B., who on all occasions, and by every means in his power, forwarded the objects of the expedition, and by his and his lady's kindness during my frequent visits to Singapore, has placed me under infinite obligations. To Drs. Oxley and Martin, and C. Carnie, Esq., with many other friends in Singapore, I am indebted for many favours; but I am only one of many who have had occasion to record their kindness.

I need not mention the name of Mr. Brooke, as his amiable character is too well known; but to the other gentlemen of Sarawak I may express my thanks for their kindness, and assure them that in whatever manner the remainder of my time may be spent, the period I passed in their company will ever be remembered with pleasure.

I return my thanks to the gentlemen of the British Museum for the list of Zoology in the Appendix, and very much regret that family affliction has prevented E. Doubleday, Esq., of that Institution, from furnishing the Catalogue of the Lepidopterous Insects. Many other skins and animals than those enumerated have been sent to England, but have not yet been examined.

HUGH LOW

UPPER CLAPTON,
Dec. 22*d*, 1847.

CONTENTS.

a

CONTENTS.

CHAPTER III.

CHAPTER IV.

CHAPTER V.

CHAPTER VI.

CHAPTER VII.

CHAPTER VIII.

a 2

CHAPTER IX.

CHAPTER X.

CHAPTER XI.

CHAPTER XII.

CHAPTER XIII.

INTRODUCTION.

It has been suggested, that a short notice of Mr. Brooke should precede this work; since it is to his exertions that the details contained in the following pages will owe their chief interest. This concise memoir is offered without comment, for a reason which a glance at the title-page will enable everybody to understand.

Mr. Brooke was born on the 29th of April, 1803, at Coombe Grove, near Bath. He was the second, but is now the sole surviving son of the late Thomas Brooke, Esq., who was long employed in the civil service of the East India Company; and, descended by both parents from ancient families, is the lineal

representative of Sir Robert Viner, Baronet,
Lord Mayor of London in the reign of
Charles II. Sir Robert was honoured by an
intimacy with his Sovereign, of which a pleasant story is told in " The Spectator," and
did the Crown many great services. Such
was his loyalty, that he willingly permitted
a great portion of his large fortune to find
its way into the Exchequer of the Merry
Monarch, to whose memory he raised a
monument in Stock's Market.

Designed for the military service of the
East India Company, Mr. Brooke received
a suitable education; and went out to India
at a very early period as a cadet. He spent
the first years of his active life in Bengal,
where he held several advantageous appoint-
ments ; and on the breaking out of the Bur-
mese war he accompanied his regiment to
Assam. In an action with the enemy his
gallantry was so conspicuous that he received
the thanks of the Government; but, being shot
through the lungs, his native air was deemed
necessary to his recovery, and he returned
to Europe.

Once more at home, he resumed the studies of his boyhood, and made himself master of several modern languages. He travelled also through France, Switzerland, and Italy, a tour which his recent literary pursuits had prepared him to enjoy.

The period at length arrived when it was necessary that he should return to India, and he embarked, but the ship was wrecked on the Isle of Wight. This mishap occasioned such a loss of time, that when he reached Madras, his leave of absence had expired, and he found that to regain the position he had involuntarily forfeited, a prolonged and tedious correspondence with the Home Authorities would probably be necessary. Accordingly, he at once relinquished the service, and decided on proceeding with the ship to China.

This step was the most important of his earlier life. Then, for the first time, he saw the islands of the Indian Archipelago, with their natural riches and incomparable beauty. The notion of one day visiting and exploring them insinuated itself into his mind, but the resolve was not suddenly made. The value and variety of the products of the Archipelago were in some measure disclosed to him during his stay at Canton. He returned to Europe, by this time full of his design, and in con-junction with another gentleman, fitted out a ship of large burden, and proceeded once more into the China seas; but circumstances, which, considering his ardour and the pur-pose he had at heart, must have been numerous, or indeed deterring, prevented at that time the accomplishment of his wishes. He gave up the idea of carrying out his plan in company with another, and again visited Europe, to " bide his time, to wait a happier hour."

On the death of his father, Mr. Brooke succeeded to a handsome fortune; and in October, 1838, eight years after his first entrance into the China seas, he set sail from England in his yacht, the 'Royalist,' a handsome schooner of 142 tons, with a picked crew of more than twenty men. The sailing qualities of his vessel, and the thorough seamanship of his crew, he had previously tested in a voyage up the Medi terranean.

On reaching Singapore, where he stayed nearly two months, Mr. Brooke saw reason to modify his original intention, and to restrict his researches for a time to the north-west coast of Borneo. He learned that Borneo Proper was under the rule of the Rajah Muda Hassim, who was represented to be humane and generous, and well-affected to the English. Muda Hassim was then at Sarawak— his occasional residence only—but at which he was detained by a rebellion in the interior. Taking with him such presents as were likely to prove most agreeable to the Rajah, Mr. Brooke stood down the Strait, visited Borneo, and proceeded up the river Sarawak, anchoring abreast of the town of that name on the 15th of August, 1839. He was received by the Rajah with courtesy and kindness, but soon found that the rebellion, of which his host had spoken lightly, was a serious matter, and he had cause to believe that Muda Hassim wished him to stay as an intimidation to the rebels. He, however, obtained permission from the Rajah to visit parts of his country, of which he availed himself, making several excursions to various Dyak tribes.

On his return to Sarawak, he had several conferences with the Rajah, touching the establishment of commerce between that place and Singapore; and on the whole was encouraged to endeavour to effect it. Carrying with him letters for the merchants of Singapore, and a list of the imports and exports of Sarawak, Mr. Brooke took a cordial leave of the Rajah, and set sail for the former port.

Mr. Brooke's second visit to Sarawak was at the end of August, 1840. He found the civil war pretty much as he had left it, but the Sultan of Bruni (Borneo) was now bestirring himself, and his measures excited Muda Hassim to action. Still, it was found that little or nothing decisive could be achieved without the co-operation of our Englishman, which, after some persuasion, he consented to render. The rebellion was at length put down, the chief surrendering at discretion, and it was not without much difficulty that Mr. Brooke succeeded in prevailing upon the Rajah to spare their lives.

By this time the Rajah was tired of Sarawak, the government of which was handed over to his valuable associate in the extinction of the civil war. The agreement was drawn out, signed, and sealed, on the 24th of September, 1841.

After many months occupied in the arduous duties of establishing his government, Mr. Brooke, accompanied by Muda Hassim, sailed for Borneo Proper, and had several interviews with the Sultan, by whom at length he was, with all solemnity, confirmed in his government. Everything now went so prosperously in the interior of his territory, that he found he could with safety proceed once more to Singapore. In his journal he observes, " My motives for going are various; but I hope to do good, to excite interest, and make friends; and I can find no season like the present for my absence. It is now two years since I left Singapore, ' the boundary of civilization.' I have been out of the civi-

lized world, living in a demi-civilized state,
peaceably, innocently, and usefully." He
sailed on the 8th of February, 1843.

The Honourable Captain Keppel, on the
termination of the war with China, was ordered by his commander-in-chief, Sir William
Parker, to proceed with his ship, the ' Dido,'
to the Malacca Straits, to protect the trade
and put down piracy. Borneo was included
in the station, and the captain, being on
duty at Singapore, made the acquaintance
of Mr. Brooke, who returned with him in his
vessel to Sarawak. At Borneo, the captain
found enough to do, and did much towards
the suppression of piracy, with the assistance
of his friend; but he was recalled to England
in August, 1844. Mr. Brooke in his journal
thus speaks of that event, " The departure
of the ' Dido' left me sad and lonely, for Captain Keppel had really been my companion
and friend; and he so thoroughly entered into
my views for the suppression of piracy, and
made them his own, that I may not expect
any successor to act with the same vigour and
the same decision. Gallant Didos! I would

ask no further aid or protection than I received from you."

Shortly after Captain Keppel's departure, H.M.S. 'Samarang' and 'Phlegethon' visited and inspected the island of Labuh-an, of which final possession has since been taken, and which is now a British settlement.

In February, 1845, H.M.S. 'Driver' brought Captain Bethune to Sarawak, bearing a letter from Lord Aberdeen, appointing Mr. Brooke confidential agent in Borneo to Her Majesty. This letter enclosed one to the Sultan and the Rajah Muda Hassim, replying to their request for the assistance of the British Government to extinguish piracy. The captain and Mr. Brooke instantly proceeded to Borneo (Bruni) city, where the letter was received by the Sultan with firing of guns and streaming of banners, and every personal demonstration of respect. The Sultan exclaimed, " it was good, very good,"—wanted to know when the English would occupy Labuh-an, and observed that he wanted to have the Europeans near him.

Hearing of hostile demonstrations on the part of certain formidable pirates, Mr. Brooke went to Singapore, and had several interviews with Sir Thomas Cochrane. The admiral proceeded to Borneo Proper, accompanied by Mr. Brooke, with a fleet of seven vessels, and had an interview with the Sultan and Muda Hassim, and an action was shortly after fought with the pirates, in which they were completely routed, but not without some loss on the English side. " Never," said the Borneons, " was such a war in Bruni." All tendered their submission to Muda Hassim, and the Sultan and Mr. Brooke returned in triumph to Sarawak.

Scarcely had these events taken place, when the Sultan, who had been accounted imbecile and a mere cypher, was discovered to be not without treachery, and the means of effecting it. He caused Muda Hassim and many others to be murdered, because they were friendly to the English; and he had employed a wretch, Mr. Brooke's greatest and most inveterate enemy, although his life had been three times interceded for by his intended victim, to poison him, or to get him dispatched by any cowardly and safe means. On hearing of these occurrences, Sir Thomas Cochrane lost not a moment in taking measures to bring the Sultan to account, unmoved by an apologetic letter which the traitor transmitted to him.

The fleet ascended the river, which was stoutly defended from forts and batteries, but on reaching the city it was found that the inhabitants had deserted it, and that the Sultan had effected his escape. In a few days, the dispersed inhabitants became reassured, and returned to their homes, when a proclamation for the Sultan was confided to the chief person in the town, reminding him how utterly he was at the admiral's mercy, and warning him of the consequences, should he again offer hostilities to England. Sir Thomas Cochrane then left Captain Mundy to complete such operations as might be necessary.

This officer, accompanied by Mr. Brooke, made some vigorous and successful demonstrations against the pirates, at the termination of which, the Rajah of Sarawak returned to Bruni, for the purpose of restoring order, a task which had been confided to him by the admiral. Thence he returned to Sarawak, taking Muda Hassim's son with him, and the rest of the ill-fated Rajah's family.

In about a month after his flight, the Sultan was permitted to return to Bruni, whence he wrote Mr. Brooke a penitential letter, imploring forgiveness and promising amendment. A similar letter was also despatched to Her Majesty Queen Victoria, but his power, as a source of offence to the British Government, is gone for ever.

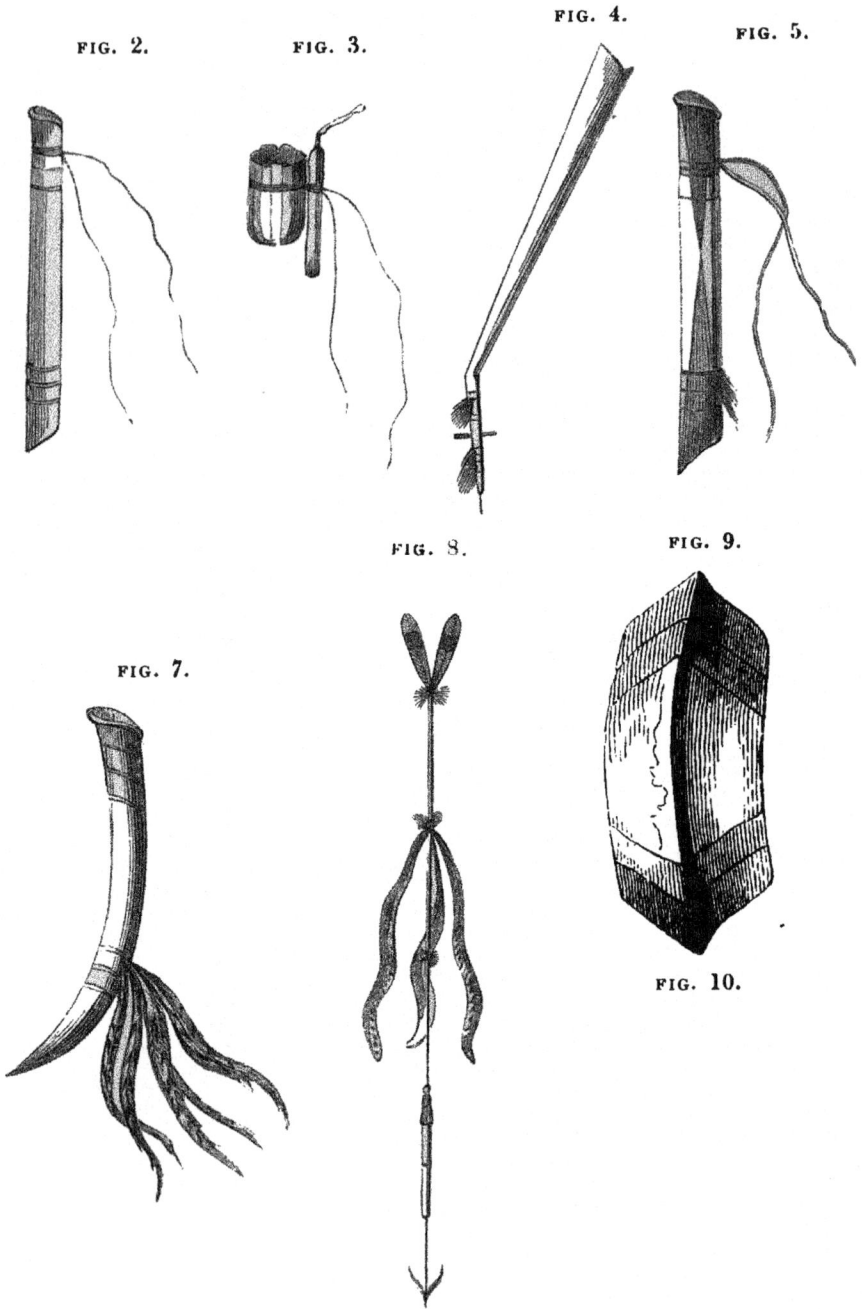

FIG. 2. FIG. 3. FIG. 4. FIG. 5.

FIG. 8. FIG. 9.

FIG. 7.

FIG. 10.

EXPLANATION OF THE FIGURES.

y Dyak Parang, or chopping knife, sometimes used in war.
of the same
ambuk, or small basket, and worn on the left side, and for carrying Sirih leaves, betel-nut,
yak sword.
th.
ak sword.
ath
nted spear of the Sadong Dyaks.
of the Dyaks.
basket, carried on the back by the strap which crosses the forehead.

FIG. 12.

FIG. 13.

FIG. 14.

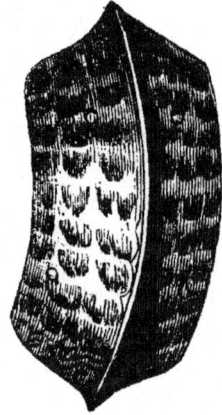

FIG. 17.

FIG. 16.

FIG. 18.

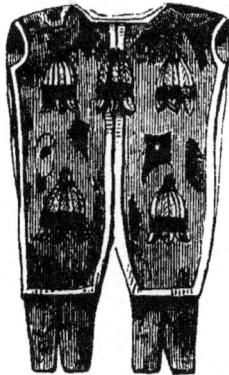

EXPLANATION OF THE FIGURES.

word, called by the Malays Parang Ilang, showing its ornamented convex side.
of the Ilang, beautifully carved, with belt and fastenings.
-an, with sight and spear as used by the Kyans.
of the Kyan chiefs, ornamented with human hair.
f the darts of Sumpit-an, with charms, and small case for the poison.
from the Sumpit-an.
war-jacket, made of tiger-cat's skin, and ornamented with tail feathers of the Rhinoceros bill.
the Kyans when going to war.

S A R A W A K.

CHAPTER I.

BORNEO, one of the largest islands of the world,
occupies portions of both the first and second grand
divisions of the Eastern Archipelago, as established by
Mr. Crawfurd; the eastern boundary of his first or
western division, 116° of east longitude, running
through the island a little to the eastward of the
town of Bruni, more commonly known as Borneo
Proper, so that the western and greater portion of the
island belongs to his first and most favoured division,
which includes also Sumatra, Java, and the Malayan
peninsula.   That part, east of the above-named me-
ridian, is comprised in the second division, which also

B

includes the island of Celebes and others, to the meri-
dian of 124° east, and to the parallel of 3° north
latitude. A portion of the island enters the fourth
geographical division of the above-named author, but
this appears to be a superfluous one, as the inhabitants
and productions of Magindanau, Soolu, &c., very
much resemble those of the second division; the
vegetables on which stress is laid, particularly the
nutmeg and sago, being abundant on those parts of
Borneo which are included in the former divisions:
the first of them, however, is not the kind so valued
for its aromatic flavour, and though there are several
species, they are all valueless in commerce, the fine
ones being confined to the Moluccas.

The name Borneo, by which the island has been
always distinguished on European charts, and which
was probably applied to it by the Portuguese from
information received previously to any of their visits
to the island, is a corruption of the word Burni, the
name of a kingdom and town on the N. W. coast of
the island—Bruni being called by the inhabitants of
the Malayan peninsula, where the Portuguese first
settled after their conquest of Malacca, under the
celebrated Albuquerque, in 1511, Tanah Burni, the
land of Burni, it being rarely the custom of the
natives to apply a distinguishing name to the whole
island collectively, but to designate each part by
the name of the most powerful kingdom situated
in it. Thus it is said that the southern part of this
island is named by the Javans, Tanah Banjarmasin,

from the Malayan or rather Javanese kingdom of that name. The natives of Borneo in general have no idea that their country is an island : it is only the Malays and inhabitants of the sea-coasts, whose maritime pursuits have necessarily forced upon them the knowledge of its insular position, who have one comprehensive term for the countries which compose it. These call it Tanah Kalamantan, and occasionally Pulo Kalamantan, or the island Kalamantan ; but this term is usually restricted to what we should call an islet, large countries being designated Tanah, or land—a word nearly similar in signification to our term continent—their language having no other expression equivalent to that geographical term, and consequently more appropriate to this land, than the term Pulo.

Though this large island has been long known to Europeans, settlements were not for many years after its discovery attempted upon it, and it is remarkable that the Portuguese, Spanish, and Dutch, who so long contended for the spice trade of the Moluccas, should have so neglected the rich island of Borneo, the productions of which must have been well known to them all. In 1747, the Dutch made a settlement at Banjar, on the southern coast, which was abandoned by Marshal Daendels, the Governor-general of Netherlands, India, in 1810 ; the sultan paying them, by agreement, the sum of 50,000 Spanish dollars for the forts and buildings. They had previously, in the year 1687, attacked Sucadana, at the instigation of the Sultan of Bantam, for the purpose of replacing the

disinherited sultan, Gura Laya, on his throne. This
territory was afterwards ceded to the Dutch by the
then Sultan of Bantam in 1778, in which year they
established a fort and factory at the neighbouring
flourishing Malay settlement of Pontianak, from which
they destroyed the rival flourishing and independent
states of Mampawa and Sucadana. Pontianak itself,
says Mr. Crawfurd, "soon fell in consideration under
their influence, until their removal and unrestricted
trade once more restored it in our times." They occupied it at this time during fourteen years. In 1823,
they again possessed themselves of Pontianak, which
they now retain. Soon after the Dutch had left Banjar, in 1810, the Earl of Minto received at Malacca
an embassy from the sultan, requesting the English to
settle, which was accepted ; and when Java was taken
possession of by the British in 1811, a factory was
established there. This settlement was delivered over
to the Dutch on the restoration of Java, and they
still retain it. The remaining Dutch settlement is at
Sambas, on the western coast : it was formed in
1823, the Hollanders paying a sum of money to the
sultan for the monopoly of the trade. It had previously
been a nest of pirates, who were destroyed by English ships of war, sent from Batavia for that purpose,
in 1812. With the exception of a British residency
formed from Balambangan during our short occupation
of that island, at Bruni, and which was soon afterwards abandoned on account of internal commotions
in that state, these are the only settlements which

have been established by Europeans on the island, and none of them have ever prospered; even those which the Dutch now maintain being reported to be an annual expense to the government. The English, in the year 1773, formed a settlement at Balambangan, an island off the northern coast of Borneo, which had been ceded to them by the Soolus, together with a portion of the opposite coast, from the river Kimanis on the west, to the great bay on the eastern side of the island. Two years after the settlement had been made, the English were attacked by the Soolus, and driven from the place in February, 1775. In 1803 the settlement was again attempted, but soon voluntarily abandoned. The above comprise the whole of the settlements which had been made on the island previously to the establishment of Mr. Brooke at Sarawak, and the failure of all of them is to be attributed to the monopolies and illiberal principles of the European nations or companies which formed them.

In consequence of the languid state of the European settlements, the true geographical position of the points and headlands of its shores has to this day remained unascertained; but the recent survey of Sir E. Belcher, of H.M.S. 'Samarang,' which has lately returned, and Lieut. Gordon, of H.M.S. 'Royalist,' who is now engaged on the northern part of the island, will soon enable the Admiralty to furnish a more correct chart of the western shores, though the eastern are still unexplored. These, however, cannot long remain unknown, as the settlement to be formed at Labuh-an

will probably soon find it necessary, for the extermi-
nation of the piratical inhabitants, to have them fully
investigated.

In geographical features this island presents us
with great variety. It has high mountains, magnificent
rivers, extensive lakes, and probably, in the northern
part of the island, considerable plains. The mountains
are disposed in a range which traverses the island
from its N. E. extremity in a south-westerly direction;
in the northern division they are very high, Kina Balou
being nearly 14,000 feet. They appear gradually to
decrease in height as they approach the south-western
shore; about the middle of the island they are
observed inland of Tanjong Barram 8,000 and 9,000
feet high; but westerly, in the Pontianak country, as
they approach the sea, they are from 2,000 to 4,000
feet in height.

The heights of many of the principal peaks of the
northern part of the island have been recently ascertained by Lieut. Gordon, but as his observations are
not yet published I am unable to avail myself of them.
Kina Balou (the Chinese widow), which is situated
about eighteen miles inland, and at the foot of which
is Malludu Bay, is supposed much to exceed any of
the others in height. I have been informed by the
Rajahs of Borneo that it derives its name from the circumstance of its summit having been in former times
the residence of a female spirit of great beauty, of
whom it is said a Chinese prince of Bruni (before the
time of its conversion to the religion of Mahomet),

became enamoured, and, wishing to obtain her in marriage, made a journey intending to visit her residence, but, losing his footing, fell over one of the rocky precipices near the top, and was killed. Hence the spirit has been denominated the Widow of the Chinaman, and the mountain, after her, named Kina or China Balou; the Borneans not pronouncing the *ch* soft, as is the practice amongst Malayan nations.

From these mountains issue innumerable rivers, which empty themselves into the sea on all sides of the island. On the north coast the largest are those of Bruni, Rejang, Sarebas, of Sakarran, and of Sarawak; on the west coast are the enormous rivers of Sambas and Pontianak; on the south the great river Banjar; on the south-east that of Passir; and further north that of Coti: beside these are very many others, all of which will be found of the greatest service hereafter, in diffusing trade and civilization from our new settlement; but those above named are selected on account of their great size. Between the province of Sarawak and the town of Bruni are upwards of twenty considerable mouths of rivers, with settlements frequented by Malay boats, for the purposes of trade; indeed, it is probable that, with the exception of the west coast of Africa, no country in the world is better watered than this island. The purposes of navigation will be greatly facilitated in these rivers by tides, which, for a great distance, flow up the larger of them; those of the greatest size being found in the flattest parts of the island. This is the case particularly with the Rejang on the north-west, and the Banjar on the south, side of the island: the same applies also to the Sambas and Pontianak, together with all the other rivers which, as on the north coast, do not immediately descend the mountains to the sea. These have frequently fresh water at their mouths, not having to traverse any level country before they disembogue.

Lakes of considerable extent are asserted by the natives to exist in the interior of the island. One called the Danau Malayu, or Malay Lake, situated on the head waters of the river of Pontianak, was visited by an expedition from that Dutch settlement in the year 1823. It ascended the river to the distance of 250 miles, when it was found to open out into a lake of twenty-five miles in length, and nine in breadth, but of no considerable depth, the average being three fathoms. It was abundantly stored with excellent fish, and in the centre were two islands, to which European names were attached by the expedition; one being that of the Baron Van der Capellen, the then governor of Netherlands, India. Before arriving at this lake they had passed many falls, one of the height of twenty-five feet; the lake itself was not estimated to be situated more than 100 feet above the level of the sea. The great river Batang-Lupar, of which the Sakarran is a branch, takes its rise very near this lake, on the banks of which one or more Malay states are established, with which, if the disturbances of the Sakarran river were settled, a lucrative commerce would be carried on by the Malay traders of Sarawak. A large lake is also said to exist amongst the ranges of mountains near Kina Balou; and on the Dutch charts a chain of lakes is laid down between this and the Danau Malayu already noticed, and consequently stretching across the island; but, as no one has visited any of them, they must be laid down from native information, which they alone have been able to obtain, or, what is more probable, they have been placed there without any information at all respecting their existence.

In surface the island is usually low and undulating towards the sea shore, and for a long way into the interior in the north-west, and south, and south-east parts of the island. The belt of undulating land on the west coast is not so broad, as the general and continuous ranges of mountains of the north are here much broken, and at first sight appear to be scattered about in a solitary manner, and without any order; they approach nearer to the sea than in the centre of the island, so that the west coast, particularly approaching the territories of Sarawak and Sambas, has a mountainous appearance at a little distance inland, quite foreign to the southern and western districts. The sea shores are all of fine sand, and lined with a hedge of the beautiful arroo tree, (Casuarina,) which, from their resemblance, are usually called firs by the Europeans. The mouths of the rivers are generally muddy and overflowed for some few miles by the tides; here the nipah palm and the mangrove delight to grow, and forests and swamps of these useful trees abound in all such situations : they give shelter to innumerable mosquitoes, which render it impossible to sleep at night in their vicinity.

Situated in the centre of islands, most of which abound in volcanoes of the most frightful activity, one would expect earthquakes and other indications of their vicinity to be frequent in Borneo; but as far as has yet been discovered, no volcanoes or other indications of subterraneous fire are found, and if they ever existed, it must have been at a period so remote that even to tradition the remembrance of them is lost. The Philippines to the north, and Java and other islands to the south, are frequently disturbed by these fearful phenomena, and I have seen many inhabitants of the western coast of Borneo, who perfectly recollected the great eruption of the mountain Tomboro, in the island of Sumbawa, which happened in April, 1815,* the effects of which are distinctly stated to

* The following interesting account of this eruption, given by Sir Stamford Raffles, is extracted from his excellent History of Java :—

" In order to give the reader some idea of the tremendous violence with which nature sometimes distinguishes the operations of the volcano in these regions, and enable him to form some conjecture, from the occurrences of recent experience, of the effects they may have produced in past ages, a short account of the extraordinary and wide spread phenomena that accompanied the eruption of the Tomboro mountain, in the island of Sumbawa, in April, 1815, may not be uninteresting. Almost every one is acquainted with the intermitting convulsions of Etna and Vesuvius, as they appear in the descriptions of the poet and the authentic have been perceptible at Sarawak, though distant, in a straight line, 800 miles.

I have been told that on the Samarhand river is a small spring of warm water, and at Borneo are one or

accounts of the naturalist, but the most extraordinary of them can bear no comparison, in point of duration and force, with that of Tomboro. This eruption extended perceptible evidences of its existence over the whole of the Molucca Islands, over Java, a considerable portion of Celebes, Sumatra, and Borneo, to a circumference of 1000 statute miles from its centre, by tremulous motions, and the report of explosions ; while within the range of its more immediate activity, embracing a space of 300 miles around it, it produced the most astonishing effects, and excited the most alarming apprehensions. On Java, at the distance of 300 miles, it seemed to be awfully present. The sky was overcast at noon-day with clouds of ashes, the sun was enveloped in an atmosphere, whose ' palpable' density it was unable to penetrate ; showers of ashes covered the houses, the streets, and the fields, to the depth of several inches ; and, amid this darkness, explosions were heard at intervals, like the report of artillery or the noise of distant thunder. So fully did the resemblance of the noises to the report of cannon impress the minds of some officers, that, from an apprehension of pirates on the coast, vessels were despatched to afford relief. Superstition, on the other hand, on the minds of the natives, was busily at work, and attributed the reports to an artillery of a different description to that of pirates. All conceived that the effects experienced might be caused by eruptions of some of the numerous volcanos on the island ; but no one could have conjectured that the showers of ashes which darkened the air, and covered the ground of the eastern districts of Java, could have proceeded from a mountain in Sumbawa, at the distance of several hundred miles. Conceiving that it might be interesting and curious to preserve an authentic and detailed account of the information that could be gained of this wonderful phenomenon, while the event was still recent and fully remembered, I directed a circular to the different residents, two small mineral springs, and one of naphtha, but this will not be thought sufficient to prove the present existence of subterranean fires.

Coal is exceedingly abundant in Pulo Labuh-an,

requiring them to transmit to the Government a statement of the facts and circumstances connected with it, which occurred within their own knowledge. From their replies, the narrative drawn up by Mr. Assey, and printed in the ninth volume of the Batavian Transactions, was collected; the following is an extract from that paper.

" ' The first explosions were heard on this island (Java) in the evening of the 5th of April: they were noticed in every quarter, and continued at intervals until the following day. The noise was, in the first instance, universally attributed to distant cannon; so much so, that a detachment of troops was marched from Djocjocarta, under the apprehension that a neighbouring post had been attacked; and along the coast boats were in two instances despatched in quest of supposed ships in distress. On the following morning, however, a slight fall of ashes removed all doubt as to the cause of the sound; and it is worthy of remark, that as the eruption continued, the sound appeared to be so close, that in each district it seemed near at hand, and was generally attributed to an eruption either from the mountains Merapi, Klut, or Bromo. From the 6th the sun became obscured; it had everywhere the appearance of being enveloped in a fog. The weather was sultry and the atmosphere close, and still the sun seemed shorn of its rays, and the general stillness and pressure of the atmosphere seemed to forbode an earthquake. This lasted several days. The explosions continued occasionally, but less violently and less frequently than at first. Volcanic ashes also began to fall, but in small quantities, and so slightly as to be hardly preceptible in the western districts. This appearance of the atmosphere continued, with little variation, until the 10th of April; and till then it does not appear that the volcano attracted much observation, or was considered of greater importance than those which have occasionally burst forth in Java. But on the evening of the 10th, and the kingdom of Borneo Proper, on the mainland, being situated near the surface of the earth in thick and apparently inexhaustible veins, it will prove of the greatest value to our increasing steam communi-

the eruptions were heard more loud and more frequent; from Cheribon eastward the air became darkened by the quantity of falling ashes; the sun was nearly darkened, and in some situations, particularly at Solo and Rembang, many said that they felt a tremulous motion of the earth. It was universally remarked in the more eastern districts, that the explosions were tremendous, continuing frequently during the 11th, and of such violence as to shake the houses perceptibly. An unusual thick darkness was remarked all the following night, and the greater part of the next day. At Solo candles were lighted at 4 P.M. of the 12th; at Mágelan in Kédu, objects could not be seen at 300 yards' distance. At Grésik and other districts more eastward, it was dark as night in the greater part of the 12th April, and this saturated state of the atmosphere lessened as the cloud of ashes passed along and discharged itself on its way. Thus, the ashes that were eight inches deep at Banyuwángi were but two in depth at Súmenap, and less in Grésik, and the sun does not seem to have been actually obscured in any district west of Semárang.

" ' All reports concur in stating, that so violent and extensive an eruption has not happened within the memory of the oldest inhabitant, nor within tradition. They speak of similar effects in a lesser degree, when an eruption took place from the volcano of Karang Asam in Bali, about seven years ago; and it was at first supposed that this mountain was the seat of the eruption. The Balinese in Java attributed the event to a recent dispute between the two Rajahs of Bali Baliling, which terminated in the death of the younger rajah by order of his brother.

" ' The haziness and heat of the atmosphere, and occasional fall of volcanic ashes, continued until the 14th, and in some parts of the island until the 17th of April. They were cleared away universally by a heavy fall of rain, after which the atmosphere became clear and more cool; and it would seem that this seasonable relief prevented much injury to the crops, and removed an appearance

cation with the East. It has been tried by various
government steamers, the engineers of which pronounce
it to be of the finest quality, superior to that imported
to Singapore from England, and in all its properties

of epidemic disease which was beginning to prevail. This was
especially the case at Batavia, where, for two or three days preceding the rain, many persons were attacked with fever. As it
was, however, no material injury was felt beyond the districts of
Banyuwángi. The cultivators everywhere took the precaution to
shake off the ashes from the growing padi as they fell, and the
timely rain removed an apprehension very generally entertained,
that insects would have been generated by the long continuance
of the ashes at the root of the plant. In Rembang, where the
rain did not fall till the 17th, and the ashes had been considerable, the crops were somewhat injured ; but in Banyuwángi,
the part of the island on which the cloud of ashes spent its force,
the injury was more extensive. A large quantity of padi was
totally destroyed, and all the plantations more or less injured.
One hundred and twenty-six horses and eighty-six head of cattle
also perished, chiefly for want of forage, during a month from the
time of the eruption.

" ' From Sumbawa to the part of Sumatra where the sound was
noticed, is about 970 geographical miles in a direct line. From
Sumbawa to Temate is a distance of about 720 miles. The
distance also to which the cloud of ashes was carried, so quickly
as to produce utter darkness, was clearly pointed out to have
been the island of Celebes and the districts of Grésik on Java :
the former is 217 nautical miles distant from the seat of the
volcano ; the latter, in a direct line, more than 300 geographical
miles.'

" The following is an extract from the reports of Lieutenant
Owen Phillips, dated at Bima on the island of Sumbawa. ' On
my trip towards the western part of the island, I passed through
nearly the whole of Dompo and a considerable part of Bima. The
extreme misery to which the inhabitants have been reduced is
shocking to behold. There were still on the roadside the remains
of several corpses, and the marks of where many others had

having the greatest affinity with the best canal coal. One great advantage it has over English coal for a hot climate is, that it requires but little " stoking," as it does not cake about the bars of the furnace, but burns

been interred ; the villages almost entirely deserted and the houses fallen down, the surviving inhabitants having dispersed in search of food. The Rajah of Sang'ir came to wait on me at Dompo, on the 3d instant. The suffering of the people there appears, from his account, to be still greater than in Dompo. The famine has been so severe that even one of his own daughters died from hunger. I presented him with three coyangs of rice in your name, for which he appeared most truly thankful.

" ' As the rajah was himself a spectator of the late eruption, the following account which he gave me is perhaps more to be depended upon than any other I can possibly obtain. About 7 p.m. on the 10th of April, three distinct columns of flame burst near the top of the Tomboro mountain (all of them apparently within the verge of the crater), and after ascending separately to a very great height, their tops united in the air in a troubled confused manner. In a short time the whole mountain next Sang'ir appeared like a body of liquid fire, extending itself in every direction. The fire and columns of flame continued to rage with unabated fury, until the darkness caused by the quantity of falling matter obscured it at about 8 p. m. Stones, at this time, fell very thick at Sang'ir ; some of them as large as two fists, but generally not larger than walnuts. Between 9 and 10 p. m. ashes began to fall, and soon after a violent whirlwind ensued, which blew down nearly every house in the village of Sang'ir, carrying the ataps, or roofs, and light parts away with it. In the parts of Sang'ir adjoining Tomboro its effects were much more violent, tearing up by the roots the largest trees and carrying them into the air, together with men, horses, cattle, and whatever else came within its influence. (This will account for the immense number of floating trees seen at sea.) The sea rose nearly twelve feet higher than it had ever been known to do before, and completely spoiled the only small spots of rice land in Sang'ir, sweeping away houses and every thing within its reach.

away to a clear white ash. In using it, however, there is no saving in quantity, as the 'Nemesis,' in steaming from Bruni to Singapore in June last, used nearly the same quantity as she would have burnt of English coal. It is probable that the whole of the sandstone formation of the north and east coasts will be found to produce this useful mineral in abundance, it having been already found by the Dutch on the great Banjar river, but in such a situation, and at such a distance from the coast, as to render it unavailable on account of the difficulty of transporting it. One of the principal reasons which has caused our government to form the settlement at Labuh-an is the value that this mineral will prove both in time of peace and in case of war.

Next in abundance to the coal, as far as is yet

The whirlwind lasted about an hour. No explosions were heard till the whirlwind had ceased, at about 11 A. M. From midnight till the evening of the 11th, they continued without intermission; after that time their violence moderated, and they were only heard at intervals, but the explosions did not cease entirely until the 15th of July. Of the whole villages of Tomboro, Tempo, containing about forty inhabitants, is the only one remaining. In Pekáté no vestige of a house is left : twenty-six of the people, who were at Sumbawa at the time, are the whole of the population who have escaped. From the most particular inquiries I have been able to make, there were certainly not fewer than 12,000 individuals in Tomboro and Pekáté at the time of the eruption, of whom only five or six survive. The trees and herbage of every description, along the whole of the north and west sides of the peninsula, have been completely destroyed, with the exception of a high point of land near the spot where the village of Tomboro stood.' "

known, is the antimony ore; it is found in several parts of the western coast, in the interior of Sambas, at Sarawak, and several other places; but, from the wild state of the inhabitants, its distance from the coast, and other causes, it can only be at present effectually worked at Sarawak. It was first brought to Singapore, soon after the establishment of that settlement, by some people who had touched for water at Sarawak on their return from a voyage to Bruni. The ore being of a much richer nature than the antimony produced in Europe, the Rajahs of Borneo were soon informed that it would readily find a sale at the British settlement; and being encouraged by some merchants of that place, the needy rajahs were not long in visiting a part of their dominions hitherto neglected, and the Pañgeran Der Makota, who governed Sarawak, caused the Dyaks, unaccustomed to such labour, to work at the antimony mines: beads and brass were distributed to a very small amount as the price of their labour, the Pañgeran with the Princes of Bruni sharing the profits of their reluctant work.

From this time are to be dated the troubles of the Dyak and other populations of Sarawak: all were obliged to labour to satisfy the demands of the nobles, to whom the Europeans regularly advanced large quantities of goods. After ten years of this oppression the inhabitants rebelled, and were still at war with their rajahs on Mr. Brooke's arrival, as will be hereafter stated. The trade in antimony of course

ceased from the beginning of the rebellion till peace
was restored.

In Sarawak the antimony is found in the limestone
districts, both in large boulders of rock, upon the
surface of the ground, and in rich veins in the limestone rock a little below the surface: it is worked by
the Chinese and Malays, who split the upper rock by
fire until the vein of antimony is laid bare ; the heat
causes beautiful chrystals of sulphur to form amongst
the antimony, which abounds with this mineral: in
smelting the ore, nearly eighty per cent. of the sul-
phate of antimony is obtained. A manufactory for
reducing it to this state has been for some time
established at Sarawak ; but the metal undergoes
another smelting to reduce it to regulus of antimony,
which is the metal pure, all the sulphur being extracted by a chemical process.   It is in this state, in
which it resembles silver, that it enters into the composition of type-metal, the various descriptions of
plate, &c.   The ore of the richest quality is obtained
from a limestone hill called Batu Bidi, on the
western branch of the Sarawak ; here it is worked by
Malays, but the greatest works are in the neighbourhood of the Chinese settlement at Tundong, on the
same branch of the river.

Iron in various forms is found in abundance
over the whole island. It is said to have been
smelted in former times by the Chinese, who cast guns
from it ; but it is not of sufficiently good quality
to lead us to suppose that it will ever engage the

capital of the European. It is said still to be dug and smelted by the Kyans, a people afterwards to be described, who inhabit the interior of the island. Their weapons, which, it is asserted, are manufactured from the native iron, are of excellent quality and temper, and are in general valued by the other tribes, who form theirs of bar-iron brought from Europe.

Tin has been recently discovered in the alluvial soil in the country of the Suntah Dyaks, on the eastern confines of the Sarawak territory: it is of that description called stream tin, which is so abundant in Malacca, and the Malayan peninsula. By digging, a vein of it will probably be found; and it is likely to be a valuable metal to the island, as the working of it generally pays the European miner a greater profit than gold.

Nickel is found over the whole territory of Sarawak, particularly in the tin and gold districts: in the former it is very abundant combined with iron and cobalt: it has not yet been worked.

Quicksilver is known to exist in several parts of the island, but has not yet been obtained in sufficient quantities to render it an article of exportation; it is, perhaps, common in the unexplored Kyan countries up the Rejang and Bintulu rivers, as a weapon which I received from them has its sheath ornamented with it.

Of the precious metals, gold is abundant; silver being unknown in the East in these latitudes, though it abounds in China and Japan. The gold is found in three situations;—in crevices of limestone rocks, in

alluvial soil, and in the sand and gravel of the
rivers : it is found chiefly on the western and southern
portions of the island, but is not obtained in any
quantities to the northward.   In Sarawak, Sambas,
Sangow, and Banjar, it appears most to abound.
In Sarawak it is found in all parts of the country on
the right-hand, or western branch of the river, beyond
the influence of the tides : it is found also in the
southern branch, but in less considerable quantities.
In the crevices of the limestone above mentioned, it
is worked by Malays.

Last year I accompanied Mr. Brooke on a visit to
the rocks.   The place they were then working was
about four miles inland from the river, and about
that distance from Seniáwan and Tundong.   This
place was called Battu Kaladi, and was a limestone
hill about 200 feet in height, the surface of which
was worn, like all the limestone rocks of the country,
apparently by water, into ridges so sharp that it
would have been exceedingly dangerous to have
fallen upon them.   Amongst these ridges were holes,
very small, continuations of which penetrated into
the heart of the mountain, some of them being forty
or more feet in depth.   The only difficulty appeared
to be in the labour of making the aperture sufficiently
large to admit the miner; but, this accomplished, on
his descent he found the bottom, which invariably
opened to a cave, covered with earth of a loamy
nature.   This, on being brought to the surface in
baskets, was washed, and we were told produced a

bengkal of gold, about one and three quarters of an ounce, from each bushel of earth; from six to ten or twelve bushels being found in each cave, according to its size. It was accordingly a very gainful speculation, and the working it was carried on by all the idle and poorer classes of the community of Sarawak; so much so, that it was difficult to hire men for ordinary work.

Gamblers repaired to this employment, and a few weeks' exertion soon repaired their ruined fortunes; so that, by supplying them with funds to encourage them in this vice, it is, perhaps, no advantage to the settlement. The Chinese, who were not permitted by the Malays to work in the rock, were quietly trenching the earth at the foot of the hill, which they had long worked for the same purpose, and with more certainty of profit, as it is not always that the caves, after the labour expended in getting into them, are found to produce the coveted metal.

How the gold should be discovered in these fissures at all is very remarkable, and perhaps may afford a curious fact for the study of geologists and mineralogists: it cannot have descended from any place higher, as the caves are found on the highest as well as on the lowest parts of the surface of the flat-topped hill; nor, after repeated examinations of the limestone, is the slightest trace of the metal discoverable in it: the surface of the rock is but scantily furnished with earth, and that is of a vegetable nature. It is true that the whole of the soil of the surrounding district is alluvial, and strongly impregnated with gold, but not to nearly so great an extent

as that found in the fissures above described; hence
the soil in these differs in the relative quantities it
contains. The golden shower into which Jupiter is
fabled to have transformed himself, appears to have
fallen here.

Antimony is found in a vein in the same rock, the
fissures of which produced the gold above described.

The gold which is found in alluvial soils is that of
which the supply is most to be depended on. This is,
in Sarawak, found and worked in many places principally by the Chinese, though the Malays also occasionally work it on a smaller scale. The earth in
which it is found is a yellow clayey loam; this being
removed to a series of large troughs, into which the
water of a pond, previously dammed up for the purpose, is turned, the heavier particles of earth are
removed. What remains is washed away by hand in
small shallow wooden dishes, until nothing, or very
little, but the pure gold remains,—the refuse in melting that which is cleaned by the Chinese never exceeding the $\frac{1}{32}$ part. It is not found in veins in any part
of Sarawak, but in small particles distributed through
the soil; nor does it extend to any great depth. In
particular cases, the smaller grains are preferred by
purchasers to the larger, as they are generally much
cleaner than the latter, the crevices of the granulated
particles of which render them more difficult to be
thoroughly cleansed.

The gold which is found in the river is of the
same description as that last mentioned, and is
probably washed from the alluvials during heavy

rains. It is sought for by numberless Malays during the dry season, when the water of the river is low. They are much exposed to agues, from their manner of standing up to their waists in water during the time they are washing it; which is for the convenience of having the strength of the stream to carry off the gravel and sand, the gold, by its greater weight, falling to the bottom of the flattish implement before described. This is usually a profitable employment, and suits the indolent Malays much better than the method followed by the Chinese.

The following account of the state of productiveness of the gold mines of Borneo is extracted from the work of Sir Stamford Raffles, who, from his high official position, had the best means of arriving at an accurate computation :—

" GOLD.—From a calculation recently made, it appears that the number of Chinese employed in the gold mines at Mentrada and other places on the western side of Borneo, amounts to not less than 32,000 working men. When a mine affords no more than four bengkals (weighing about two dollars each, or something less than a tahil) per man in the year, it is reckoned a losing concern, and abandoned accordingly. Valuing the bengkal at eighteen Spanish dollars, which is a low rate of estimation, and supposing only four bengkals produced in the year by the labour of each man, the total produce is 128,000 bengkals, worth 2,224,000 Spanish dollars, equal to 556,000l., at the rate of five shillings the dollar. But it is asserted, that upon the general run of the mines, seldom less than six bengkals per head has been obtained, and in very rainy seasons seven. Taking the medium at six-and-a-half bengkals, the 32,000 Chinese will procure 208,000 bengkals, which, at eighteen Spanish dollars the bengkal, is 3,744,000 Spanish dollars, equal to 936,000l. Such is the result of a very moderate calculation of the produce of these mines. According to an estimate made in the year 1812, the annual produce of the mines on the west coast of Borneo was estimated at 4,744,000 Spanish dollars, being an excess of a million sterling. The quantity of gold procured in Sumatra, the supposed golden Chersonesus of the ancients, is, according to Mr. Marsden, about 30,800 ounces, which, at 4*l.* sterling the ounce, is worth 123,200*l.*, equal to 492,800 Spanish dollars.

" With respect to the disposal of the gold from the mines of Borneo, it may be observed, that every native Chinese, whether employed in the mines, in agriculture, as merchant or artificer, manages every year to remit at least the value of one tahil, more or less, of gold to his relations in China. These remittances are generally made by the junks in gold, as it saves freight, is more easily smuggled on shore without the notice of the rapacious mandarin, and remitted overland to the residence of their families. Taking the Chinese male population who can thus remit at double the number employed in the mines, and supposing one half to be born

the country, most of whom may not remit to China, this remittance would amount to 34,000 bengkals or tahils, which at eighteen Spanish dollars is 612,000 dollars, or 153,000*l.*

" It is calculated that, one year with another, at least 500 Chinese return in the junks to their native country with a competency. Several have been known to take away 1,000 bengkals of gold, many from 100 to 500 ; but very few return before they have cleared a competency of 2,000 dollars, or from 100 to 120 tahils of gold. This goes partly in gold ; though they prefer investing a part of it in tin from Banka, opium, and other articles. Say, however, that they remit one half in gold ; 500 men, at 1,000 dollars each, will give 500,000 dollars, which added to the small family remittances, accounts for an amount exceeding 1,000,000 dollars, or 250,000*l.* This calculation, however, seems to be far within the mark, and gives less by one-half than what is usually stated to be remitted to China from the Bornean mines, which has been estimated at a loose guess at 2,000,000 dollars, or 500,000*l.*

" A further amount of not less than the value of 1,000,000 dollars, or 250,000*l.* is supposed to find its way annually to Western India, and principally to Bengal, *viâ* Batavia, Malacca, and Pinang, for the purchase of opium, and piece goods. The surplus enriches Java and some of the other islands, in exchange for salt, tobacco, coarse cloths, &c.

" As the mines are worked with so little expense of machinery, the funds necessary for commencing an undertaking of the kind are small ; and as the property of the soil belongs to the first occupant, almost every Chinese would become a proprietor, but for the mode by which their services are, in the first instance, secured by the council of proprietors, or kongsis. A parcel of half-starved Chinese, enchanted with the prospect of wealth on the golden shores of Borneo, readily find a passage in the annual junks that sail from the mother country to Borneo at ten dollars a-head. On their arrival, being unable to pay the passage-money and the tax of a dollar per head established by the native authority, while their immediate wants for food and habitation are urgent and imperious, the proprietors of the mines find it easy to engage their services for three or four years. In some other cases, agents are employed to obtain men from China, on stipulated agreements, to work for a number of years : the usual rate of payment to the miners so engaged is not considered to average less than five Spanish dollars a-month. No sooner, however, are these engagements concluded with their masters, than a number of them club together with the funds they have been able to save, and commence a new mine upon their joint account, in a few years acquiring a competency to return to their native country.

This computation at that time would have included the gold produced by Sarawak, with the exception of such portions of it as were collected by the Malays ; the Chinese who work its gold being all members of the great Kung Si, or company of their countrymen settled in the territory of Sambas, and to whom all their collections are remitted four times a-year ; the Kung Si having officers in all the districts it occupies, who manage all their affairs, and are in constant communication with Montradak and Sambas. It is probable that the export of gold from Sambas has been rapidly decreasing since 1823, as immigration from China has in a great measure ceased, on account of the bad understanding which exists between the Dutch and Sultan of Sambas, and the Chinese, the former holding the monopolies of the opium, salt, tobacco, and other things, without which the Chinese cannot exist. The export of gold from Sarawak has, on the contrary, greatly increased; but as no duties or taxes are levied by its government on the mines, and no notes kept of the quantity exported, it is impossible to arrive at anything near the true result, each person taking out and bringing into the country what he pleases. One of the nakodas (merchants) of Sarawak who deals in gold very extensively, told me that he considered that quite one picul of gold was annually exported from the settlement by Malay traders to Singapore; and as this includes very little gathered by the Chinese, which finds its way to Batavia and Singapore by way of Sambas, I have no doubt that four times this amount is collected in this little country. I should suppose, from the number of men employed (about 700), that at least 7,000 ounces are annually collected.

The diamonds of Borneo have long been celebrated as equal to any from India or Brazil in abundance and beauty. They are found principally in the greatest numbers in Sangow, Landak, and Banjarmasin. They were also formerly worked at Sarawak, but never very extensively: a few years since, some fine ones were obtained by the chief Patingi Ali, in a large hole during a very dry state of the river. At the other three places they are worked to a small extent by the Chinese and Malays.

The mines of Landak have supplied the Malays with diamonds ever since their first settling on the island; those of Sangow and Banjar are more recent. It is said by Sir Stamford Raffles, that "few courts of Europe could perhaps boast of a more brilliant display of diamonds than, in the prosperous days of the Dutch, was exhibited by the ladies of Batavia, the principal and only mart then opened for the Bornean diamond mines." The diamonds are found in a gravelly stratum, at various distances below the surface: in Sarawak the gravel in which they are found is in some places not more than six feet, in others as much as eighteen below the surface. They are found in abundance in the soil, but are generally small in size, though of the most brilliant water. Large ones are also occasionally met with, and it is said that at Sangow and Landak, diamonds of from twelve to sixteen carats are not uncommon. The diamond of the Sultan of Matan is known to be one of the largest in the world. It is as yet uncut, and weighs 367 carats, so that if cut and polished it would be reduced in size to $183\frac{1}{2}$ carats. Its value is stated by Mr. Crawfurd to be 269,378*l.*, being less by 34,822*l.* than that of the Russian diamond: and 119,773*l.* 10*s.* more than that of the Pitt diamond: its present shape is that of an egg indented on one side. I have been informed by a person, who supposed himself to be a good judge of diamonds, that the sultan possesses the real stone, which he had seen, but that a crystal is shown to strangers, as the sultan, who has been already robbed of his territory, fears that this last emblem of royalty will be also taken from him by his powerful and avaricious neighbours at Pontianak.

The mines which I have seen at Sarawak are of the most simple construction : shafts are sunk in the earth to the stratum that contains the diamonds (which varies in thickness from two feet to much more), at the distance of about twenty feet apart; the soil is then extracted from each by the miner, who excavates it for ten feet on each side of the shaft, so that the workers in the different shafts communicating with each other; the whole of the gravel is removed; this is passed up in baskets and washed in troughs, as already described, in the gold mines, or rather ditches, as the native word signifies (parit).

The Malays of Banjarmasin and Landak are very anxious to work the diamonds at Sarawak, but being generally very bad characters, the government has not thought proper to encourage their immigration. Many diamonds are, however, obtained by the people, who wash for gold in the river; and on one occasion I saw a person get three small ones at one washing, together with a considerable portion of gold. With capital, and proper superintendence, it would pro- bably turn out a gainful speculation if properly con- ducted, more particularly as gold is found in the same soil, though not in such abundance as in some other kinds of earth.

Though in the neighbourhood of Siam and the Birman

Empire, which are said to produce rubies and sapphires superior to those of Ceylon, neither of these or any other precious stones have yet been discovered in Borneo. A beautifully resplendent sand, the particles of which resemble amethysts and topazes, and which is used in the adulteration of gold dust, may perhaps be thought to indicate the vicinity of other gems : it is found at Lingah, a branch of the great Batang Lupar river, not far from its mouth.

The above metals and minerals are, I believe, all that are as yet satisfactorily proved to exist on the island, though, doubtless, many more remain to be yet discovered. Copper, it is said, has been produced by the Dyaks of the Sambas territory; but the ore has not hitherto been examined by Europeans. Besides the metals and minerals, many coloured earths and valuable clays are in abundance. In the neighbourhood of Sarawak is found a white clay of great purity, such as is used in the manufacture of the finest porcelain. It is used by the native goldsmiths for the purpose of making the crucibles in which they melt the gold dust. In proper hands a profitable manufactory might, perhaps, be established for the purpose of making coarse China ware, so much valued by the Dyaks, from it; but as this is bought at a very low price, and in very large quantity, at Singapore, it would be difficult, on account of the higher price of labour, to compete with the manufacture of China.

CHAPTER II.

THE climate of Borneo, like that of most of the
Eastern islands, has been found exceedingly healthy
to persons whose avocations do not render great
exposure necessary. The north-east monsoon, or that
which blows from April to October, is the rainy period;
but a day rarely passes during the south-west, or fine
monsoon, without a refreshing shower: this, with the
constant warmth, causes every thing to grow during
the whole year, the forests being clothed with a per-
petual verdure, which gives the islands, when seen
from the sea, a beautiful appearance, possessed by no
country in the world to so great an extent; shrubs
(Hibiscus) and flowering trees (Barringtonia) always
overhanging the margin of the ocean, and the inland
mountains are observed covered to their summits with
a dense and luxuriant vegetation.

In temperature it has never been found by Euro-

peans to be oppressively hot; the thermometer generally averaging 70° to 72° Fahrenheit in the mornings
and evenings, and 82° to 85° at 2 P.M., which is
generally the hottest part of the day; and though in
the dry season the mercury has sometimes ascended as
high as 92°, and occasionally 93°, it has not been felt
so inconveniently oppressive to Europeans as a hot
summer day in England. The houses of the Europeans being built near the rivers, are kept cool and
pleasant by the breeze which generally prevails in
those open situations.

As in all countries within the tropics, thunder and
lightning are so very frequent as to be but little
regarded by the inhabitants, though the former is
more sonorous, and the latter more vivid, than in
Europe. The lightning is, also, very destructive,
several instances of damage and loss of life by it
having happened, although from the smaller number
of inhabitants these are of less frequent occurrence
than in Europe. One of the men belonging to
H.M.S. 'Samarang,' who was cutting wood in the
jungle, near the Santubong mouth of the Sarawak
river, was killed by a tree, which had been struck,
falling upon him. The 'Hazard,' in 1846, was also
struck, and the upper works and masts considerably
injured; fortunately there was no loss of human life.
In all the quiet seas of the East the lightning is very
much dreaded by European shipping, many vessels
having been lost in the Straits of Malacca and the
Java seas by its effects. A heavy shower of rain is

always preceded by lightning and thunder, and generally by strong wind.

Though the vegetation of no country in the world
is so luxuriant as that of the Eastern islands, it has
been proved by many writers that the soil of some of
them is not so fertile as the appearance of the forests
would lead the cultivator to expect.   This remark
particularly applies to Sumatra, the forests of which
are supported in their luxuriance, in a great measure,
by the moisture of the surrounding atmosphere.   Java
has, however, been proved to be, in the very highest
degree, fertile, and capable of producing every thing in
the greatest perfection suitable to a tropical climate;
and in this respect, from what I have observed of the
soil of Borneo, I should imagine it to be equally productive.

The soil of Sarawak, with which I am best
acquainted, and which, from the similarity of productions over the whole island, may probably be fairly
taken as an example of its whole extent, is of a rich
strong yellow loam, covered to a depth of from six
inches to a foot with black and very productive
vegetable mould, which has been formed by the
decayed vegetation of the forests.   Beneath the loam,
which is generally from ten to twenty feet in depth, is
found a stratum of gravel in the districts where
diamonds are found; in others, it rests upon the
sandstone and limestone rocks, in their particular districts.   It is admirably suited for the production of
the sugar-cane, which here grows amongst the Dyaks

without the slightest cultivation, to greater perfection than I have seen it in Ceylon under the care of Europeans. The cultivated cane of the Chinese in Sarawak I have frequently seen eighteen feet in length, and abounding in saccharine juice of the richest quality. The natives grow several kinds of sugar-cane, some of which they assert were formerly found wild in the island; but the golden yellow cane, which appears to have been imported by the Chinese, and is now cultivated by them, is the most esteemed by the Malays. It is not cultivated for the purpose of making sugar, but, the outer skin being thrown off, the inner is chewed by them much in the manner followed by the orang utan of their woods, the fibrous part being throw away after the sweet juice has been extracted.

Some nutmegs, which were planted for experiment by Mr. Brooke, grew, without manuring or any attention, remarkably well; they were left entirely to nature, the weeds not being once cleared away; and the result is satisfactory proof that the cultivation of this valuable spice, which in Singapore and Penang is pursued at so great an expense, may be here carried on with the ordinary cost of cocoa-nut, or other cheap plantations, merely at the cost of labour sufficient to clear away the weeds.

Some plants of the cinnamon, nutmeg, and clove, together with oranges and many other exotic plants, now growing in the beautiful garden of Mr. Heutig, an English gentleman resident at Sarawak, afford abundant testimony of the suitableness

of the soil and climate for the production of the finer
spices, should their cultivation be attended to with
ordinary care.

The heat of the climate, and the constant growth
consequent on its moisture, render it difficult to raise
European fruits and vegetables, though, when roads
are cut through the island, the mountains will be
found to produce these in perfection. In the low
lands it is useless to attempt the cultivation of the
former, though, by great perseverance on the part of
the gentleman above referred to, some kinds of vegetables have been obtained in considerable abundance :
of these, French beans, cucumbers, endive, tomatoes, and
asparagus, have succeeded best; when I left, in June
last, many others, however, were looking very promising.
As on the mountains, the sides of all of which are
covered with productive soil, any climate and temperature may be obtained, it is probable that the new
settlement of Labuh-an will not be left in the same
destitute state for vegetables as Singapore, where
the few cabbages which are produced are cultivated in
flower-pots, and with great care.

The Chinese in Sarawak have several gardens for
the production of native vegetables near the town. In
these are grown, in great perfection, the egg plants,
the fruit of which, under the name of ' brenjal,' is a
favourite vegetable; a large kind of radish, which,
cooked, very much resembles the turnip in flavour.
Sweet potatoes, yams, earthnuts (Arachis hypogœa), and
various kinds of leguminous plants (kachang), cucum-

bers, and some herbs, are also furnished from these gardens for the tables of the Europeans. In them are also grown abundance of sugar-cane and pine-apples for the Malays, who rarely take the trouble of cultivating these things themselves. Some kinds of fern (paku), the yet unopened fronds of which when boiled become an excellent vegetable, and, with the exception of the cabbage of the various palms, are preferred to most others of the production of the island by European residents. The fern which produces it is a strong growing species, (Marrattia) plentiful on the banks of the rivers: several kinds are eaten, but this is preferred.

Of all the vegetables produced in the island, the cabbage of the palm, called ' nibong,' is the most esteemed ; it is taken from the heart of the tree, being formed of the unexpanded leaves, which are of a delicate whiteness, and of a very sweet, nutty flavour. It is preferred to that of the cocoa nut, but is inferior to that of the ' pinang,' or areca nut, which, however, on account of the value of the tree, is very rarely used, the extraction of the edible part, in all cases, causing the destruction of the tree. The nibong is found in great numbers near the mouths of all the rivers, and besides producing the esteemed vegetable above described, is very useful to the natives in house-building, for forming their posts, flooring, &c. The stem being perfectly round, and of about six inches in diameter, no more trouble is necessary than to cut down the tree, and divide the stem into the requisite

lengths. Its outside has a rind, and is hard to the
thickness of an inch; the inside, being, as in all palms,
the most recently formed fibre, is soft, and couse-
quently soon decays. These trees are used principally
by the poorer sort of inhabitants, the richer generally
employing hard wood posts. The posts of nibong will
last from three to four years, so that they have, at the
end of that time, to be either renewed, or the houses
supported by extra ones, when it may be made to
stand for some time longer, though, as house-building
of this description is not at all expensive, the greater
part are pulled down, at the end of this period, and
rebuilt. It forms the rafters to which the roof-cover-
ing and the open flooring are tied. The stems of the
nibong are split into laths, the outer, or hard part,
only being retained for flooring. These are kept
together by rattans interwoven amongst them, each
lath being placed at the distance of about two inches
from that on each side of it; by this arrangement all
the dirt and rubbish passes below the house, which is
generally cleansed by the river at high tides.

The bamboo, the shoots of which are also an
esteemed vegetable, and which, in the hands of
Europeans, make a most excellent pickle, is as useful
to the Dyaks as the nibong is to the Malays, the
one being as abundant in the interior as the other
is on the coasts. There are many kinds of bamboo,
but that most valued is the large kind, called by
the natives ' boolu ayer,' or the water bamboo; it
grows to a very large size, attaining the height

of sixty feet, and appears to thrive best on the sides of mountains, in very rich soil. The other kinds, of which there are six, are much smaller, but are very useful to the natives, as they grow in more attainable situations, generally on the banks of the rivers, and their stems are said to be of a harder nature than those of the large bamboo. They are used, as in India, and in all countries where they are produced, for an infinity of purposes, and in house-building they take the place of the nibongs, except in their permanent habitations, which have hard wood posts; the smaller kinds are used as cooking pots by the natives when in the jungle, and by those whose poverty prevents them purchasing the pots of earth or brass, called ' priuck,' which the Malays bring to them for sale.

The rice called ' pulut,' hereafter to be described, is always cooked by the Malays and Dyaks in a green bamboo, this mode of preparing it being most esteemed amongst all their tribes. For the purposes of cooking, the bamboo is cut into lengths of about two to three feet; these being filled with the rice or meat cut into small pieces, and having a sufficiency of water, are placed over the fire in such a position that the joint of the bamboo does not come in contact with it, but rests upon the ground beyond it, the fire being placed under the green and harder part of the cane, which resists the effects of the heat and flame until the provisions are sufficiently prepared; a bundle of leaves placed in the mouth of the cane answers the purposes of the lid of an ordinary cooking pot. This cane is of such value to them that, like the fruit trees, those which are planted in the vicinity of their villages, are individual property.

Next in order of the vegetable productions, and equal to either of the above in the estimation in which it is held by the natives, is the cocoa-nut, which has been so often and so well described that I shall not here repeat its well-known uses ; though in countries where cordages of other kinds abound, and where better thatch for their houses can be easily procured, the husk of this fruit is not used for the one purpose, nor its leaves for the other. The wars of the inhabitants have almost exterminated this useful plant from the western coast of Borneo ; it is, however, abundant to the northward ; and the Natunas on the west, and the Sooloo islands on the east, are said to be covered with these palms. The supply of Sarawak and the west coast is drawn entirely from the Natunas islands, the inhabitants of which trust principally to this commerce for their supply of rice, which they do not themselves produce. About fifty of their boats, carrying from six to twenty tons each, arrive annually at Sarawak, during the fine monsoon, loaded with nuts, oil, and sugar, the productions of this tree. The sugar is a coarse kind, resembling molasses, and is made by boiling the sap extracted from the flower stem of this palm ; it also may be procured in less quantities from the gomuti, nipah, and many others.

The sago palm (Metroxylon) is grown in great per-fection in some parts of the island, and the rough sago is exported in large quantities from the west coast to

Singapore, and also by the Bugis boats from the eastern and southern sides of the island. The sago of commerce is the well-known substance forming the heart of the plant, and in those parts where it is most abundant it forms a great portion of the food of the inhabitants ; but, notwithstanding its nutritive proper- ties, the natives, who are not so expert in preparing it as those farther east, much prefer rice; and the Milanowes, who live on the rivers Egan, Hoya, Mocha, and Bintulu, and are the principal cultivators of the tree, always import considerable quantities of grain for their own consumption. The tree grows in marshy places, and rarely attains a greater height than thirty feet.

The time for collecting the sago, and in which state it is most productive, is just before it begins to show its large and spreading terminal spike of flowers. It attains this state in from seven to eight years from the time of planting. While young, it is beautifully provided by nature with strong and lengthy spines, which serve to protect it from the wild pigs which would otherwise destroy it. On its attaining a greater size, the outer shell of the trunk becoming sufficiently hard, the spines drop off, the hard wood protecting the farina of the centre from their attacks ; after the flower and fruit have perfected themselves, which occupies a period of two years from their first appearance, the pith of the centre is found dried up, the leaves have fallen, and the plant is dead. It is rarely propagated from the seed, which is generally unproductive ; but as it freely produces offsets, the supply is easily raised. Amongst the Dyaks, who grow rice, sago is very rarely used as food except in times of scarcity, from oppression, or other causes. The whole of the sago exported from Borneo is in a rough state, manufactories being established at Singapore and Batavia for its preparation and refining. In its rough state it is an ungainly-looking and ungrateful-smelling substance, and one unacquainted with its properties would be at a loss to conceive that the pearl sago of the shops is prepared from it. The manufacture of the medulla into sago is fully described by Mr. Crawfurd and other writers.

In general appearance the gomuti-palm (Arenga saccharifera,) very much resembles the sago, but the pinnæ of the leaves, which are erect in the latter, droop in the former like those of the nibong and many other palms. It is valued by the Dyaks, as producing the best toddy, and in the greatest abundance. It is extracted from the plant by cutting off the large lateral bunches of fruit. When these are about half-grown, they are severed close to the division of the peduncle or stem, and bamboos being hung to them, a good tree with two incisions will produce about a gallon daily for two months; a fresh surface being constantly kept on the severed part by a thin slice being daily cut off the stem or peduncle, so that at the end of the above-named period it has altogether disappeared. The toddy is taken from the bamboo twice a-day, and, when fresh, has a very agreeable taste, and is a re-freshing drink; but the Dyaks always place a piece of a bitter kind of bark in the bamboos which contain it, and this communicates its flavour to the toddy. The cordage it produces from the hairy-like filaments, which are interwoven round the stem and about the axils of the leaves, is of excellent quality, and of great service, on account of its durability, in the house-building economy of the Dyak. This substance is also plaited into ornaments for the arms, legs, and neck, and its deep black and neat appearance renders it, to the eye of an European, a much more agreeable ornament than either the brass or beads with which they abundantly adorn their persons, as will be explained hereafter.

The graceful betel or areca-nut (Areca catechu) palm is one of the greatest ornaments of Eastern gardens. It is not here planted in sufficient quantities to form an article of exportation; indeed, considerable quantities are imported, as, like the cocoa-nut, the trees were destroyed during the wars which, previous to the arrival of Mr. Brooke on the western coast, desolated the country. The nut is used for no other purpose but that of being chewed with the sirih leaves (piper), lime, and gambier; this practice of the other natives of India and the Archipelago being quite as universal among the Dyaks as the Malays.

This beautiful tree is also much prized by the natives on account of the delightful fragrance of its flowers, which, taken just before opening from the sheath or spathe, in which the inflorescence is enveloped, and called myang, is requisite in all their medicines and conjurations for the purpose of healing the sick : it is also used with other sweet-scented flowers at bridals and all occasions of festivity. This delightful perfume,

and its fine head of plume-like leaves, supported on
a slender and graceful stem, render it the universal
favourite amongst its beautiful tribe.

Of the remaining articles useful to the natives,
either in their own economy or for exportation, the
numerous kinds of rattans and canes are of the greatest importance.　They are produced from many
species of the genus Calamus, and abound in all the
old and dense jungles in damp situations.　The leaves
of many of them being furnished with a long and
slender mid-rib, which extends far beyond the pinnæ
of the leaf, and furnished with strong curved spines,
are particularly troublesome to persons travelling in
the jungles.　Their slender form rendering them in-
visible unless carefully watched, they frequently catch
the clothes, or person, and cannot be detached except
by walking back a pace or two, and carefully un-
hooking them.

The different kinds of rattan vary very much both in
size and in the appearance of the leaves; some of them
being smooth and spineless, with leaves like those of
the bamboo; others rough, with spines covering the
stems and ribs of the leaves: of the former class
are all the smaller rattans, such as bear that name in
commerce, while to the latter belong the Malacca cane,
and other strong varieties.　The rattans of Borneo are
esteemed finer than those produced in any other part
of the world, and are exported to Singapore and
Batavia in immense quantities from the Coti and
Banjar rivers: on the south and eastern parts of the
island they are collected, and brought down these

streams on rafts by the Dyaks for a very small remuneration; they are principally exported finally from Batavia and Singapore to India and China.

To the natives themselves they are very useful in the manufacture of baskets and mats, of great durability, and very fine workmanship; they are also of the greatest importance as cordage, where nails are not known, and the timbers of houses are secured by them: for this purpose the outer and hard parts only are used, the rattans being split, and the inner part carefully removed. The drug called Dragon's Blood is procured from one of the large species of rattans; but as its manufacture in Borneo is peculiar to the southern parts of the island, which I have not yet visited, I can give no satisfactory information respecting the method of preparing it. Large quantities of it are annually exported from Banjarmasin to Singapore and Batavia, and thence to China, where it is held in high estimation.

The nipah (Nipa fruticans), though in growth amongst the humblest of the palm tribe, in its value to the natives of this island is inferior to few of them. It is found on the margins of the rivers as far as the salt water extends, and large salt marshes at the mouths of rivers are covered with it to the extent of thousands of acres; its chief value is for covering houses, the leaves of which for this purpose are made into 'ataps,' and endure for two years. Salt is made in some places from its leaves by burning them, and in others sugar is extracted from syrup supplied

by its flower - stem. The fruit, though tasteless, is
esteemed by the natives, and is said to make an excellent preserve. Its leaves, on luxuriant plants, are
occasionally twenty feet long, all growing from the
centre, the plant having no stem, unless a kind of
rhizoma, which is found on the ground, like that of a
fern, and attached to the old plants, may be called
such.

The mangrove, which abounds in situations similar
to the nipah, is valued on account of its timber,
which is used as the best firewood; from the aerial
roots of this tree a bitter and coarse salt is made,
similar to that from the nipah.

Such are the principal products of the vegetables
of the island which are used for home consumption.
We will now notice those which are principally collected for exportation; of these perhaps the first in
rank is camphor, or, as it is called by the natives and
in commerce, the ' kapur barus,' or Barus camphor,
to distinguish it from the production of the Laurus
camphora, or Japan camphor. It derives its name of
Barus from a place in Sumatra, where it is produced,
and whence it was probably first exported. The
true Dryobalanops camphora, which produces it,
has not hitherto been found on any of the Indian
islands, with the exception of those of Borneo and
Sumatra, and only on the northern parts of these
islands: the tree is said by Mr. Marsden to be
very common in Sumatra, in the country of the
Battas, but not to be found to the south of the line.

On Borneo it is found at present towards the north; but as I once discovered these trees in Sarawak, near the Santubong entrance of the river, I think it probable that they have once been abundant here, but have been destroyed in extracting the camphor. That it has been once collected there appears, the more probable, as one of the three trees above named, on being felled, was found to have had a large notch cut into the tree, as is the custom to the northward, to see if it is likely to produce the camphor. On Labuh-an it is common, and is one of the noblest trees in that, the finest jungle I ever saw: it has a fine straight stem, from which the bark comes off in large flakes; the foliage is very dense, forming a well shaped head to the tree, the stem of which is frequently ninety feet to the first branches.

A tree of another species, which had fallen down, measured nearly 120 feet to the branches, but none of these at all equal the Tapang, of which mention is made in another place. Nearly all the kapur trees, excepting such as were young, had large notches cut almost into the centre of the tree: this was for the purpose of ascertaining whether, on being felled, it was likely to be productive, as it is said that not one in ten is found to produce it; so that its appearance must be caused by a particular state, probably of vigour or disease in the tree. It is said that in those which produce it, the younger and smaller trees are often found to be quite as prolific as the old and larger trees. The camphor is found in a concrete state in the crevices of the wood, so that it can only be extracted by felling the tree, which is afterwards cut into blocks and split with wedges, and the camphor, which is white and transparent, is then taken out. An essential oil is also found in hollows in the wood, which the natives crystallize artificially, but the camphor thus obtained is not so much esteemed as that found naturally crystallized. The tree is found on all the northern parts of Borneo, and is said to be particularly abundant in the country of the Kyans, in the interior of the Bintulu and Rejang rivers. The produce, though so valued by the Chinese, is not used much by the natives, though it is occasionally taken inwardly as a medicine. The price in China of the Bornean camphor is said to be higher than that of Japan, in the proportion of twenty to one: it has been supposed that this disproportion is caused more by some superstitions of the consumer, than any real distinction of properties, for though the trees which produce them are so dissimilar, the chemical properties are said nearly to approach each other.

Several trees of the genus Dipterocarpus produce a nut, that, when compressed, yields a fatty oil, which having been recently sent to England, has been used extensively under the names of vegetable tallow and vegetable wax. Three species of this genus are common in Sarawak, under the name of 'mencabang;' one of them, 'mencabang pinang,' is valued for its close-grained timber; the others do not grow so large in size, but have larger leaves and fruit. The one most valued for producing the oil, is a fine tree growing on the banks of the Sarawak river; it attains the height of forty feet; the leaves being large, and the branches drooping towards the water, give it a very beautiful appearance : its fruit is produced in the greatest profusion about December and January, being as large as a walnut, with two long wings to the seed. These nuts are collected by the natives, and yield a very large proportion of oil, which, on being allowed to cool, takes the consistence of sperm, and in appearance very much resembles that substance. The natives at present only value this as a cooking oil; but when the demand for it in Europe becomes better known to them, they will doubtless increase their manufacture of it.

In England it has proved to be the best lubricating substance for steam machinery, far surpassing even olive oil; and it has been used in Manilla in the manufacture of candles, and found to answer admirably. As it becomes more common, it will doubtless be applied to many other purposes. From the quickness of its growth, and the great profusion with which it bears its fruit, it will, should the demand for it continue, become a profitable object for cultivation, by which the quality and quantity would most likely be improved and increased. It is also found in Java and Sumatra, and a similar substance has been lately sent from China. In Borneo it is called by the natives indifferently ' miniak mencabang,' or ' miniak tankawan.'

Another oil expressed from the seed of a tree, called ' katiow ' by the natives, and much valued for cooking, is, as far as I have been able to learn, entirely unknown to Europe; but as the tree which produces it is not found in Sarawak, I have never had an opportunity of seeing it. The seeds are oblong, pointed, and of a shining rich brown colour; the oil which they produce, on compression, is of a yellow colour, with a perfume precisely resembling that of almond oil; and, as it is very cheap and abundant in the places where it grows, it would perhaps be serviceable to soap-makers and perfumers. It is a very fine oil for lamps, burning with a bright and clear flame, at the same time emitting an agreeable odour; it is produced chiefly on the Sadong, Lingah, and Kallekka rivers, and exported to Sarawak and other places under the name of ' miniak katiow.'

The ' miniak kapayang ' is another oil held in esteem for cooking amongst the natives: it is produced by a tree called by botanists Pangium edule. The tree grows to about forty feet high, and is not found wild, but has been planted by the Dyaks: the leaves are large, dark green, on long petioles, and the large fruit is terminal. On opening the fruit it is found to contain many large seeds embedded in a slight pulp, which is said by the natives to be deleterious. When the fruit is ripe, these seeds are extracted, and when compressed, produce an oil which is much scarcer than any of the other kinds before enumerated: the tree bears fruit all the year, and is a very ornamental plant.

Wood oil, called by the natives of Borneo ' miniak kruing,' is extracted from the trees which produce it, by simply cutting a large hole in the tree, into which fire being placed, the oil is attracted. The tree probably belongs to the order Myrtaceæ, but I have never seen it; it is found plentifully to the eastward, in the interior of the Samarhand, and Sadong rivers : it is used by the natives to mix with dammer for paying the seams of boats, and also instead of linseed oil in mixing their paints, and is of great assistance in preserving wood from the effects of the weather.

The seeds of many of the forest trees, as the niato, or gutta percha, of the Malay peninsula, produce edible oils of fine qualities; but the natives, possessing such a choice, rarely take the trouble to express them; but in future it will be well worth the study of our merchants and others whose occupation and opportunities will permit them to make inquiries respecting these and many other totally unknown products.

The gutta percha, or niato, is a plant which has been lately brought before the attention of British merchants by Dr. W. Montgomerie and Dr. D'Almeida, the former of whom communicated some information respecting its application to surgical purposes to the Bengal Medical Board, in 1843. In April, of the same year, Dr. D'Almeida presented specimens of it to the Royal Society of Arts in London, who, at the time, merely acknowledged the receipt of the specimens. Its character and properties have since been more fully given to the public by Dr. Oxley, the senior surgeon of the Straits settlements; a gentleman whose kindness and valuable assistance all who visit the East for scientific purposes have gratefully to record.

Dr. Oxley says of it, that it is called, properly, the gutta suban—the percha being an inferior article—and is a tree of considerable size, being from sixty to seventy feet in height, and from two to three feet in diameter; in general appearance, much resembling the genus Durio, which produces the celebrated durian of the East.   It is said to be found in all the forests of the peninsula of Malacca, of Borneo, Singapore, and the adjacent islands; but the quantity is much diminished, as, to procure the gutta, the natives fell the trees, and ring the bark at distances of from twelve to eighteen inches; a cocoa-nut shell, or some other receptacle, being placed to receive the sap which exudes from each incision : this sap is afterwards collected in bamboos and boiled, in order to drive off the watery particles and inspissate it to the consistence it finally assumes.   Although in large quantities the boiling may be necessary, the Doctor observes, it will consolidate and assume the same appearance without it.

The quantity of gutta obtained from each tree varies from five to twenty catties, each catty being equal to to $1\frac{1}{3}$lb. English.   Its great peculiarity, and that which renders it so very useful, is the effect boiling water has upon it; for, on being immersed in water above the temperature of 150° Fahrenheit, it becomes soft and plastic, so as to be capable of being moulded into any required form, which it retains on cooling. The Malays have manufactured it into whips, baskets, basins and jugs, shoes, traces, vessels for cooling wine, and several other domestic uses.

It has been found by Dr. Oxley to be of the greatest value in surgery, particularly as splints for fractured limbs. Many interesting particulars connected with it will be found in the original paper from which these remarks are extracted, and which will be found in the first or July number of a little but highly interesting work, published monthly at a trifling expense, under the superintendence of Mr. Logan of Singapore. It is entitled the ' Journal of the Indian Archipelago, and Eastern Asia,' and the numbers already published contain some valuable and new information on the interesting countries of which it treats.

As has been stated above, the gutta percha has been found in Borneo, and the same substance is said by the natives, who know at present nothing of the manner of collecting it, or of its uses, and who call it by a different name, ' gutta niato,' to be produced by several different trees. The same name is mentioned by Sir Stamford Raffles, in his ' History of Java,' (vol. i. page 42, 4to edition), but he confounds it with the miniak kawon, or tankawan, already described; but the name being the same as that used by the people of Borneo, it is very likely that both the trees are found in Java. The gutta percha has been recently referred by Sir W. Hooker to the order Sapotaceæ, and to Dr. Wight's new genus, Isonandra, under the name of Isonandra gutta.

Another substance, similar in all respects to caoutchouc, might be obtained in quantities in Borneo, as well as in many other of the islands and on the peninsula : it is the produce of a climbing plant of the genus

Urceola, which grows to the size of a man's body. The bark, which is soft and thick, with a very rough appearance, on being cut, emits the sap in the greatest abundance, and without destroying the tree; very large quantities might be obtained from a single trunk.

There are three kinds in Borneo, called by the generic name of 'jintawan' by the natives; two are common in Sarawak, viz. the J. susuh, or milky jintawan, and the J. bulat, or round-fruited jintawan. They equally produce the caoutchouc, which, having been analyzed, is found to differ in no respect from that produced by the Ficus elastica and other trees. The natives of Borneo use it to cover the sticks with which they beat their gongs and other musical instruments. The fruit, which is large, and of a fine apricot colour, contains ten or twelve seeds enveloped in a rich reddish pulp, and though but a jungle plant, is one of the most grateful fruits of the country to the European palate.

Many of the other trees produce sap from their soft and spongy bark, which, on being drawn from the tree, assumes a concrete form, but they are not known to the natives as of any use. Perhaps, as in the case of the oils, the skill and enterprise of Europeans will discover amongst them properties analogous to those of gutta percha; and when a mode of extracting them less injurious to the tree than that pursued in the case of the tuban is followed, will prove a source of permanent wealth to the island.

The celebrated upas tree, Antiaris toxicaria, is found upon the island, but not very common. Of a tree which I had an opportunity of observing through the kindness of Captain Bethune, R.N. C.B., who allowed me to accompany him to Borneo, in May, 1845, and gave me every facility for examining the jungles which the disturbed state of the country would admit, and which were in his power, many absurd stories were related to me by the natives, similar to those published by Mr. Foersch, of the Dutch East India Company, in the 'London Magazine' for September, 1785; and it seems very curious that, having this tree before them, which was surrounded by their graves, they should tell me it was impossible to go under it without dying.

On my insisting, however, I got one of them to climb up to get me some specimens, but they were neither in flower nor fruit. The poisonous sap flows freely from the bark when tapped, and Dr. Horsfield, whose admirable account of it was first published in the Batavian Transactions (vol. vii.) and afterwards by Sir Stamford Raffles, (Hist. Arch. vol. i.) tells us that it is equal in potency, when thrown into the circulation, to any animal poison yet known. Several interesting experiments with it, in prepared and natural states, are detailed in the paper alluded to. The tree is called 'Bina' by the Borneans, and has a fine appearance. The specimen at Borneo was about sixty feet high, with a fine stem, the bark of which was of a very white colour: it was supported at its base by those processes resembling buttresses, which are so common to the trees of tropical jungles.

A poison of greater potency was said to be manu-

factured from a climbing plant which grew in the
neighbourhood of Bintulu : it is perhaps the same as
the ' chitik,' of Java—the botanical name of which is
not yet ascertained. This was called upas by the
natives of Borneo, but I think, with other authors,
that upas is a name for vegetable poisons in general.

Dammar is a resinous gum produced by many kinds
of trees quite different in their character and habit
from the Dammara orientalis figured in Marsden's
' History of Sumatra.' The dammar is of several
kinds : the white, which is used for the same purposes
as gum copal, is called ' dammar mata kuching,' or
the cat's eye dammar ; it is the least common, and
most valuable, being beautifully transparent. The
' dammar daging,' or flesh-like dammar, takes its name
from its veined appearance, which causes it to resemble
some kinds of agate ; it is not set apart, but used
with the common kinds for paying the seams of boats
and prows ; for which purpose it is pounded and boiled
with wood oil until it becomes of a pitchy consistence.

The various kinds of dammar form an article of
considerable trade between different places in the
Archipelago, and are exported to India and China from
Singapore, at a very low price : they exude spouta-
neously, and are collected after having fallen to the
ground. The Dyaks and Malays form torches of this
inflammable substance, by filling the interior of small
bamboo canes with it, which have been previously
dried for the purpose ; such torches are used only by
the poorer classes of Malays, those in better circumstances preferring the more expensive oil of the cocoa-

nut, which is burnt in tumblers by means of cotton wicks generally floating in the oil.

The 'kulit lawang' of commerce is the aromatic bark of a wild species of cinnamon, and is produced in abundance in all parts of the island : it is the true Cinnamomeum kulit lawan, but I think that other varieties are also found. It was probably this plant which induced the earlier voyagers to imagine that the true cinnamon of Ceylon, which this much resembles, was found in the Archipelago. The bark is well known for its clove-like aromatic flavour, and for the essential oil it produces, which, however, is never extracted by the natives of Borneo.

Cotton is grown by the Sea Dyaks sufficient in quantity for their own use, and to make cloths for exportation. Some of the same kind produced in the garden of Mr. Hentig, and which was sent to Liverpool as a sample, was found to be of superior quality. Its cultivation will hereafter, probably, form an important feature in the agricultural pursuits of the island, as it can be exported to China with great advantage. Indigo has not been tried on the island; but as it succeeds in Sumatra and Java, there can be no doubt that its culture might be successfully pursued.

Pepper has been long exported in great quantities from several ports in Borneo, particularly from Bruni and Banjar. During the disturbances of Bruni, since the withdrawal of the English factory, the trade has very much declined, as the Chinese—who, it is said, to the number of 30,000, cultivated pepper in the neigh-

bourhood of the capital—have all been obliged to
leave, neither their lives nor property being secure;
the few who are now in Bruni, and who do not probably exceed twenty in number, being detained as
slaves.   The pepper at present exported from Bruni is
grown by the Kadyans and Meroots, a race of people
resembling the Dyaks, who inhabit the interior of the
Borneo river.   It is a curious fact, remarked by all
writers on the East, that this aromatic is universally
esteemed, except by the inhabitants of the countries
which produce it; the Malays never use it in their
cookery, as they ascribe a heating quality to it: the
small kind of capsicums they use largely, and attribute
to them a contrary effect.   In 1801 the district of
Banjarmasin alone, on the south coast of Borneo, was
capable of producing 1,500 tons of this spice.

Coffee has been tried in the gardens of the Europeans, and thrives remarkably well, producing a fine
and well-flavoured berry.   I have been told by the
Malays that it is grown by the Dyaks of the Pontianak river, for the use of that settlement, but its
cultivation on an extensive scale has not been encouraged; the government probably not wishing it
to come in competition with Java, which so largely
produces this berry.   The hills on the main-land
opposite Labuh-an, would be well adapted for its cultivation, since here, as in Ceylon, it might be grown
without the trouble and expense of raising trees
amongst the plantations to protect the bushes from
the sun, as is done in Java.   In Ceylon the best
elevation for the coffee estates is from 3,000 to

4,000 feet; the berries produced at this height being of much finer quality and richer flavour than any others.

Gambier (Uncaria) is not cultivated in the island, though found wild in many parts of it: that used by the Malays is brought from Singapore, the Dyaks contenting themselves with chewing the leaves together with their Sirih, &c. The gambier plantations in Singapore are said so much to exhaust the land, that nothing can be grown on their site for many years after they are abandoned.

Tobacco is grown in small quantities by the Dyaks and people of Bruni; but they are unskilful in its manufacture, though the flavour of that of Bruni is much esteemed by Europeans. Under skilful management, and by introducing a better kind—if the one now known should not prove a good one—it might become as profitable to the island as it now is to the neighbouring ones of the Philippines, Java, and Bali. The Dyaks might be more readily induced to cultivate this plant, the nature of which they know, than indigo and other plants which are strange to them.

Besides the articles above imperfectly enumerated, many others, it is highly probable, might be introduced with advantage. The success attending the partial cultivation of the spices of Amboyna, and the Banda islands, has been already mentioned, and it is probable that they may be cultivated at so cheap a rate, as to be able to compete with the productions of their native islands, even if all restrictions on the commerce in them were removed by the government. Vanilla, should the climate not prove too damp, is a valuable spice, and of easy cultivation. The cocoa-tree of Manilla (Theobroma cacao) has been proved to be in every way suited to the soil and climate, producing fruit of excellent quality. Cotton, it has been already said, might be cultivated with advantage; as also the plantain, (Musa textilis), of which the fine Manilla cordage is made. Ginger grows well in all the native gardens, and turmeric is found wild in abundance. Many kinds of oils might be produced in perfection, and most of the valuable vegetable productions of India and the tropics, it is supposed, might be here success-fully grown, and profitably exported. Now that the British settler will be cared for and protected by his own government, the national enterprise will soon develope some of these immense vegetable resources.

While treating of the vegetable productions, the many valuable kinds of wood produced by the vast and magnificent forests of the island must be noticed. The botanical characters of but few of these are yet ascertained, so that I am unable at present to furnish their scientific names. The wood most esteemed amongst the natives, on account of its hardness and durability, is called by them ' balean ' or ' kyuh balean,' the term kayu, meaning wood, being always appended to the names of timber trees.

The balean is a tree of the largest size, and although its wood is so hard as to be almost incorruptible, the tree is of quick and vigorous growth: it is found most abundantly in the low damp forests in the neigh-

bourhood of the sea and of large rivers. It is much
used by the natives for posts of their houses, which,
amongst the Dyaks, are handed down from father
to son for many generations. Many specimens
which I have seen, and which must have been in the
river for ages, are as hard when cut as those fresh
taken from the forest, and I have never met with a
piece of this timber in a state of decay. The water
worm (Teredo) is the only insect which attacks it when
in the water; and though its channelling the wood must
necessarily much weaken the post, the water being
admitted into it does not cause it to rot. On land or
under the earth it equally resists the effects of atmosphere and white ants, so destructive in tropical
countries to most other species of wood. This valuable
timber was formerly an article of export much sought
after by the Chinese; and in those ports which they
still frequent, is still a source of considerable trade.

Next in value is the 'kayu kapur' a close-grained and
durable timber, much valued by the natives for boat-
building purposes. Several kinds of the puhn of India
grow here in perfection; they are called by the natives
'bintañgur,' and are well known for their value in ship-
building. The 'kayuh rasack' very much resembles the
bintañgur, is close-grained, strong, and tough, and is
used for rudders, masts, and oars for the trading boats.
The mungris is, while fresh, nearly as hard as the iron-
wood, and more difficult to be worked; though it is very
durable, it is not equally so with the balean or iron-
wood; but is a large timber and a very fine tree. The
'merbau' is a fine durable timber, very useful in ship

and house-building, being easily worked and very durable.

'Mencabang pinang' is one of the trees which produce the vegetable tallow : it is plentiful in the forests, but would be more profitable for its fruit (which is of the small kind, and produces good oil) than its timber, though for this it is also held in high esteem. The wood is close-grained, hard, of a reddish colour, easily worked, and very durable. This tree differs from the others which produce the vegetable oil, in growing to a much greater height. The timber of the Kapur barus, or true camphor tree, is also highly esteemed : excepting when charged with the valuable drug, it does not emit the camphor smell, as does the timber of the Laurus camphora, of which the Chinese manufacture trunks and boxes, which, from the odour emitted by the wood, preserve whatever is put into them, from the attacks of insects of all kinds, particularly of the small ants, which are so troublesome in hot countries.

The 'neri' is a very hard wood, growing with the mangrove in salt swamps ; its timber, which has a reddish appearance, is not large but very abundant. The 'jelutong' is a larger growing tree with verticillate leaves, and a bark which, on being wounded, emits plentifully a white milk, which is inspissated by boiling, but has not yet been discovered to be of any use. The timber it produces, though large, is not esteemed by the natives, on account of its early decay when exposed to the rain and sun : it is white, and, being very soft, easily worked ; and it is much used by the poorer Malays for the sides of their houses, which are protected from the rain by the overhanging roofs. The 'maranti,' also a quick-growing timber tree, is held in much higher esteem than the last. In grain it resembles cedar, and like it is of a reddish colour, and it is much valued for making packing-cases, planks for the sides of houses, &c. : when protected from the weather it is a good and useful timber. The 'duñgun' also belongs to this class : it grows on the banks of rivers, and though the timber is soft, the large buttress-like supports at the base of the tree are very hard, and are valuable for gun carriages, and other purposes : they would doubtless be useful in turnery.

These that I have enumerated are but a few of the trees in most general use among the natives ; indeed, I have been informed that the trees which are abundant, and produce excellent timber, amount to upwards of sixty species : many of the other kinds, not useful as timber trees, are valuable, or might be, for making charcoal, pot-ash, pearlash, &c. Several kinds of oaks are found in the forests, but being of quick growth and soft wood, their timber is not esteemed.

Of ornamental woods, though it is improbable that the island should be destitute of them, many kinds have not yet been found. The ebony is abundant in many parts of the island, particularly on the west coast, but it is said to be inferior to that from the Mauritius, although it has been found a very profitable export to China. In the neighbourhood of the Lundu river, in the Sarawak territory, are large forests of it, which the Sebooyoh Dyaks would collect with gladness, if merchants were established at Sarawak to buy it of them. The 'rungas' is a red wood handsomely veined, which takes a fine polish, and is much used at Singapore for the purposes of furniture-making: like the ebony, it is only the old wood in the centre of the tree which is of an useful colour.

Of scented woods, several are known to exist, though few are collected, the value of the others not being yet known to commerce. The 'bidarru,' a yellow wood of a very agreeable odour, is the most plentiful, and being of a very hard and durable nature, is much esteemed for posts of houses and other purposes underground: its perfume will ultimately rescue this beautiful wood from its present degradation. There are one or two others, the names of which I have not preserved, which are all very durable and highly esteemed woods amongst the natives. The sandal wood, though it grows on Timor, has not, I believe, been hitherto found on this island.

Lignum aloes, of which there are several kinds, called generically by the natives 'kayu garu,' are produced apparently by diseases in some trees, the scented and resinous parts not being procurable until the tree has been cut down and decayed. The garu has long been an article of considerable export from this and the other islands to Arabia and China, where it is burned as incense.

A curious substance called 'plye,' is collected in the forests, and is the root of a large timber tree of the same name. It is very light, more so than cork, and might perhaps be used for the same purposes. A very similar substance is the root of another tree called 'si pait,' or the bitter wood : to the taste it is, as its name implies, very bitter, and in substance, appearance, and lightness, precisely resembles its tasteless con- gener. These plants have never been as yet either commercially or botanically examined, so that their uses are at present unknown, but the bitter one may perhaps prove valuable as a medicinal drug. The timber of both these trees, though large, is white, light, and useless, resembling that of the jelutong already noticed.

Dye stuffs and tannin are the produce of many barks and fruits of the Indian islands, but from what has been hitherto ascertained of them, they are not likely to be of use except for home consumption.

The flowers of Borneo, and of the Archipelago generally, are not less grateful and beautiful than the forests are grand and majestic. It has been said, perhaps too hastily, that no country in the world pro- duces such ravishing vegetable perfumes as the Malayan islands ; and the well known and now widely distributed scents of Kananga, (Uvaria), Champaka, (Michelia), Melur (Jasminum), and many others, would seem in a great measure to sustain them in this enviable pre-eminence ; but though grateful perfumes are in such profusion, the woods also abound in shrubs and flowers, which delight the eye and attract the curiosity by their rich and gaudy colours, or their delicate and beautiful forms. As in all tropical countries, the tribe Orchidaceæ is in profusion and beauty ; and on the open banks of the rivers, where the sun can shed its vivifying influence upon them, these delightful epiphytes decorate with their fragile but showy forms the otherwise naked and unsightly stumps of decaying forest trees.

The most gaudy are perhaps the various species of Cælogyne, called collectively by the natives the ' buñga kasih-an,' or the flowers of mercy; they are all highly fragrant, and their white and orange coloured flowers are exceedingly delicate and beautiful. Several Vandas, of which the continent of India has produced so many for the ornament of our gardens, are found here inferior to none of those from India, many of which are, by one gigantic species, far surpassed in beauty. This I have been successful in introducing into England, and Dr. Lindley has done me the honour of naming it after me.

One kind of the beautiful genus Cyprepedium, or Ladies' Slipper, so named from the curious form of the labellum, far surpasses in beauty any of its tribe from other countries. The Dendrobiums, which in India are so gorgeous, here dwindle, for the most part, into insignificant flowers; while the species of Æria which are abundant, are so beautiful that, were they once seen, they would probably raise their hitherto despised genus in the estimation of the English culti-vator of these beautiful plants. Of the smaller kinds, the Cirrhopetalon Bolbophyllum, and some other genera, though not showy, are curious, delicate, and beautiful. Several new species and some genera I have had the pleasure of introducing into England.

On the banks of the rivers, and growing as underwood in the dense jungles, are found many beautiful species of the genera Ixora and Pavetta, the former with large bunches of flowers of every shade, from orange to crimson, the latter with tufts of pure and delicate white blossoms ; other genera of the order Rubiaceæ abound, and are amongst the most beautiful wild plants ; many of these are fragrant.

Perhaps the most gorgeous of the native plants are the various species of the genus Rhododendron, which here assume a peculiar form, being found epiphytal upon the trunks of trees, as in the genera of the tribe Orchidaceæ. This habit, induced probably by the excessive moisture of the climate, is not, however, confined to the Ericaceous plants, but also prevails with the genera Fagrea, Combretum, and many others, usually terrestrial; the roots of the Rhododendrons, instead of being, as with the species, inhabitants of cold climates, small and fibrous, become large and fleshy, winding round the trunks of the forest trees ; the most beautiful one is that which I have named in compliment to Mr. Brooke. Its large heads of flowers are produced in the greatest abundance throughout the year: they much exceed in size that of any known species, frequently being formed of eighteen flowers, which are of all shades, from pale and rich yellow to a rich reddish salmon colour ; in the sun, the flowers sparkle with a brilliancy resembling that of gold dust.

Four other species which I discovered are very gorgeous, but of different colours, one being crimson and another red, and the third a rich tint between these two: of the fourth I have not yet seen the flowers. Besides the curious nature of the root above noticed, botanists may learn that these species differ from others of the genus in having very small, almost imperceptible, calyces and caudal appendages to the seeds; these last greatly facilitating the attainment of a situation favourable for their growth. Four species of the Clerodendron also adorn the banks of the Sarawak river, two of them bearing white, one scarlet, and one crimson flowers; one of the white ones emits a grateful perfume.

The Clerodendron which bears the crimson flowers is the most handsome of them all; it grows to a shrub of ten feet in height, having at the point of every branch a large loose spike of rich crimson flowers; the head of the flowers is frequently three feet in height from the foliage—rarely less than two—forming with the bracts and stems, which are equally crimson, a magnificent pyramid of flowers; each being relieved by a beautifully white centre and the long protruding stamens; the foliage is also fine, being heart-shaped, very large, and dense. This fine species, which is now growing well in England, I have named after Captain C. Drinkwater Bethune, R.N., C.B., whose kindness in Borneo was of the greatest assistance to me, and who, on his return, was successful in introducing some of the finest of the Borneo plants.

When the Clerodendron has ceased flowering, the crimson bracts and calyx which remain are scarcely less gaudy than the flowers, and each calyx contains within it a four-seeded berry of the richest blue colour. Scitaminæ, an order not much cultivated in England, produces some beautiful plants here of the genus Alpinia, and others. A fine white-fringed flowered Bignonia is a beautiful and fragrant shrub. An Echites, which produces its handsome blossoms abundantly in April and May, grows also on the banks of the rivers; it emits a delightful perfume. The beautiful Melas-tomas grow everywhere in open places, and their soft and pulpy fruit furnishes a never-failing supply of food to pigeons of every colour.

Of climbing-plants, a new and undescribed species of Bauhinia is the most showy, covering the trees in December with its large bunches of gaudy crimson blossoms. The Hoya imperialis is highly beautiful, its large and rich purple flowers being relieved by the white, ivory-like centre; it is epiphytal. On trees near the river various kinds of beautiful Combretums may be added to these; and Cyrtandraceæ produces species of Lysinotus and Æschynanthus, which yield to none in beauty: that which bears the name of the Earl of Auckland, (Lysinotus Aucklandii,) far surpasses any others yet known in the size and richness of colouring of the flowers, which are produced in bunches frequently containing twenty-four corollas; it is distinguished from others by its undulate and verticillate leaves, and the woody nature of the stems, which render it more a shrub than others of its genus.

On the mountains are found plants altogether different from these: there the genus Dacrydium, and others of the order Taxaceæ, resemble the cypresses and firs of our northern clime. Herbaceous plants of great beauty are also found on the exposed and damp rocks, while in mossy places the beautiful golden-leaved Anæctocheilus and a new and more beautiful species flourish. But of all those above mentioned, though they excel in beauty, none so much attract our curiosity as the various and beautiful pitcher-plants, eight different species of which I discovered in the western part of the island.

The pitchers, which in some instances would contain upwards of a pint of water, hang from the mid-rib of the leaf of which they are a formation ; they precisely resemble pitchers, being furnished also with a lid. The Nepenthes Rafflesiania produces its pitchers singly ; they are large and generally crimson : it grows on rocky islands in the neighbourhood of Singapore, and it is easily distinguished from its near ally the native of Borneo and Mount Ophir by its inferior size, shortness of the column which supports the lid, the white and powdered appearance of its stems, and its bushy habit, never exceeding four or five feet in height, while the largest Bornean one, which I propose to call Nepenthes Hookeriana, in honour of Sir W. J. Hooker, the able director of the Botanic Gardens at Kew, is found growing in deep and shaded jungles, climbing to the tops of the trees. The pitcher is nine inches in length, having a large lid standing on a column, which is a continuation of the beautiful edge of the pitcher : that part which is broadest and turned towards the mid-rib of the leaf from which it depends, is furnished with two broad wings, which are beautifully ciliated with large ciliæ; the broad pitcher—for this, like the Rafflesiana, produces two kinds—is generally crimson; the long pitcher differs from the other in its trumpet shape and green colour, which is spotted with crimson. The flower I have not seen, but the leaves, which are moderately large and broad—at least those of them which produce the broad pitcher, and which are found near the base of the plant—are dark green above, and of a fine peach-coloured red beneath. Six plants of this kind are now in England, but have not yet produced their pitchers.

The Nepenthes ampullacea produces its green or spotted short and broad pitchers in a different manner from the last: it is also a climbing plant, and found in thick jungles. The old stems, falling from the trees, become covered in a short time with leaves and vegetable matter, which form a coating of earth about them; they then throw out shoots which become in time new plants; but apparently the first attempts to form the leaf are futile, and become only pitchers, which, as the petioles are closely imbricated, form a dense mass, and frequently cover the ground as with a carpet of these curious formations. As it continues growing and endeavouring to become a plant, the laminæ of the leaves gradually appear, small at first, but every new one increasing in size, until finally the blades of the leaves are perfect, and the pitchers, which, as the leaves developed themselves, have become gradually smaller on each new leaf, finally disappear altogether when the plant climbs into the trees. This formation of the pitcher may afford an instructive lesson to the naturalist; as, though not to the same extent, the principle is perceptible in all of this curious tribe, the leaves of seedlings and weak plants always producing the largest pitchers.

The others cannot be enumerated, but one which approaches the Nepenthes boschianus of the Dutch must be mentioned on account of the elegance of its foliage and the beauty of its purple flowers : it produces small tubical pitchers, but in the greatest profusion ; it is a climbing plant on low shrubs, generally covering them to the height of about eight feet : it grows near the sea, on rocky places, and, as I have said before, is strikingly handsome ; if it be different from the boschianus, as I have no doubt it is, I should wish it to bear the name of the celebrated botanist, Dr. Lindley, whose kindness and advice have been always most beneficial to me.

It would be out of place, were I to occupy more space in a work of this nature in enumerating all the beauties of the kingdom of Flora displayed by the forests of this beautiful land ; and as they would be uninteresting to many, I will let those already noticed suffice, as they are quite numerous enough to show any one interested in flowers that those of Borneo are inferior to very few of the neighbouring islands or other tropical countries.

CHAPTER III.

THE fruits of the Indian islands since their first discovery, have been held in the highest esteem, and though neither care nor expense has been spared in endeavouring to cultivate them in other countries, as India, Ceylon, and the West Indian islands, they have never succeeded, though the fruits of these countries grow with the greatest luxuriance in the Archipelago.

" Malaya's nectared mangustin" has been by all writers placed at the head of the native lists of fruits, its delicious and delicate flavour having gained it a place in the estimation of Europeans over the rich and luscious Durian. In my opinion, though both of these are exceedingly fine, the Lansat (Lancium), when well ripened, has a peculiar aromatic flavour combined with all the delicacy of the mangustin, which renders its firm, transparent, and jelly-like pulp much more agreeable. The ' mangustin,' or, as the natives call it,

'buah manggis,' (buah, signifying fruit, being prefixed
to all the names of the different kinds as puhu and
kyuh are to trees,) is produced terminally by a tree
which attains the height of thirty feet, called, botanically, Garcinea mangustina; it is a very handsome
tree, the foliage, which is large and opposite, being of
the darkest shining green. The fruit, as large as a
moderate apple, is composed of an outer skin of a
soft and fibrous nature, dark purple on the outside,
but when cut of a bright crimson : the snow-white
pulp which envelopes the seeds, lying within this, has
an appearance no less beautiful to the eye than the
flavour is grateful to the palate; when cultivated, as
in the peninsula of Malacca, it fruits twice a year,
being ripe in July and December. The durian (Durio
zibethinus), the strong odour from which disgusts many
Europeans, is a large fruit from nine to twelve inches in
length; when ripe it opens into five divisions, each containing several seeds, which are environed by the rich
and cream-like acid. The tree which produces it is
lofty, frequently sixty or more feet in height. In Borneo
its seasons are irregular, but in favourable seasons it
produces three, and sometimes four, crops in immediate
succession, having the flowers, young fruit, and perfect,
all at one time. The flowers are produced in bunches
from the stem and older branches.

Of this fruit there are many kinds, some of which are
without the offensive odour complained of by Europeans : the most esteemed is called by the natives
' durian esa;' its coat is furnished with longer but
weaker spines than those of the other kinds. The wild

kind is common in the woods, as is the wild mangustin in those of Malacca. A species of mangustin produces the gamboge of commerce, which exudes also in small quantities from the cultivated varieties.

The fruits of the islands have been so well described by the writers on the Archipelago, that I will here do no more than enumerate them, referring to the other works for particular descriptions of them. The lansat is one of the finest; it is small, and produced in bunches from the stem and branches of the Lancium. The bread. fruit (Artocarpus) is well known; two kinds exist in Borneo, but neither are esteemed by the natives or Europeans. The 'nañgka,' or 'jack,' and the ' champadak,' are varieties of Artocarpus integrifolia; and differ from each other in the smaller size, and hairy stems of the latter. The Jack fruit is very large, and exudes abundantly a slimy matter which makes excellent bird-lime : a single fruit sometimes weighs sixty pounds; they esteem it, as it is constantly producing its rough looking fruit from the trunks and large branches. Though the tree grows forty feet high, it will produce fruit on small ones : a wild species is found in the jungle.

The ' tampui ' is an orange-coloured fruit produced on the stems and branches of a small tree, with large dark coloured leaves, of the order Sapotaceæ; its pulp is of a sweetish acid; the fermented juice makes an intoxicating liquor much esteemed by the Dyaks. The ' rhambut-an ' (Nephilium) is produced in bunches terminally; the pulp, which surrounds a seed of the size and flavour of a cob-nut, is transparent, and of a delicate sweetish acid flavour; it is very plentiful in the woods. The varieties of mango (Mangifera) are very numerous, but the island produces none of those of the fine flavour of the Indian ones: all the species known to Borneo, probably seven or eight, are found wild. Several kinds of ' jambu ' (Eugenia) are grown, but are not held in high esteem for their flavour, though they have a beautiful appearance. The ' blimbing' (Averoah), of which there are two kinds, are used by the natives in cookery, as are also the limes for purposes where acidity is required. The ' barañgan,' a kind of chestnut, is grown by the Dyaks, and the pomegranate is found with the fruits of India and America in the gardens of the Europeans.

To the above an extensive list of fruits produced in Borneo alone, and peculiar to it, might be added, but the papers containing it, together with several others of valuable notes, were left by me in Borneo, as on my departure for England I had not contemplated publishing my remarks on the island. The fruit trees generally receive little attention from the natives, and it is probably for this reason, that the seasons are so irregular. They are surrounded by the jungle, and, except to the experienced eye, are in no way to be distinguished from the trees composing it. In Penang and Malacca, where care is taken of the trees, they always produce fruit regularly twice a year—the small crop about July, the large and general crop about December.

Having thus, as far as the limited knowledge we possess will allow, noticed the principal vegetables and vegetable productions of the island, we pass in order to the animal kingdom, which, however, is not of such an extensive nature as to detain us so long in its description, although some of its forms are highly curious and interesting.

The larger and fiercer animals are not found in this island; so that, though its jungles teem with the smaller carnivora, the tiger, which is so abundant and destructive to human life in Singapore, on the peninsula of Malacca, in Sumatra, and in Java, never molests the traveller in these wilds. Of the larger animals, the elephant is said by the natives to exist in the northern parts of the island, but as they have never been seen by any of my informants themselves, I have not put much faith in the relation. The rhinoceros exists in the interior of the country, but as it is seldom seen, it must be very rare. An animal resembling the Malayan tapir has also been described to me, but I have not seen during my travels either of the above three animals, or even traces of their existence.

The small Malayan bear (Ursus Malayanus) is found on the west coast, but must be much more common in the country of the Kyans, as their dresses are frequently made of its skin. It is a well-known species, which feeds principally on vegetables, and climbs the trees in search of honey, frequently going up to the bees' nests on the lofty tapang. Deer are abundant, and of several kinds. The large Malayan rusa, common to the whole Archipelago (Cervus equinus), is very common all over the country, and affords excellent sport to the Europeans of

Sarawak in such places as are sufficiently open to allow of an approach to it. The flesh is coarse, and, being altogether devoid of fat, it is not esteemed by the Europeans, though much sought after by the Malays. It is said by the natives to be found occasionally white; it is then called ' rajah-rusa,' or the king-deer. Its usual colour is dark brown. The rutting season is about August.

The ' kijang,' or roe, as it is commonly called by Europeans, is the Cervus muntjack, an elegant animal, the points of the horns of which are turned forwards: it is of a light brown colour, about the size of the antelope, which, with the exception of the horns, it resembles in general appearance. The elegant little ' palandok' and its varieties are perhaps the smallest of the deer tribe, some of them being only eight inches in height at the shoulder. They live in very old woods, and feed entirely, as does the kijang, on leaves and berries, and they are particularly fond of the flower-buds of the beautiful Dillennia speciosa. They are so graceful and elegant in their forms and movements as to be universal pets. Their coat is covered with fine and glossy rich brown fur, and their eyes, which are large and dark, have all that soft and melting beauty which has rendered the gazelle so famous. Had the Malayan countries been as fertile in poets as those of the west, the palandok had doubtless occupied in their delightful romances the place at present ceded to the gazelle. They are frequently eaten; and, notwithstanding their fitness to adorn the page of poetry, they are not considered out of place on a well-furnished table.

Wild pigs are very plentiful, though they are constantly beset by the Dyaks and their traps in every jungle, so that it is astonishing that they have not been long since exterminated. They are of two kinds—the large, long-legged, and bristly brown pig, which is found most abundant near the sea shore, and the white, short-legged, and round-bodied pig of the interior. This is perhaps a mere variety of the Chinese breed, which has run wild, as it very much resembles those kept by these people. The flesh of both kinds is highly esteemed by the Dyaks, particularly at certain seasons when the fruits are ripe, as then the animal becomes fat, and its flesh of a better flavour.

Though the tiger itself is a stranger to the island, a kind of panther (Felis macrocelis) exists, but it is not of a sanguinary description, nor does its size render it dangerous. In appearance it is very similar to the hunting-chita of India. Many species of cat—amongst them the tiger- cat—are found. Some of them are fine and beautiful animals. Two or three kinds of otters, the civet-cat, and the pole-cat are common. The sloth is also known by the name of ' ka-malasan,' a word having the same signification as our term, which is, perhaps, but a translation of the Malayan one. The great anteater (Manis), called by the Malays ' peng-goling,' or the animal which rolls itself up, which this animal does, like the hedgehog, being in this position better defended by the scales with which its body is covered, is also to be found here. Many kinds of Lemur are seen in the woods. Some of the flying ones, particularly a long-tailed species (a species of Pteromys)

with very rich brown fur of a fine texture, are very rare
in Europe, and others are unknown to zoologists.
Squirrels are very numerous, and some of them are of
great beauty. The little Sciurus Rafflesiana is amongst
the most common and pretty. One species is very
large, and of a black colour; another resembles in
form the hare, being also nearly equal in size. Their
flesh is much valued by the Dyaks, and they will doubtless hereafter be prized for the tables of Europeans.

Monkeys are found in infinite variety, and of the
most rare and curious kinds: the true orang utan is
a native of no other country, and notwithstanding the
fabulous accounts of its resemblance to the human
species, which have so often amused the world, there
is still a sufficient degree of similarity to render the
comparison disgusting. It is found in the old jungles
on the banks of rivers in some parts of the island,
but not in the Sarawak territory, nor in that of Sambas; the tract of country between the Sadong and
Batang Lupar rivers extending across the island
in the direction of Pontianak, are the favourite haunts
of this strange animal. Two species of it have been
seen by Europeans, the larger called ' mias pappan,'
and the smaller, or ' mias rambi.' They are distinguished from each other by the greater size, more
abundant and long red hair, and the large processes
on each side of the head of the former; though both
are found in the same forests, the breed is said by
the natives never to be mixed: they do not attain the
large size which has been attributed to them, and it is
probable they rarely exceed five feet when measured from

the heel to the top of the head; those, the heights of which have been often given to the public as exceeding this, have been measured to the toes, the foot being of very great proportionate length.

In the jungle they are indolent animals, never jumping from tree to tree, as do the more active monkeys, but carefully securing their safety by previously catching hold with their hands; they do not make houses or huts in the jungle, but live in every respect as other large monkeys. Fruits are their food, and during the fruit season many of them are destroyed by the Dyaks stealing the, to them, prohibited food; they also occasionally do injury to the sugar-cane of the Dyaks. A story was once related to me of this animal by a Malay, which, though I cannot vouch for its truth, may perhaps amuse the reader:

" A Dyak, whose farm had been visited every night by the orang utan, watched for him carefully on a clear night, armed with a spear. Soon after night-fall the mias came, and, while seated on the fallen trunk of a tree masticating and extracting the sweets of the sugar-cane, was carefully approached by the Dyak, who succeeded in wounding him with the spear; but, as these animals when wounded fight desperately, he was also provided with a sword, which, however, in this instance, was not necessary, as the mias on turning to see by whom or what he was wounded, perceived coming down the trunk of the tree towards him, a bear, probably with the intention of only sharing his meal; but the mias, who did not see the man, fancied the bear the aggressor, and began to punish him accordingly. The Dyak fearing that perhaps they might see the real offender, and both set upon him, and terrified besides at the grunting of the one, and the growling of the other combatant, ran away as fast as possible; but on returning in the morning he found the bear dead on the field, and the mias also dead not far distant, his spear wound having much disabled him." If the story be true, the Dyak might thank the bear for interfering, as a full-grown mias is quite a match for a naked man, and generally before he can be killed contrives to bite off two or three fingers, or otherwise maim the individual. I have seen several Dyaks thus mutilated by them.

The long-nosed monkey (Semnopithecus nasicus) is exceedingly rare in the collections of Europe: it is remarkable for its very long nose; it is a very fine monkey, in size approaching the orang utan, but much less disgusting in appearance. It is furnished with a very long tail, and its fur is particularly fine, and of a pretty fawn colour; its eyes are very small, and bright; its teeth sharp and long; its head is small; it feeds on fruits. The curious nose of this species is long and fleshy, the bones of it not being larger than those of other monkeys of its size; the hands and feet are short, but very powerful, and the whole frame more muscular in proportion than that of the mias.

The 'wa-wa' (Hylobates) or long-armed ape, is the most beautiful of all the monkey tribe. This species has been

introduced into England, to the gardens of the Zoo-
logical Society, but has not, I believe, lived long.
The fur of this gentle little animal is grey; its face,
hands, and feet, are jet black; in features it more
resembles those of the human race than the orang
utan, or any other I have seen; it has no tail, and
feeds on fruits and insects; is delicate, and does
not, though it becomes very gentle, live long in con-
finement. It is abundant in the jungle, and in the
morning may be heard, close to the houses at Sarawak,
uttering its peculiar note, which has been aptly compared to the noise made by water being poured out of
a bottle. The moniet is a pretty little monkey, with
a long tail and grey fur, easily tamed, and very
amusing. The brùk, (Innuus nemestrimus), is a large
and disgusting short-tailed animal of the baboon kind.

Besides these are many others not distinguished by
particular names; many of them are perfectly unknown
to the naturalist, and would be very interesting to the
learned of this country. As all kinds of monkeys are
destructive to the rice-fields, the Dyak is equally their
enemy, and as these people esteem their flesh as an
article of food, no opportunity of destroying them is
lost; they are very abundant, and at night, about
sunset, all the trees on the banks of the river are
absolutely alive with them, they are in such astonishing numbers.

Reptiles, so abounding in moist and hot countries,
are found, as might be expected, in abundance here;
and the large size of the alligators (Crocodilus

biporcatus) and some kinds of serpents, testify the suitableness of the climate for them. The alligator is in some of the rivers of the west coast plentiful and voracious. It is said, that on the Sambas river it is dangerous in the highest degree to sleep in boats: they do not swarm in the river Sarawak as in that just mentioned, though they are numerous, and occasionally destructive. Many superstitions are observed by these half Mahometans respecting them, for it is supposed that they cannot be caught without the assistance of a person who charms them, called the ‘dukun buaya,’ or the alligator doctor.

In November, 1845, two persons having been taken by the alligators, the dukun was sent for to Sadong, a town and river to the eastward: the traps were set by him, which merely consisted of a cage made of bamboo and placed on posts above the water. In this was confined a Pariah dog, that by his barking and howling he might attract the alligators to the true bait which was hung beneath: it was a dead monkey, through the body of which had been passed a stout stick with a fine small rattan made fast to the centre. During the night the bait was taken away, and the doctor, accompanied by a great many men, went to search for the rattan, which, being small, passes between the crevices of the teeth so that the animal cannot bite it, and it remains attached to the stick, which by this time the alligator, in his attempts to evacuate, has got athwartwise in his throat. The top of the rattan floating soon discovers the retreat of the alligator, and then the conjuror's work begins. The alligator is addressed by all sorts of dignified and pathetic names; and it is asserted, that he is as quiet as possible in their hands, and suffers his hands and feet to be bound without a struggle. Certain it is, that the one now referred to was soon brought down the river, slung between two large boats, and escorted by the greater part of the male population of the town, with flags and banners flying, and drums and gongs beating. No native present spoke of the beast as the alligator, but always as the rajah, addressing it in such terms as these: " Will the rajah come ashore ?" " Will the rajah please to be quiet ?"

On reaching the grand wharf a large rope was bound round the body of the already powerless rajah, and 200 or 300 people soon dragged him ashore; now all consideration with all fear of him ended, and every one considered himself entitled to play the part of the ass in the fable, and they accordingly insulted in every way the now powerless monster. A heavy ' parang,' or chopping knife, was delivered to a man whose child had been taken, and he soon revenged himself by cutting off his victim's head. Till this time the animal had shown nothing but passive endurance, but, on feeling the knife, struggled furiously, but being bound every way was dispatched by his many executioners.

This animal was seventeen feet in length; but the doctor said it was not a mischievous one, so he set his traps again, and in two days we had the pleasure of seeing another brought down the river, which the dukun insisted upon being the wicked one; and when he was killed, the prediction was verified by the bones and clothes of a man being taken from his stomach. It was not so large as the former one, being only about fifteen and a half feet in length: a large piece had been broken off its bony nose by fighting with others of its tribe, and it was probably from this outward evidence of its disposition that the doctor was enabled to pronounce so confidently on its character. Since that one was destroyed we have not been troubled with them in Sarawak, though they are still numerous.

The 'biawak' of the Malays, called by Europeans the iguana, is plentiful in creeks near houses where poultry is kept, to which it proves very destructive. In appearance it resembles the alligator, but rarely attains a greater length than six feet. A smaller animal, called by the same name, which lives in woods and climbs trees, is much valued by the Dyaks as a delicate article of food. Many other kinds of the lizard tribe, under various names, are also abundant in trees and in grassy places, amongst old houses, &c. The most beautiful are the green ones, resembling the chameleon, of which there are several kinds; they live on flies and other insects.

The flying lizard (Draco volans) is a curious and harmless little animal, which is frequently found about the pinang, and other trees, in the vicinity of the European houses. The 'chichak' is a little

lizard found in houses, running along the walls
and ceilings in search of flies; the structure of their
feet enabling them to do this by creating a vacuum
beneath the foot: this is proved by their not being
able to sustain themselves on cloth, which often forms
the ceilings of houses in Borneo. They sometimes
fall, and their tails get broken off, but, being possessed
of the power of reproduction, the loss is soon supplied
—a new tail growing in its place.

The land-tortoises are of at least two species, one
of which attains considerable size : I once had one in
my possession which was nearly two feet in length.
They are found in the thick and damp woods: their
food is vegetable; their eggs are long and linear,
rounded at the ends, hard, like that of the alligator,
not with a soft shell, as that of the turtle.

All the marshes abound with frogs, which croak
their dismal notes during the whole night; they are
fed upon by the snakes, which are in great numbers
in the same situations. Many of the snakes of Borneo
are unknown to European naturalists. The crested
cobra of India is found here, and called by the
natives ' ular tadong '—but I think that tadong is a
generic name, applied to many of the venomous ones,
—and the beautiful but deadly ' tadong matahari,' or
the sun-snake (Tortrix), and the ' tadong chinchin mas,'
or golden-ringed viper (Dipsas dendrophila), deriving
its name from the beautiful golden rings with which its
black body is adorned: this kind is very common in
mangrove swamps, ascending the trees to sleep at
high water, and descending to search for its prey

when the tide has receded. The 'ular ledong' (Trigonocephalus Waglerii), or, as it is called by Europeans, the hammer-headed viper, from the great proportionate breadth of its head, is also very venomous; its body is short and thick, and it is of very sluggish habits.

There are many other kinds which have poisonous fangs; but, notwithstanding their number, accidents rarely occur from them. Those which are poisonous rarely are large, the cobra never exceeding six feet in length, while the green hammer-headed viper does not attain that length. The largest of the snake tribe are the different kinds of the 'ular sawah' (Python), found in damp and marshy places: they are called boa by Europeans. I never met with them larger than fourteen feet in length; but while I was in the country a native killed one, which had an undigested deer with horns in its stomach, and must have been considerably larger. None of these large snakes are venomous, being provided with strength sufficient to ensure the capture of their prey: those not venomous are more numerous than the others.

Amongst them is a small one, called 'ular bunga' (Dryophis prassina), or the flower-snake; it is of the most rich and beautiful green colour above, resembling velvet, and yellow beneath, with a slender and graceful form; it is very pretty, and a favourite animal with the Malays. A very venomous one resembles it; and, during my stay, a fatal accident had nearly occurred to an European gentleman, who, having one of them brought to him, thought it had been a flower-snake, and was putting his hand

into the basket to take it out, when fortunately the
native observed it in time to prevent the fatal consequences. In the river are various kinds of water-
snakes, some of them very large; they are also
common in the sea, and of beautiful colours; many of
them are said to be poisonous.

The woods of this island, and every other part of
it, teem with insect life. The butterflies are large, and
of gaudy colours, many of them of very curious forms;
they appear to be irregular in their seasons, at some
periods being very plentiful, at others rarely seen.
Beetles are very scarce, and, excepting three or four
fine kinds, which are occasionally met with about
the lamps in the houses at night, are difficult to be
procured. Many species of garden bugs are found,
which, though beautiful to the eye, are of a very
unpleasant odour.

The spiders, so disgusting in appearance in many
other countries, are here of quite a different nature,
and are the most beautiful of the insect tribe: they
have a skin of a shell-like texture, furnished with ·
curious processes, in some long, in others short, in
some few, in others numerous; but are found, of this
description, only in thick woods and shaded places:
their colours are of every hue, brilliant and metallic as
the feathers of the humming-bird, but are, unlike the
bright colours of the beetle, totally dependent on the
life of the insect which they beautify, so that it is
impossible to preserve them.

The noisy cicadas sing their shrill notes from

every tree, and the chorus is always supplied by
the numerous varieties of grasshoppers which everywhere abound. No one who has not walked in
similar jungles, can imagine the noisy concert produced by the loud and shrill voices of so many insects
during the whole day, which is increased towards
evening by the many lizards, frogs, snakes, &c., so as
to be almost deafening. Bees, of different descriptions,
are found in the woods in great abundance, and this
is the only country of the Archipelago where those
little insects are known to be kept in a domestic
state.

Having noticed the productions of the land sufficiently
for our purpose, those of the sea and waters claim our
attention. The fish of the Archipelago are very numerous, and some of them particularly fine. The
pomfret, or 'ikan bawal,' two kinds of mullet, and the
sole are much esteemed by Europeans. The natives
seldom eat their fish in a fresh state, but it is for the
most part salted and dried in the sun, and in this
state forms an extensive article of trade between the
sea coasts and the interior country. Large fishing
establishments are found at the mouths of all the
principal rivers during the S. W., or fine monsoon;
the fishermen usually leaving them during the N. E.,
or boisterous monsoon, and returning to the town,
where they pursue other avocations until fine weather
again brings the shoals of fish to their shores. One
kind of fish, the 'ikan trobuk,' is caught in great
numbers during this season on the west coast: it is

valued for its large roe, which, being extracted, is salted and dried, and sent to those parts of the coast which do not possess it.

The 'blâchang' is a kind of fish paste of several qualities. That most in esteem is made of a species of very small shrimp, which, in the fine season, is found in enormous numbers on the borders of the sea : it is salted and pounded in a mortar, and being made up into little parcels is sent into the interior, where it is highly esteemed. The inferior kind is made of all kinds of little fish—shrimps, &c., in the same way, but does not bear so high a price : they both have an odour which renders them offensive to Europeans.

Sharks' fins and 'tripang,' or sea slug, are exported by the Bugis boats from the eastern parts of the island ; they are first sent to Singapore, afterwards to China. Tortoise-shell is also found in these seas, but not in such abundance as amongst the islands further to the eastward. The turtle is very common on the small islands off the coast. Its flesh is not eaten by the natives, but its eggs form a considerable article of trade. Shell-fish of several kinds are found upon the coasts, the oysters being of very great abundance, and of very fine flavour. The pearl and the mother-of-pearl oyster also abound, and the fishery of the Soolu islands has been long known and highly valued : in proper hands it would be the finest in the world ; but pearls are produced in plenty all along the northern coast. The prawns produced by the seas and rivers of this island are of the very finest flavour, and many other edible shell-fish are in perfection. The sperm whale is found amongst the quiet seas of the eastern coasts, and the fishery is often profitable to the American vessels employed in it. There is little doubt, should our new settlement at Labuh-an prosper, and form a colony in these seas, that to the above list of marine productions many will soon be added.

Ambergris is found in the Indian seas, but I am not certain that those of the coast of Borneo produce it. Under the fostering care of the British government, the natives themselves will in a great measure assist in developing the resources of this rich island; and when European skill and capital are employed, as they are likely to be, we may soon see its valuable productions forming a larger, and much more important item than they have hitherto done in the commerce of the Archipelago.

Of the domestic animals but few are kept on the west coast of Borneo, though the buffalo (kerbau) is well known on the south and north, at Banjarmasin and Borneo; they are probably abundant on the east coast. I have not heard of their having ever been found wild in the island, and from their scarcity should think they have been introduced. They are sometimes brought to Sarawak by the chiefs for their festivals, from the Natunas islands, where they are plentiful. The cow is of the Indian breed, having a hump at the shoulders; they are small, but prettily shaped cattle, and when furnished with good pasture afford excellent beef : they are plentiful at Bruni and to the northward, but not on the west coast, and are sold to the ships of war at a very cheap rate. The cows of this breed kept at Sarawak do not give much milk, though the little they produce is very rich.

About the river of Tanjong Barram, and on the Sangow river, is a breed of wild cattle called by the name of ' banting,' (Bos Sondiacus), they are said to be very wild and fierce, living chiefly in bamboo forests, on the young shoots of which they feed. Were they not in such inaccessible parts of the country, they would furnish excellent sport to the Europeans; and if in very great numbers, their hides and tallow might become an article of commerce. Horses, of a small breed, are also plentiful in the northern and southern parts of the island, though unknown on the western coast. In Banjarmasin, as in Celebes, they are trained to hunt the deer, which are caught by a lasso, the loop of which being carried on a light bamboo is passed over the head of the animal. This sport can only be followed in open countries, which are not found on the western coast. It is a favourite amusement with the Bugis nobles of Celebes, and has been by them introduced into the south and east coasts of Borneo.

Amongst the Kyans and sea Dyaks, and in most of the Malayan towns many goats are kept, but the land Dyaks have none of them, as their superstitious belief, hereafter to be mentioned, prevents their using the flesh of these animals. They are of a small breed, and are killed by the Kyans and sea Dyaks on festival days; but their flesh is not so much esteemed as that of the pigs, which they keep in large quantities. The Dyak pig very much resembles the breed of China, being short and broadly made little animals; when fattened and kept by the Chinese, who purchase them from the Dyaks, their flesh is valued at the European tables on the west coast, where neither beef nor mutton is procurable except at rare intervals. The Dyaks have also a small kind of currish looking dog, which is very useful to them in the jungle, in hunting the wild hog, the deer, and the palandok: these little animals are of a reddish colour in general, though they vary as do the dogs of Europe. The Chinese settlers have a larger breed, which, when young and well fattened, form an esteemed dish at their tables.

The cats of the Malays have been mentioned, and described by many writers, their peculiar tails having always attracted attention. The joints of the tail are crooked, so that the tail appears, as it were, tied in a knot, nor can the animal itself straighten it: this breed being mixed with the European for some generations does not entirely lose this remarkable deformity.

Of domestic poultry both ducks and fowls are kept by the Malays, the latter only by the Dyaks. Mr. Brooke has attempted to introduce others, and has for this purpose distributed many geese among these people. He has also endeavoured by the introduction of the larger Cochin China breed of fowls to improve the small race now kept by the Dyaks. Pigeons are occasionally, though rarely, seen amongst the Malays; but I have never seen them in the Dyak villages.

CHAPTER IV.

HAVING in the foregoing chapters given a general
description of the island of Borneo, or Kalamantan,
and having enumerated such of its vegetable, mineral,
and other productions, as cannot with equal propriety
be introduced into other parts of the work, it becomes
necessary to notice the political divisions of the land,
and to inquire, as far as our at present very limited
knowledge will allow, into the situation of the many
tribes inhabiting it, and their relations to each other.

The island has been, from its first discovery by Europeans, separated into several kingdoms, the limits and
power of which have been constantly changing, their
extent and influence generally depending on the talent
and tastes of their respective chieftains.   The Malays,
who settled here on the north coast during the flourishing periods of the kingdoms of Singapore, Malacca,
and Johore, have become so mixed with the Javans
who colonized the western and southern shores, as to

have given their name to the whole of the people in
these districts; but though it is very common to
call the people of each town or kingdom the Malays
of such or such a place, it would be much more correct to designate them by a term derived from the
name of the town or kingdom of which they are
inhabitants; for though they have a very considerable
general resemblance to the Malays of Sumatra and the
peninsula, any person accustomed to see both people
can readily distinguish one from the other. Though this
distinction is so perceptible, that even the descendants
of the different races which have colonized the various
parts of the island are to this day easily separated, it is
more difficult to reduce it to writing. No person
conversant with these people would be for an instant
at a loss to distinguish one of the natives of the town
of Bruni from a person descended from the Javan
colonists of Sarawak, and yet these differ from the
present natives of their parent island, as much as from
the people of Bruni.

The kingdom of Bruni is said by the natives
themselves to have been first formed by large settlements of Chinese; and in Forrest's Voyages he
relates that the brothers of Serif Ali, the first
sultan of Magindanau, of the Mahommedan religion,
became King of Borneo towards the latter part of the
fifteenth century. It is probable that these brothers,
with another who became Sultan of Soolu, had in
their capacity of zerifs, or descendants of the prophet,
gathered many followers on their road from Mecca at

the Malayan kingdoms on the peninsula, and thus
have appeared, at the kingdoms of which they afterwards became the sovereigns, not only as spiritual
teachers, but also as temporal princes. It is not likely
that the three came at one time, but the Sultan of
Magindanau being himself successful, perhaps invited
the other two.

There still existed during the lifetime of the late
rajah, Mudah Hassim, the genealogical tree of the
royal family of Borneo, and annals of its history,
but after his lamented death I could not learn what
had become of them; and the surviving brother,
the present rajah, Mudah Mohammed, feared that
these relics, which had been preserved through generations with the most religious care, had perished in
the flames of the houses of the murdered pañgerans.
These Mahometans, being more proud of their ancestry
than those of the eastern world will allow themselves
to be, take the greatest possible care of the histories of their families. On returning to the island
I shall not fail to try by every means to obtain these
papers, or copies of them, if they should be found
still to exist.

The Arab xerif, or serif from Mecca, is said to
have married the daughter of the last of the infidel
kings, and thus the Malays were established in this
part of the island; but it is curious, that, if this
had been a powerful Chinese settlement, so few
traces of their language or customs exist; and I
should rather be inclined to suppose, in the absence of
authentic documents, that the Chinese population was

not considerable, nor, previous to the arrival of the
Arabs and Malays, the kingdom either extensive or
influential.   Abundant proof exists, both in the tra-
ditions of the inhabitants, and the written histories of
Java, that colonies from that island were' the first
foreign settlers on the southern and western coasts, as
far north as Sarawak; and during the thirteenth
century we find the whole of the southern and western
shores of Borneo, which are described as having at that
period no regular government, protected by the sultan
of the powerful Hindu state of Majapahit, in Java,
against the piratical inhabitants of Lampung in Sumatra, who thus early appear to have been dangerous
in those seas.

After the fall of Majapahit, and the triumph of
the Mahometan religion in Java, A. D. 1478, the
colonies of the coasts of Borneo are said to have become independent; but in 1643 we find the chief of
the Javanese colony of Banjarmasin, and in 1653 the
Sultan of Sucadana, sending missions of homage to the
then Sultan of Motarem in Java.   In 1687 the Dutch
attacked Sucadana at the instance of the King of
Bantam, whose right to interfere in their country
was, however, denied by the people of Sucadana.

As has been previously observed, the descendants of
the Javanese colonies are all now denominated Malays,
and they call themselves ' orang Malayu,' and ' orang
laut'—meaning, respectively, Malay men, and men
from the sea.   These descendants of Javans have
mixed more with the aborigines of the countries than
any other tribes of the coast, and it is probable that

it is this mixture of race which serves to distinguish them in person, as already noticed, from the present inhabitants of Java, as the mixture with the Chinese may have altered the race of the kingdom of Borneo from the true Malay of Sumatra. The east coasts of the island appear to have been occupied by the Bugis people of Celebes, who have kept themselves more distinct, and their blood more pure than the other races, so that the Bugis of Pasir or of Coti is in no way distinguishable from his countryman on the opposite island of Celebes. These are all the tribes inhabiting the sea-coast : they profess the Mahometan religion, and from the power given to them by being in possession of the mouths of the rivers, they have always continued to hold the Dyaks, the Kyans, and other aboriginal tribes in some degree of subjection, though in general, when the weakness of the Malayan governments, or other causes, presented opportunities of throwing off their allegiance, these have been duly seized; and the Kyans of the Barram, Bintulu, and Rejang rivers, and the Dyaks of Sarebas and Sakarran, at present allow of no coast government's interference.

The aboriginal inhabitants, which, doubtless of the same race as their more civilized and power-ful neighbours, but now differing much from them, have, though divided into several families, so great a general resemblance as to mark them undoubtedly equally the offspring of the great Polynesian race. At present they are distinguished by the Malays, and after them by the Europeans, as the orang Dyak and

H

the orang Kyan; the orang Milanowe, Tedong, Kadyan, Idaan, and Merut, and some others, being smaller
divisions, and differing in some particulars from either
of the two first and greatest divisions. The peculiarities
of each will be described in portions of the work which
will be devoted to them; and as here it is more our
object in mentioning them to facilitate our description
of the division of the country into Malayan kingdoms,
it will suffice to say that, independent of their similarity of language and many customs, the great and
distinguishing feature of their character—the barbarous
custom of taking and prizing as objects of pride and
triumph the heads of their enemies—is equally common
to all the ramifications of their tribes.

The descendants of the Malays of the peninsula
appear to have formed no other kingdom in the island
than that of Bruni, which has been of sufficient importance to have caused strangers to apply to the whole
island the appellation of Borneo, a corruption of the
name of this state.   During the time of its greatest
power, in the 16th and 17th centuries, it governed the
whole of the north-west coast, from Tanjong Dattoo, in
long. 109° 41' east, and lat. 2° 5' 22" north, to the opposite or eastern shores.   All the tribes of the many rivers
in this extensive district are said to have acknowledged
its sway; and it was divided into provinces, each of
which was governed by wise though rigorous laws,
administered under the immediate superintendence of
a pañgeran, or noble, sent directly from the capital,
which, when visited by Pigafetta, the companion of the

celebrated Magellan, about the year 1521, contained 25,000 families. He says of it, that " La ville est bâtie dans la mer même, excepté la maison du roi et de quelques principaux chefs. Elle contient vingt-cinq milles feux ou familles. Les maisons sont construites de bois, et portées sur de grosses poutres pour les ga-rantir de l'eau ; lorsque la marée monte, les femmes qui vendent les denrées nécessaires traversent la ville dans des barques." (Pigafetta, extracted from Mr. Crawfurd, vol. i. p. 172.) Excepting in size, and the wooden structure of the houses, the description is suitable to the present town.

In 1645 the Malays of Borneo, in conjunction with their allies, the people of Soolu, attacked the Spanish settlements in the Philippines, doing much damage. This was in revenge for the repeated but unsuccessful attacks of the Spaniards on the Soolu islands. Soon after, the Spaniards burnt the city of Borneo, and took many of the inhabitants prisoners, but were disgrace-fully beaten by the Soolus in 1751, in their last great attempt upon that island. Since that time the kingdom has gradually lost its importance.

In 1776 we find, by Forrest's account, that the Soolus were the deadly enemies of the Borneans, these latter alleging that the former had encroached upon their territories ; which was doubtless the case, as the people of Soolu had ceded to the English the whole of the northern part of the island, from the Kimanis river on the west, to the great bay on the east, to which territory they had no other right

than that of conquest.   In 1774, we find one of the
terms of agreement between the Sultan of Borneo and
the government of Balambangan,—the settlement
established by the English in the previous year,—
respecting the establishment of a trading factory in
Bruni, to be, that the English should protect his
kingdom against his enemies the Soolus, on condition
of having the monopoly of the Bornean pepper.
Neither parties, it is said, fulfilled the agreement
contracted by Mr. Jesse, though the residency at
Borneo was continued for several years after the abandonment of Balambangan.   It was finally withdrawn,
the intestine troubles of the state, and consequent
anarchy, rendering it unproductive.

Of the Javanese settlements on the west and southern coast, Sucadana and Banjarmasin have been the
most considerable.   The territory of the former was,
as has been previously mentioned, ceded to the Dutch
by the Sultan of Bantam in 1778.   It was destroyed
by them, and the new and rival state of Pontianak,
where they established a fort and factory, was encouraged, but soon fell into insignificance under their
protection, and was abandoned by them after an occupation of fourteen years.   In 1823 they again returned
to Pontianak, and purchased the monopoly of the
diamond mines of the sultan for 50,000 dollars:
they have since retained possession of the place, though
it is not supposed to be profitable to them.

Banjarmasin, in the south of Borneo, is another
Javanese state which, on account of its exports, has

always enjoyed consideration; and, notwithstanding the occupation of the Dutch, is still a place of great trade, exporting quantities of gold, diamonds, pepper, rattans, and dragon's blood. In 1706 the English attempted to establish a factory at Banjar, but before their forts were finished their haughty and insolent behaviour brought down upon them the vengeance of the sultan, who attacked and burnt their settlement in the night with 3,000 men; but as the Europeans had received notice of his intention, they had retired to their ships, which, to the number of four, were in the harbour; but these also were attacked by the infuriated sultan and his injured subjects, so that though the larger two escaped, the two smaller ones were burnt, together with the greater part of their crews. Soon after, the sultan, finding the loss of trade affected his revenues, informed the English that a free trade might be carried on with his dominions, but that he would never suffer them, nor any other nation, to fortify themselves in his country.

In 1714 the English company, wishing to restore its trade and factory at Banjar, sent Capt. Daniel Beeckman, a gentleman of great discretion and ability. This person had an opportunity of seeing the great odium in which the company was held; but by his conciliatory conduct, and by giving the natives to understand that the ships were in no way connected with the company, but private traders, he succeeded in getting cargoes of pepper, though he found it impossible to get permission to re-establish the factory. In

1747 the Dutch succeeded in establishing a settlement, which, as has been before stated, was continued till 1810, when it was formally abandoned by the then Dutch governor-general, Marshal Dændals; it was soon after re-occupied by the English from Java, at the invitation of the sultan, and was, together with the other possessions of the Dutch in the East which the English had occupied during the war, delivered over to that nation at the general peace.

Coti, the largest of the Bugis kingdoms on the island, has been but little known to Europeans: the inhabitants are of the same commercial disposition as those of their countrymen in the other parts of the Archipelago. In 1825 the Dutch sent an expedition for the purpose of exploring the river, which is said to be one of the largest in the island. It was commanded by Major Muller, a gentleman who had been long employed surveying on the western coast, but it was unfortunate in its termination. The major and his attendants were murdered by the Dyaks at the instigation of the Bugis who accompanied him, after having ascended the river upwards of 300 miles from its mouth.

It is said that Major Muller, on his first arrival, had made an arrangement with the sultan, by which the latter had agreed to permit the Dutch to settle, and monopolize the commerce of the place, they paying annually the sum of 80,000 guilders into the royal treasury. When this compact became known to the nobles, with whose interests it would have seriously interfered, they remonstrated so strongly with the sultan that he regretted having made the agreement, and, to destroy all evidence of it, caused the Dyaks to assassinate Major Muller and his party. Since then the unfortunate death of the Honourable Mr. Murray, in 1845, while gallantly fighting his two ships down the river, has brought the place under the notice of the English and protection of the Dutch, as the sultan, fearing that Mr. Murray's death might be revenged by the English, consented to the establishment of a Dutch residency, and a gentleman of that nation now resides at Semerindem, the Bugis capital. The Sultan of Coti does not appear to have been to blame in his conduct to Mr. Murray, that gentleman appearing to have insulted him grievously, and by his conduct to have brought upon himself the displeasure of the nobles and other orders in the place.

Pasir is another Bugis settlement, a little to the south of Coti, but has never been so important. The remainder of the eastern coast to the northward of Coti, is nominally tributary to the kingdom of Soolu, the people of which have large settlements on it; but there are also several wild and independent tribes.

Besides the kingdoms of the coast above enumerated, there are several other small settlements of more recent formation on the south and western coasts; of Bugis, and the Javanese Malays, who are the chiefs of them, as of the settlements of Soolus and Magindanau. Pirates on the northern and eastern parts of the island frequently arrogate to themselves the title of sultan, though their states are of little power or consideration.

Sambas, on the western coast, formerly a piratical station, but destroyed by the English, has become a kingdom of some consideration: the Dutch established themselves there in 1823, for the purpose of hemming in, and thus stopping all the supplies of the refractory Chinese gold-workers of the country situated between the Sambas and Pontianak rivers, whom they could not otherwise reduce : they pay the sultan an annual sum for the monopoly of the trade, which they farm out to the Malays at a great profit.

From the preceding sketch of the several—and as they are generally called collectively and to distinguish them from the Aborigines—the Malayan nations, it will be seen that the principal kingdoms on the western coast are those of Sambas and Pontianak, to the latter of which the large settlements in the diamond and gold districts of Landak and Sangau are nominally tributary.   On the southern coast Banjarmasin is the most powerful, Sucadana having fallen into insignificance, and on the eastern the kingdom of Coti; and on the northern and north-western the state of Bruni, or Borneo Proper, of which the principality of Sarawak is a large and flourishing settlement.

As it is not our wish or in our power to furnish complete histories of these kingdoms, we shall pass on to the description of the inhabitants of the island, in their different classes, merely premising, that what is said of the Malays applies more particularly to the descendants of the Javanese on the western coast, except when it is stated expressly to the contrary;

these people being selected from the other Mahometans, since they are those with which the English have had the greatest communication, and whose habits they have in consequence had the best opportunities of observing.

It is certain that none of the Mahometan kingdoms of the island possess at present so much influence, or such extensive territories, as during the flourishing periods of their history,—the first and second centuries after their conversion to Islamism. The power of Pontianak, the pet settlement of the Dutch, is considerable, but its sultan is a mere puppet in the hands of that nation. Had the talented rajahs of Borneo, who, in the beginning of last year, fell a sacrifice to their patriotic exertions for the rescue of their country from its fallen state, been spared, we might have hoped to have seen it soon restored in some measure to its ancient power and consideration; but as if Providence had ordained that it should not be at this time renovated, every one of the royal family possessing the least good sense, principle, or talent, fell a sacrifice to the cruelty of the most ignorant and brutal of princes that ever disgraced even an eastern throne.

Some hope, however, yet remains for Borneo, from the family of the murdered rajah, Mudah Hassim; his sons, though still young, showing indications of a high order of intelligence ; and as they are residing at Sarawak, where the European missionaries will shortly be established, it is to be hoped that these gentlemen will have opportunities, and be successful, in instilling into their minds such principles as will hereafter enable them to fill, with profit to the nation and honour to themselves, the high station in it which they are born to occupy. The great fear is, that should the life of the present unprincipled and idiotic tyrant be long continued, his maladministration, or, more properly speaking, that of his corrupt advisers, may reduce the country to so low a state, that to raise it again will be impossible; but the talents and energy of Mr. Brooke, the governor of the new settlement at Labuh-an, are a sufficient guarantee, that if it should be thought advisable to continue Omar Ali in the government, he will be surrounded by advisers who will have at heart more than their master the interests of the kingdom and of the heirs to the throne.

We have seen that at the visit of Pigafetta the capital alone was estimated to contain 25,000 families : 200 years after, it was computed to be only 40,000 persons, with a Chinese population in its neighbourhood, employed in the cultivation of pepper, amounting to 30,000 persons. At present the town may be said to be in ruins; the houses being no longer built of wood, and on those strong posts described by Pigafetta, but of atap leaves and on nibong posts, which are frequently in a very tottering condition.

The present native population is not estimated to exceed 12,000, and the Chinese have altogether disappeared, the very few that are occasionally seen having been reduced by the Borneans to slavery; thus by the dissensions of the nobles and princes has a once powerful and flourishing state been reduced to the condition of a miserable village. Before the abandonment of the town by the Chinese, several large junks annually visited Borneo, and many were built at the town, of the fine timber with which the country abounds. These were sent to China loaded with the produce of the island, and on being sold in that country, realized a profit exceeding 300 per cent.; as timber, fit for the purposes of ship building, is very expensive in China.

The government of Borneo appears to have been despotic, or oligarchical, according as the power and talent of the prince or the nobles prevailed. The great officers of state appear usually to have been selected from the royal family. The title of the prince was formerly Iang-de-per-tuan, which has been translated, "The lord who rules;" but "the ruler" appears to be equally appropriate. The second person in the kingdom was formerly styled the Rajah Mudah, and was the successor to the throne; but the present sultan, Omar Ali, has never been properly invested with the supreme title of Iang-de-per-tuan, and is, consequently, only styled sultan by courtesy—a title foreign to the court language of Borneo.

The character of the present ruler of Borneo has been frequently before the English public during the last few years. He is a man of upwards of fifty years of age, of dark complexion, and stupid features. On his right hand he has a malformation resembling a thumb, which stands at an angle from the true thumb. This

alone, according to the laws of Borneo, would have
disqualified him for the throne; for these provide that
no person in any way imbecile in mind, or deformed
in person, can enjoy the regal dignity, whatever title
his birth might have given him. His mind also is
weak, approaching to idiotcy; he is, nevertheless,
possessed of a wicked disposition, by encouraging
which his worthless advisers have held their sway over
him; amd by these means it was that the insolent
rebel, Pañgeran Usnf, possessed his undue influence in
the councils of the kingdom. His weakness of intellect, combined with the depravity of his disposition, causes him to be swayed by the advice
of the last speaker, and the worst and most wicked
counsels are sure to be the most acceptable to him.

His object being immediate gain, his covetous disposition eagerly seizes upon all means of supplying
his cupidity; and it was by their knowledge of this
trait in his character that the pañgerans, who insti-
gated the murder of those rajahs that insisted upon
the suppression of piracy, gained the consent of their
avaricious lord. These unprincipled men are reported
to have laid before the sultan a statement of the riches
which would accrue to him from murdering his relations; and the weak old man is said so eagerly to have
coveted the goods of his kinsmen, that so soon as the
murder and pillage were accomplished, his agents carried the plunder to the anxiously expecting sultan.

This consisted principally of the presents which had
been made to the rajahs by Mr. Brooke and the

English government through Captain C. Drinkwater Bethune, R.N. C.B. The whole of the property for which this man murdered eleven of his relatives could not have exceeded the value of a few hundred dollars; the rajahs during their absence, while attempting to quell the insurrection of Sarawak, having been despoiled of the revenues of their estates by the sultan and the Pañgeran Usnf, then his prime minister.

He has been happily described by a person who saw him and knew him in Borneo, as possessing the " head of an idiot, and the heart of a pirate." He has frequently said, that provided he be supplied with money, and his harem be filled with women, he does not care who governs the country, or in what manner it is done.

The two men who are called by the sultan his sons, Pañgeran Hassim and his brother, are the well-known offspring of two Bornean nakodahs, or merchants, introduced to the harem by the sultan himself, nature having fortunately denied this imbecile the power of propagating his like. Neither Pañgeran Hassim nor his brother have had at any time thoughts of being successful in any attempts to succeed the sultan, though it had been the declared intention of Pañgeran Usnf,—who was driven from Borneo by the admiral, in 1845, for having detained slaves, and for having fired at the admiral's own ship, and who was afterwards killed by the Pañgeran Bed-er-ed-din, at Kimanis,—in the event of the sultan's death to endeavour to place himself on the throne. Since

the murder of the rajahs, and the attack on Borneo
in consequence, by Admiral Sir Thos. Cochrane,
last year, the sultan has been quiet, and has given
repeated assurances of protection to the two surviving brothers of Bed-er-ed-din and Mudah Hassim,
if they will return from Sarawak to Bruni: in his
letters to them he has also stated, that the murder
of their relatives took place against his wish, and that
it was perpetrated by Pañgeran Hassim and the others
of the party friendly to the late Pañgeran Usnf and his
piratical practices, and of consequence inimical to their
relations with the English.   The sultan has moreover
promised to govern according to the councils of the
Pañgeran Moulmein, the brother-in-law of the late
Rajah Mudah, and the other nobles recommended
to him by Mr. Brooke on the part of the British
government.   The country is now quiet, and the near
vicinity of our new settlement will probably keep it so;
but the intriguing and restless nature of the Borneans
will probably cause petty disturbances to be of frequent
occurrence.

The flourishing settlement of Sarawak promises
soon to eclipse in power and importance the capital
of the kingdom to which it is tributary.   Through
the work of Captain Keppel, the enterprise and character of Mr. Brooke have been laid before the public;
and the hero of the work is now in London, receiving
the rewards and honours which a country proud of his
achievements and character are liberal in bestowing
on him.   The discovery of the antimony ore, the

oppression to which it gave rise, the rebellion in consequence, its continuance and suppression, are all related in the above work in the words of the Rajah of Sarawak. His principality, which is situated in the north-west corner of the island, extends from the Tanjong Dattu on the west, to the river Samarhand on the east, comprising an extent of coast in a straight line of about seventy geographical miles in length: it varies, but the average depth is between seventy and eighty miles, being bounded on the west by Sambas, on the south by Sangau, and on the east by Sadong and Samarhand; but though this country is the actual principality and property of the rajah, his influence and government extend over a much greater space, but weaker, of course, in proportion to the distance at which the respective countries are situated from his residence.

Samarhand, Sadong, and Lingah have equal or nearly equal reason with Sarawak to rejoice in his government; for, by the authority granted to him by the rajahs of Borneo, and at the prayer of the natives themselves, he has been enabled to correct many abuses, and in particular to stop the kidnapping of the Dyaks for slaves in the Sadong territory, which formerly prevailed to as great an extent as in the immediate territory of Sarawak. This province, not being cursed by an indigent nobility, as is the capital, where princes, nobles, and their slaves and followers, form a large proportion of the population—but the people being in a more inartificial state, and of more simple and less intriguing natures—has been brought by the perseverance of Mr. Brooke into the prosperous and peaceful state it now enjoys.

The people of Sarawak (we are now speaking of the viceroy, the Malays of the town), at the retirement of the former Pañgeran Makota, formed a population of about 2,000 souls. At present the town is supposed to contain nearly 8,000 inhabitants; this great and increasing population having flocked from the misgoverned towns along the coast to a settlement where their persons were inviolate and their property secure. The town is situated on the river of the same name, and was called by the natives Kuching; but the name of the river is now universally employed also to designate the town. The houses of the natives are built on each side of two reaches of the river, and are divided into kampongs or clusters, which are generally named after the chief or other principal person about whose house the others are collected; they are also frequently named from other circumstances, as the 'kampong bharu,' or the new kampong, and the 'kampong Pa-mutus' or the kampong inhabited by the people who settled here from Pa-mutus in the Batang Lupar river, on its destruction by Captain Keppel.

The Chinese occupy a kampong on the bank of the river, opposite to the residences of the Europeans, which occupy hills on the left bank. The fort is a six-gun battery, commanding the reach immediately below the town, being situated on the right-hand bank, below the Chinese houses: it is garrisoned by twenty-five Malays under the command of a native officer formerly in the Ceylon rifle regiment. Their business is very light, their principal duty being to hail and report every boat which passes the fort during the twenty-four hours : they are armed with muskets and bayonets, and have barracks adjoining the fort: they are each paid six Spanish dollars per month, and found with a certain portion of rice ; the jemadar and corporal having proportionately higher pay.

The town is governed by three native chiefs called Dattus, whose authority is derived from the rajah for the time being; though their office is not strictly hereditary, the son of a chief, if he be of age, and otherwise fitted to conduct the business of the office, usually succeeding his father ; or, if the deceased chieftain has not children of the requisite age, another relation is appointed, who enjoys it for life ; but, on his decease, it reverts to the family of his predecessor.

The principal native chief of Sarawak is styled Dattu Patiñgi Gappur ; he is a fine character, and high in the confidence of Mr. Brooke, to whose intercession he owes his life, forfeited to the Rajah Mudah Hassim on account of his having been one of the chief rebels in the Seniawan war. It was with great difficulty that Mr. Brooke prevailed upon the rajah to spare the lives of this and the other chieftains, although, when they had submitted, he had stipulated for them. The Dattu Patiñgi was one of the greatest sufferers by the oppression of the Pañgeran Makota, the pañgeran having seized all his revenues, and destroyed the Dyaks by whom he gained his subsistence as chief.

The patiñgi was, during all the troubles of Sarawak, the friend of the Dyaks, and assisted them by every means in his power, and for this the Dyaks have a grateful remembrance of him, never mentioning him but with respect. He is now a firm friend and active supporter of Mr. Brooke's government; and, being a person of good ability, is of great service in carrying out his views, and during Mr. Brooke's absence is of the greatest assistance to Mr. Crookshank, the gentleman in charge of the settlement, from his knowledge of the customs and usages of the people.

The second chief is the Dàttu Bandar, a young man of mild, pleasing, and elegant manners, the son of that brave chief, the Dattu Patiñgi Ali, who, together with Mr. Stuart of Sarawak, perished with an advanced party of the expedition up the Sakarran river. At present the young Bandar does not interfere much with the affairs of the state: though he regularly attends the court, he always defers his opinion to the more experienced patiñgi. The Bandar is very anxious to learn English, and provided the missionaries do not at first interfere with his religious belief, of which he is a strict observer and zealous advocate, they will find this young chief of great service to them.

The chief third in rank in the Sarawak river is the Dattu Tumungong, a hale old man, and finely and strongly made, but heretofore of very bad charaeter, and still of very questionable loyalty. He delights in telling stories of his adventures and narrow escapes from the Dyaks and Chinese in his numerous marauding expeditions against them; and he would doubtless, had he the opportunity, act over again the whole of his former achievements. On account of his many injuries to them, the Dyaks hold him in abhorrence, and probably nothing but the fear of the rajah's displeasure would allow them to permit him to return safe out of any of their countries; but the old man wanders about amongst them, constantly trading, as he fortunately has no wish to interfere in the government, and when he visits a tribe which he has in former times severely injured, he never fails to remind them of the different circumstances under which he had previously seen them: during all his relations of this nature, he laughs as if he were recounting an excellent joke, and any successful piece of treachery or duplicity practised on the Dyaks calls forth an increase of his merriment.

These officers it has been Mr. Brooke's wise policy to perpetuate in their offices, in preference to trusting the affairs of the province to Borneans or other men of hereditary rank. Their revenues have been duly secured to them, and more considerable profit and dignity is now attached to their offices than they ever before enjoyed, or than probably ever previously appertained to the rank of Dattu. Nor have the chiefs alone to congratulate themselves on this better state of things; but the nakodahs, or merchants—who are of great respectability, and though without any definite place in the councils, are always allowed to give an opinion—have their properties secured to them, which were previously taken from them by their rajahs; and of what these, their principal oppressors, left, their followers despoiled them.

During the residence of the Pañgeran Makota at Sarawak, and generally under the native princes, their wives and daughters were frequently taken from the respectable classes of the people to gratify the passions of these tyrants. On the return of the rajahs to Bruni, a great number of women, daughters of the chiefs and most respectable people of Sarawak, were left behind with their own families at Mr. Brooke's request. This favour was obtained for the parents with difficulty from the rajahs, who prefer the women of the Sarawak as concubines before the women of the north, those of the western parts of the island being more fair and beautiful from their mixture with the Dyak races.

The nakodahs of Sarawak are now men of wealth and traders on a large scale, some of the boats recently built being as large as 100 tons. They sail annually to Singapore, carrying sago and the other productions of the coast, which they exchange for European goods, Javanese cloths, and brass-work, and the coarse basins and earthenware manufactured in China, and brought down by the junks. Until within very recent times, none of these people would have been known to possess money sufficient to build a boat, knowing that it would assuredly have been taken from them. Their improved condition is also seen in the appearance of their houses, which, three years since, were built entirely on nibong posts and of atap leaves; but, finding that the European influence is likely to be permanent—which at first they feared might not be the case—all the better classes have, within the above-named period, raised houses on posts of balean, and with wooden sides, which would be considered palaces in the capital city of Bruni. Roads along the town to the court-house and offices of business have been constructed, so that the natives can now communicate with each other by land, whereas formerly the only method available was by water.

The other classes of the inhabitants of Sarawak comprise the poor people who are free, and the slaves and slave debtors. The amba raja, or followers of the princes, are not known here. In Sarawak the poorest man can always without difficulty ensure to himself a comfortable subsistence, as at present the amount of labour is not in proportion to the demand; but as the Malay is averse to working for hire, and much prefers gaining a livelihood by trading, it generally happens that having gained a few dollars as a servant, or labourer to the Europeans, these are laid out in a stock of beads, salt, and brass wire, with which he starts up the country on a trading expedition to the Dyaks; and though, notwithstanding the competition caused by so many pursuing the same course of life, the profits are usually very large, and no expenses are incurred beyond the first purchase of the trading stock, as the trader always expects to be fed

by the village at which he is staying, he contrives to
live easily and idly.

Another means of livelihood to which those of the
poorer classes have often recourse—at least such of
them as are not averse to a little exertion—is the
never-failing gold mines.   As no tax is put upon the
produce, and no restrictions are laid upon the working of them, the extravagant, the dissipated, and the
gambler, always supply their exhausted funds, so that
Malayan labour, such as European settlers would require, would never be available, and it would, in the
event of large settlements being made, be necessary to
introduce the Malabar or Chinese labour, similar to
that employed by the proprietors of the Pinang and
Singapore estates.

Slavery in the east has always been of a more mild
and gentle character than that which in the west has
so disgusted the intelligent nations of Europe.   The
slaves (ulun-ulun) in Borneo are generally Dyaks and
their descendants who have been captured by the
rulers of the country for the purposes of slavery, and
swelling the number of their immediate dependants.
During the misgovernment of the western provinces
of the kingdom of Bruni by the Arabs, Sereib Saib,
and his brother, Sereib Muller, and their relations, it
was no uncommon thing for these tyrannical chiefs,
heretofore, and in Sadong after Mr. Brooke's arrival,
to send up parties to the Dyaks to bring down all the
young girls and boys they could catch.   I have been
told by Dyaks, and by dependants on the sereib, that

300 girls and boys have frequently been brought down at one time ; such of these as the chief selected as likely to be suitable to his purposes were reserved, the remainder were sold to whoever would buy them, the chief taking a considerable share, though his servants who had kidnapped the poor children generally contrived to cheat him of a considerable portion of the produce, to which they had perhaps as good a right as he.

With regard to slavery, the Malays strangely disregard the instructions of the Koran, which tells them that no true believer can be retained in slavery, so that the nations of the west are always obliged to find some method of proving that their prisoners are not of the orthodox faith before they keep them in slavery. The Malays, on the contrary, rarely allow infidels who have by any means come into their hands long to remain in ignorance of the true faith. The first act of their masters is to cause them all, both men and women, to be circumcised ; nor do the Dyaks in general exhibit the least reluctance to embrace Islamism, considering it more as consisting in the use of the better clothes of the Malays than as a ceremony affecting their future state, of which, during their adoption of their new faith, they hear very little ; but they look upon the Malays always with respect, and consider that an appeal to the book— as the Koran is called—is unanswerable, though it is believed that no person residing in the town of Sarawak, priest or layman, could translate a single chapter of it.

It follows from the listlessness they display in embracing the Mahometan religion that, should they by any chance return to their tribe, they soon throw it off, and, without the least thought on the subject, embrace their old habits of life. This, however, rarely happens. Those Dyaks who have long resided with the Malays, appear to fall into their ways of life, and the women particularly, to whom the finer clothes and less hard work are great temptations, seldom return to their tribes, even when opportunities are afforded them.

The slaves generally in Sarawak belong to the Dattus and merchants, and are treated with great liberality. Their duties consist in assisting their master, who always works with them, in his house or boat-building occupations, accompanying him on his trading expeditions, assisting in the navigation of his boats, &c. Their masters generally allot them wives from amongst their female domestics, and in this respect, where wives are not to be obtained without money, and where love is seldom a cherished and pure natural affection, they are much better off than their free but poorer neighbours, who are often obliged to pledge their own persons to obtain the object of their choice. Many slaves acquire so much of the confidence of their masters as almost to turn the scale, and become the masters of their lords ; but amongst a people so naturally sagacions and clever as the Malays, this undue influence less frequently occurs than amongst the more enervated Asiatics of the continent.

When the male slaves are not wanted by their masters, they are at liberty to hire themselves by the day to other employers, and the proceeds are kept by themselves. The price of a slave in Sarawak is from thirty to sixty dollars, but as the trade is being as gradually and quickly suppressed as possible, without too much shocking the prejudices of the inhabitants, they have of late become very scarce and difficult to be bought. The slave boys purchased by Europeans, who bring them up as servants, are necessarily free as soon as they enter the settlement, but are not often anxious to go away, as, being without friends, they might be again captured and sold to some other place, whereas with the Europeans they get, in addition to their freedom, their clothes, food, and two or three Spanish dollars per month pocket money.

Slave girls are frequently more harshly treated than their husbands and brothers, the Malayan ladies whom they serve being more commonly difficult to please than their lords. Should a girl be so unfortunate as to be possessed of personal attractions, so as to excite the jealousy of her mistress, her case is, indeed, pitiable; but, under the circumstances, the girl has generally redress by causing herself to be purchased by another person, if her proofs of bad treatment are sufficiently clear. Any slave girl having been used as a concubine is free by the law, and she can, if she likes, accordingly depart; but as virtue amongst the lower classes is but little regarded, they find it better to live at the expense of their master, though they receive the constant attentions of a lover equally favoured. The price of a girl varies according to her age and other quali-

fications, from thirty to 100 dollars, but at Sarawak
they are even more difficult than men to be obtained.

Slave debtors differ but little in the estimation in
which they are held, and in their duties, from slaves,
but they have the privilege of freeing themselves if
they can raise the money to pay the debt with its
enormous accumulation of interest.   Another privilege
is, that they cannot be sold or transferred but with
their own consent.   No institution of the Malays has
been more abused than this system of taking the persons for slaves of such as have become indebted to
them.   I have seen instances where, for the trifling
amount of a very few dollars, borrowed from the pañgeran to pay perhaps an exaction of his own, which by
the accumulation of interest, perhaps fifty per cent.
monthly, had increased to so large an amount that
whole families were obliged to submit themselves
as slave debtors to their creditor.   As it is impossible
for them ever to raise the constantly increasing amount,
this state of slavery is hopeless.   I need scarcely add
that this abuse of the practice of usury, as also the
state of the slaves in general, received the prompt
attention of the Rajah of Sarawak, and many are
the slaves in the settlement whom he has freed by
the sacrifice of his money.

CHAPTER V.

THE Malays of Sarawak are all of the Mahometan
religion, and having received the faith through missionaries from Arabia, are all of the orthodox or Sunni
sect. The Princes of Borneo, and of the other Malayan nations of the coasts, though professing the
religion of Islam, were always very neglectful of its
tenets, the only precept strictly observed being the
destruction and reducing to slavery of their infidel
subjects and neighbours. The Arabs, who were at
one time numerous on the coasts, and are still so at
Pontianak, all pretending to be sereibs or seriffs,
descendants of the Prophet, have always been held in
high consideration. They are always addressed by
the title of tuan-ku, or "your highness," and on state
days and festivals occupy a position more eminent
than that of the highest hereditary nobles. These

priestly hypocrites, constantly interfering for the purpose of promoting their own ends, caused more of the
troubles which have afflicted the Malayan kingdoms of
this island than have been produced by any other
means. On one occasion a man of rank, who ought to
have known better, informed me seriously that a certain vagabond of this class, called Mulana, who had
cajoled the rajah out of the government of the Kalekka river, had only been prevented by the earnest
entreaties of Sereib Sahib from removing the island of
Pulau Barong, opposite the Sadong river, to the neighbourhood of the Kalekka river. As this threat and
entreaty took place before a large assemblage of people, it is probable that the two hypocritical Arabs had
contrived the scene to impress the vulgar with an awe
of their persons. The generality of the natives of
Pa-mutus believe, or pretend to believe, that had not
Sereib Sahib so earnestly entreated him to desist, the
Tuan Mulana, as he was called, would have ordered the
island to remove, and that it would accordingly have
stationed itself opposite Kalekka. This Mulana, who
died last May, was discovered to be an Arab, who,
having arrived poor at Pinang, was befriended by a
rich countryman, who advanced him goods to the
amount of 4,000 dollars that he might go on a trading
voyage to the Archipelago. It is useless to add that
the friendly merchant never heard again from his holy
debtor ; but having accidentally found out the place
of his residence, he sent his son to demand the debt.
It was not denied, and a box was offered to the young

man which was said to contain jewels, &c., to the amount. The merchant could never recover any of his money, the Tuan Mulana having spent it on his numerous concubines and slaves. He was in the habit of sending charms and jackets which were inscribed with the verses of the Koran to the chiefs of Sarawak as presents, of course expecting a valuable consideration in return, but of late years the old gentleman did not find this plan of raising money at all productive; and as the Rajahs of Bruni had removed from Sarawak, he was able to draw but little revenue from the natives of the settlement, who, though in general they pretend to be good Musselmen, never contribute, if they can possibly avoid it, to the support of their religion. Until very recently the only mosque in the town was in such a dilapidated condition that it was dangerous to enter it, and when the inhabitants were called upon for subscriptions to raise a new one, not a fourth of the necessary sum could be procured by the priests.

The Klings, or natives of the Malabar coast, who have a flourishing bazaar in the town, have recently built a respectable mosque, being, though few in number, very zealous for their religion. I believe they are of the Shiah sect, which is that prevalent in Persia, and between the advocates of which and the orthodox sect so deadly a hatred subsists on the continent of Asia; but here, if the distinctions be understood, the hostile spirit does not exist, though the Malays rarely worship in the same building with them.

That doctrine to which the Malays of Sarawak most rigidly adhere, is the aversion in which the unclean animal is held. The Princes of Borneo do not scruple to drink wine when it is procurable, and I have frequently seen them partake of it before the Malays, their dependants, without the least sense of impropriety, or fear of their being openly seen thus to violate the inculcations of the Koran.

From what has been stated respecting their religion, it will be easily seen that the intolerant bigotry of the western Mahometan is entirely unknown to these people; and I am strongly inclined to believe that a rigid Turk, being set down in their country, would scarcely allow that they had a chance of safely skating over the narrow bridge into the paradise of the Prophet. Many superstitions are mixed with their religious belief, such as charming out the spirits which are supposed to possess a sick or mad person; these, and many others, the relics of a former idolatry, are unknown to the purer precepts of the Koran.

Their marriages and burials are performed according to the ceremonial ritual of the Koran, but as far as I have been able to observe, the respect paid by most of the Mahometans to the graves of their ancestors does not prevail here, as their graves are neglected, and frequently all traces of them taken away without the slightest remonstrance on their parts. A little stone, or a piece of wood which soon decays, are the most frequent and only memorials of the persons, the sole indications of the tenements of the dead. The modern burial-place at Sarawak is kept in better repair, and the graves have various attentions shown them, being frequently planted with flowers; of these the pinang appears to be the most esteemed. I have never seen the buñga kambôja in such situations, though it is so commonly employed for this purpose in other Malayan countries.

The Malays, natives of the western coast of Borneo, do not practise many of the vices for which their nation in general has become so famous. In their character they are a mild and quiet people, devoid of the cunning and treachery of the natives of Sumatra, whom the dissolute inhabitants of the capital more nearly resemble. They are not, like the inhabitants of the piratical states, fond of desperate adventure, and not being possessed of a great share of physical courage, and their tastes inclining them to follow the more peaceful pursuits of trade, under a government which will encourage commerce, they live happy and contented. In capacity the Malays are probably not inferior to any of the nations of Europe, and in their trading expeditions, and other intercourse with foreigners of several nations, particularly the Chinese, their ability in managing their affairs protects them from the frauds which are constantly attempted by these unscrupulous traders.

In the government of Sarawak Mr. Brooke has generally found the view of a political question taken by the principal natives and chiefs to be the most sound and profitable which, under the circum-stances, could be adopted. Piracy, which is considered in Europe to be proper to the nature of every Malay, has never been carried on by the na- tives of the western coast of Borneo. It is true that formidable fleets were sent from Sambas, and that many ships were taken at Bruni, but the chiefs of both these towns, the inhabitants of which are by far the most dissolute on the island, were Illanons, or at least intimately connected with them. The son of one of the most formidable of the chiefs who defended Sambas against the English in 1812, is now living a peaceable inhabitant of Sarawak : his father came with his followers from Magindanau and settled at Sambas, as did those to the northward which have been more recently destroyed by Sir Thomas Cochrane.

Though the pirates were encouraged by the rulers of the west coast, it does not appear that they have succeeded in inducing the natives of it themselves to go on piratical cruises. Teluk Serban, a bay inside of Tanjong Dattu, and opposite to the islands Telang Telang, was a station occupied during the S.W. monsoon by the pirates of Soolu and Migandanau. Here their principal fleet lay anchored, while small and fast cruisers in the offing constantly communi- cated to them the appearance of a sail : a force deemed sufficient was immediately sent out to cap- ture it, when, if it proved to be from a distance, the slaves or goods were sent into the Sarawak or Sadong rivers to the sereibs, who then governed this part of the coast, in exchange for provisions and other necessaries, of which their long absence from home had exhausted their stock ; the prisoners captured in the neighbourhood were handcuffed and bound until their captors were ready, on the approach of the boisterous monsoon, to return to their island homes. Thus the whole trade of the coast was destroyed, and it was for protection against these people that the government of Borneo stipulated with Mr. Jesse, when it granted to the settlement of Balambangan the monopoly of the pepper of Borneo.

Piracy does not therefore appear to have been proper to the native inhabitants of the west coast of Borneo, though frequently carried on from its ports; at present the coast is annually infested by the fleets from the Soolu Archipelago, which, leaving their own islands, situated on the N.E. of Borneo, about the middle of the N.E. monsoon, sail round the island with a fair wind, stretching across to the coasts of Java, Banca, Singapore, and the peninsula, and visiting all the islands in the way, attacking all the trading boats they meet, and carrying their crews into slavery, frequently landing and capturing the whole of the inhabitants of small villages.

They generally pass the western coast of Borneo about June or July, arriving in August at the Soolu islands laden with plunder. The number of boats which sail from this Archipelago cannot be accurately ascertained, but they must be very numerous, as not less than six squadrons of from five to eleven boats each, were seen to pass the Sarawak river during the past season. A large trading boat belonging to a native merchant of Sarawak was captured a little to the eastward of the river; her valuable cargo being taken out, she was scuttled and sunk; the crew saved themselves by their boats. This was in April last. Another boat, coming from the Natunas to Sarawak laden with oil, was chased by five boats to the small island Satang, opposite the western entrance of the Sarawak river, and two large boats, the property of merchants of this town returning from Singapore in March, sustained an action which lasted several hours, but the boats being well armed, and containing cargoes which rendered them worth defending, succeeded in beating off the pirates.

The action of the 'Nemesis' in June last is fresh in the recollection of our readers; of eleven boats which were caught by that ship in the act of piracy, chasing a small merchant-man near the mouth of the Borneo river, five were sunk, and of the six which escaped three only were enabled to reach Soolu from the damages they had received. This action, conducted by Captain Grey, of H.M.S. 'Columbine,' and Captain Wallage, H.C.'s steam-ship, 'Nemesis,' has been the severest lesson the pirates have ever received at sea, of the force of European nations, and their determination to suppress piracy: by this action the pirates suffered very severely, and several slaves which were bound in the boats were released. The pirates, who deserted their sinking boats and fled into the jungle, were captured by the parties sent against them by the Sultan of Bruni, in his anxiety to convince the English of the goodness of his intentions. It is rumoured that the fine frigate lately commissioned by

Captain the Honourable Henry Keppel, who has previously so much distinguished himself in those seas, is
intended to act particularly against the people of
Soolu and Magindanau, though from the nature of
their strong-holds, their numbers, and the confidence
they have from having hitherto defeated all the expeditions sent against them by the Spaniards, a large
additional force will be necessary to insure success.

The natives of the coast of Borneo are not addicted to
the vice of gambling, which amongst the natives of
Celebes and the Malays of the peninsula and Sumatra,
is carried to so great an excess ; it is, however, much
practised in the two capitals of Bruni and Sambas,
together with opium smoking and other kinds of
debauchery. In the town of Sarawak, gambling, except
to a trifling extent by the Chinese and other foreigners,
is unknown ; the natives of Sarawak, or those of other
coast towns which have settled there, never being
known to indulge in either of the above-named vices.
Cock-fighting is not practised, except amongst the
debauched nobles and their followers in the capital
towns, and thefts and robberies are always traced to
the natives of Sambas and Borneo. During a residence
of upwards of two years in Sarawak, no native of the
town was ever convicted of either gaming, using
opium, or stealing ; and were it not for the strangers
and traders from other towns, the magistrate of Sarawak would, perhaps, not have to adjudicate on half-a-
dozen cases in a year.

The government of Sarawak is carried on, in the

rajah's absence, by his deputy, Arthur Crookshank, Esq., assisted by the three Dattus; but, as has been previously noticed, the Dattu Tumungong seldom attends. These magistrates try, in the court-house, all cases brought before them, in the presence, generally, of a large assemblage of natives, who have free access during the hours of business. The class abang-abang, who are the merchants and respectable people, and from whom the dattus are chosen, are permitted to offer any proper and pertinent remark they please after the evidence has been heard. The rajah, after summing up the case to the chiefs, leaves them to return the verdict, which, as justice is here administered, free from the subtleties and technicalities of law, is generally unanimous, and according to evidence. When it happens that a Dyak, or any of the more simple classes of inhabitants, are brought before this court, they always make, immediately on being called upon, a simple and artless confession; but the Borneans, and people of Sambas, and the Chinese, who are much more frequently the accused, always most stoutly deny the charges, even in the face of the most positive evidence, and sometimes those known to be the greatest rascals will appeal to the court in the most impudent manner, and inquire whether the people present could conceive them capable of the actions laid to their charge.

The punishments awarded by their laws were very severe, resembling those of the Javans, from whom they are descended; but these have been all modified, and tortures and mutilations are now totally abolished. Formerly the slightest and most paltry theft, if, during the supremacy of the native rajahs, the culprit had no powerful friend to protect him, was punished by the loss of his hand; and, at the present day, many of these mutilated objects may be seen at the town of Bruni, where, notwithstanding thefts are of daily occurrence, the followers and slaves of the Pañgerans of Borneo were formerly allowed, and are still— excepting in countries under the influence of Sarawak— to commit any excesses, without the fear of punishment, as followers—' amba-raja'—of the princes and powerful nobles, who frequently themselves employed them in robberies and extortions on the poorer and industrious classes of the people.

Murder is, at present, the only crime in Sarawak punishable with death; and, during its recent history, occasions which have called for this extreme penalty are of very rare occurrence: for the most part the crimes are of so light a nature, that fines and banishment are considered sufficient punishments; the money collected from the former is spent on the extension and improvement of the roads and government buildings, though the rarity of fineable offences prevents this fund from ever becoming sufficient to be of any considerable service to the purposes to which it is applied.

No duties or exactions are levied on any ships or boats entering the port, all being allowed to come and go as they please, provided only that they report their arrival and departure to the government. The trade of the place has increased in the same proportion as its size and population, and, during the year, there are now upwards of 120 boats of large tonnage enter the river of Sarawak for the purposes of trade. Before the present government was established, the trade was carried on by about one-tenth of that number. A schooner sails monthly to Singapore, carrying the produce of the settlement, and it is visited frequently during the year by junks, and other merchant vessels, from Sambas, Java, Bali, &c. Besides the above-named trading vessels a great number of small boats are employed in the coasting trade, which is, as is also the foreign business, steadily and rapidly on the increase. The exports from Sarawak are antimony, gold, diamonds, sago, bees'-wax, birds'-nests, tortoise-shell, sharks' fins, vegetable tallow, dammar, rice, ebony, rattans, Malacca canes, salt fish, and many other articles, as the valuable camphor, which are brought here by the coasting vessels from the eastward. They import, salt, opium (consumed by the Chinese), silks, cocoa-nut oil, brass wire, and brass cooking-pots; with Javanese handkerchiefs, and European cloths and earthenware, and also much of the coarser earthen manufacture of China. The Klings have a well-stocked bazaar in the town, and make expeditions from it to all the towns along the coast. These people and the Chinese, who cultivate gardens and work the gold and antimony mines, are always found where the Europeans residing afford them protection. The Klings successfully compete with the native merchants for goods of European manufacture, which they bring over, of a damaged description, they having been sold at Singapore at less than their original cost. This the Klings buy from their correspondents at Singapore cheaper than can the Malayan traders who visit that settlement ; and as they are not at the expense of sailing ships of their own, but get their things on freight by the schooner, the Malays generally leave this branch of the commerce to them, and confine themselves to trading in the goods of Javanese and Chinese manufacture, the prices of which do not fluctuate. The Kling merchants, after living here for two or three years, become so rich that they are soon enabled to return to their own country, which, as they bring no wives with them, and have no ties in the island, they are all anxious to do.

The vessels belonging to the Malayan nakodahs of Sarawak are sailed at an inconsiderable expense. A person having the capital to build a boat, when it is finished finds no difficulty in getting sailors to navigate it; the sailors, being all merchants on a smaller scale than the owner and captain of the vessel, engage with the nakodah to sail with him, and assist in navigating and keeping the ship in repair, on condition of having a certain quantity of the tonnage of the vessel for their own purposes. Thus, if a nakodah gives out that he intends to sail his boat to Singapore, all the persons wishing to go to Singapore apply to him, and he grants them passages, or such of them as he has room for, on the above conditions. Quarrels respecting amount of tonnage allowed to each are very rare, and every thing proceeds quietly and orderly during the voyage. The most experienced persons, under the captain, are the juro-batu, or pilot, and the juro-mudi, or steersman; these act in the capacity of officers of the prauh. As the Malays are never in a hurry, they remain at one place as long as any trade can be carried on, when they either sail to another port, or return home as circumstances seem to render most profitable. The nakodahs sometimes have wives at each of the different places they are in the habit of visiting annually, so that wherever they go they have a home for their reception. Their taste for the pursuits of trade is quite a passion, and during all their early life they look steadily and anxiously forward to the time when they shall be able to indulge it with profit to themselves. It is from this principle being so rooted in their natures, that the kings and princes have been found, in all periods of their history, to be the greatest merchants in their state; and a tomb a little below the town of Bruni is that of one of the most powerful sultans who governed the kingdom in its flourishing times, and who is called by the natives by no other name than that of nakodah Ragam, or captain merchant Ragam.

The people of Sarawak, and the west coast generally, possess none of the disgusting and cringing servility of the natives of continental India; but their manners are distinguished for their politeness and freedom. The peasantry of Europe would lose much by comparison on this head with the poorest of the

Malays, whose manners are rendered attractive by
a natural courtesy quite unknown to the lower orders
of Europeans : excepting in places where their intercourse with foreigners has corrupted them, as in
Bruni and Sambas, an impertinent person is unknown.
Europeans visiting these countries are frequently
astonished at the elegant manners and dignified
bearing of the higher classes of Malays. The late
lamented Pañgeran Bed-er-ed-din displayed an air and
carriage which would have adorned an European
prince ; and the gentlemen who had opportunities
of seeing him, delight in recounting anecdotes of the
high generosity and considerate feeling which occurred
in their intercourse with him.

From what has been said of the character of the
people of Sarawak and the west coast of Borneo
generally, with the exception of those in the immediate vicinity, and under the influence of the de-
banched natives of the capital,—it will be easily seen
how susceptible their condition is of improvement, and
with what facility they may be brought to become
useful members of society under the influence of a
good government. The reader will also notice, that
the terms of treacherous, and other equally abusive
epithets, are no more applicable to them than we may
suppose they would be to European nations in circumstances when, reduced by oppression, they could
not revenge themselves by open and honest means.
Though the natives of Sarawak are quiet, and accordingly easily governed, it is not to be supposed that on

this account they will long endure oppression without complaint, or that they will allow themselves to be entirely trodden down without resistance. The history of the settlement proves the contrary, and the tyrannical sereibs and pañgerans, who formerly governed the country, now perhaps regret the measures they pursued, and envy the prosperity of the settlement which they had well nigh ruined by the civil wars their extortions occasioned. At the present time, Sarawak presents the rare prospect of a government, the people living under which are prosperous, contented, and happy; and when the state in which it was found by its rajah nine years ago is considered, the English nation may well admire the energy and enterprise of Mr. Brooke.

Many schools are established in Sarawak for the education of the children, as the neglect of providing instruction for those of the better classes reflects disgrace upon the parents. The sons only are educated in these establishments, which are generally kept by priests : their course of instruction comprises the reading and writing of their own language, the reading of the Koran in Arabic, and the repetitions of the various forms of prayer enjoined by the Mahometan religion. The children are not supposed to understand a single word of the book, nor could their teachers translate it; and as it cannot be translated into any language and remain pure, according to the instructions of the prophet, the forms of the religion are preserved by the oral precepts of the hadjis who have visited the holy city. The children in the schools

are only taught to give it in reading the proper intonation, and to repeat its precepts in the singing, chant-
ing method supposed to be practised in the temple of
Mecca. The great use of their learning to read the Koran at all is, that by using a chapter of it they pretend
to be able to drive away the spirit which is supposed
to possess an insane person, or one in a fit. The different
periods of the progress of the sons' advancement in edu-
cational knowledge afford the parents an opportunity
of giving feasts to their relations, when the son is examined by the master in the presence of his family and
connexions, who, in consideration of the liberal and
expensive feast usually provided for them, congratulate
the father on the splendid talents of the son ; at these
entertainments the principal part of the feast consists
of rice, fish, and fowls. The rice is brought up in large
dishes, some of which contain the grain coloured, and
disposed in fanciful combinations. The dishes are
also garnished with sweet-scented flowers ; the fish
and fowls are curried with vegetables, and in the
number of different flavours given to these two articles
consists the principal secret of their cookery. They
have so many of them, some of which are, however,
only to be distinguished by the nicest palate, that I
cannot give their numbers, nor is it probable that they
themselves know. The Malayan curries, when made
by the natives, have a flavour which is frequently preferred to those made by the natives of Madras, into
the composition of which, I believe, the cocoa-nut, so
liberally employed by the Malays, does not enter.

On occasions of great festivals, goats are killed, and buffaloes, which are brought from the Natunas islands : the woods also are ransacked for the different species of deer. The Malays in general are abstemious in their eating, and not partial to animal food. Fowls and ducks are rarely killed by them excepting on high occasions; of eggs, both of the fowl and the turtle, they are very fond; the former, coloured variously, and having flowers and other patterns upon them, formed by the colouring matter being picked off so as to expose the white shell of the egg, are a part of all their entertainments. Salt fish is preferred by them to fresh, in which state it is seldom eaten : the Malays eat none of the animals of the jungle which are not used by the Europeans, and are equally clean and particular in the preparation of their food. Their rice is beautifully boiled, as is generally the case in the East, where it forms so great a portion of the food of the inhabitants.

The Dattu Patiñgi of Sarawak, and many other Malays, eat no flesh whatever, declaring that the flavour of it is coarse, and not equal to that of fish, of which they constantly partake, and which is caught in abundance during the fine season or south-west monsoon, at the mouths of all their rivers. Few of the Malays eat more frequently than twice a-day, though those of the higher classes frequently partake of tea out of small cups, in the manner of the Chinese, from whom they have adopted the practice : all classes and sexes use the sirih and betel, which they are constantly chewing; this renders their teeth black, and spoils the appearance of their mouths : an exciting effect is attributed to its use.

In person these people, together with those inhabiting the other islands, are below the average stature of European nations : they are, however, finely formed, and well made in their persons, and of a strong, robust constitution, which renders them capable of enduring, when called upon, excessive fatigue; their women, at least those of the higher classes, are, as in other countries where the profession of Islamism prevails, carefully excluded from the gaze of strangers; some whom I have had opportunities of seeing have astonished me by the fairness of their complexion, and the comparative beauty of their features. They are generally short in stature, but of the most beautifully symmetrical figures, and their long and slender fingers, with the small and pretty hands, wrists, feet, and ankles, are seldom seen amongst the western fair ones in any thing approaching such perfection. Their long black hair, which falls on their backs in the greatest profusion, and in many cases reaches nearly to the ground, has, if we may believe the reports of the vendors of oils and unguents said to be used by them, been long the envy of the ladies of the west. But, notwithstanding these advantages of figure, and of the greatest ornament of female beauty, they can never approach the combination of perfection which constitutes loveliness in the west ; their too flat noses, and the want of clearness and brilliancy in their complexions, and of anima-

tion in their features, are the great natural bars to
their successful rivalry ; while their totally uncultivated
minds, and the absurd practice of blacking their
teeth, to heighten, as they imagine, their beauty,
renders them disgusting to intelligent Europeans :
should the Malays themselves become more improved,
it is probable that these women, who at present are
in so ignorant and debased a state, will also rise in
the scale of civilization ; but unless they can be persuaded to relinquish the religion of Mahomet, it is
much to be feared that neither of these desirable results
can take place.

The women adorn their hair with beautiful and fragrant flowers, of which they are passionately fond. The
sweet unopened buds of the buñga melur (Jasminum
sambae), and the buñga gambir, both of them species of
jessamine, are the favourites for this purpose ; the buds,
being gathered in the morning, are strung in wreaths by
the girls, who afterwards weave them into their hair, also
concealing amongst the folds some flowers of the buñga
kanañga (Uvaria), and of the delightful golden cham-
puka, both of which trees they cultivate for this purpose.
The strong but ravishing perfume of the flower called
sundal malam, or harlot of the night, the tuberose of
European gardens, is also esteemed by them, as is the
ganda suli, a species of Hedychium, and the Gardenia
florida, a variety of the Cape jessamine : these, with
many other flowers, are usually planted by the women,
or their slaves, near to their houses. As the Malays
of Sarawak do not make gardens, the flowers are often

difficult to be procured, except by purchase, when they
are very expensive. A garden or two at Sarawak, for
the purpose of supplying the Malays with sweet-scented
and other flowers, would pay well if the Chinamen
could be induced to undertake it, and so refined a taste
amongst these people it would be well to encourage.
At present the families of the chiefs are supplied with
flowers from the bushes and trees in the garden of
their rajah, the liberty of taking which they value
highly. The Malay women are also, like their sex in
general, fond of fine clothes and jewellery, and their
extravagance is the frequent cause of unpleasantness
between them and their husbands. Their dress is
simple, and consists of the kain tapé, or cloth, which
has been described as a wide sack open at both ends;
this extends from below the breast to the ground. It
is fastened by being merely folded and tucked in; it
is of silk or satin amongst the higher orders, and of
cotton cloth of their own, or European manufacture,
amongst the poorer classes. The jacket is the next part
of their dress; this also is of dark-coloured satin, and
made to fit close at the neck when fastened, and with
tight sleeves for the arms; it reaches to the waist, so
as to cover the folds of the tapé: it is buttoned at the
wrist with nine large gold buttons, which extend up
each sleeve towards the elbow, and is fastened at the
neck with a large gold clasp. The front, which covers
the breast, is also adorned with a profusion of gold
plates of various shapes and patterns, so as with rich
people entirely to conceal the jacket, or badju, as it is

called.   The only other article of apparel is the kain
sarong.   This is worn by them loosely folded round
the waist when in the house, but abroad it is opened
so as to cover the whole upper part of the person, as a
veil, being extended over the head, and supported by the
hands.   It is of the same form as the cloth first described, but when not of a rich silk of a tartan pattern,
it is made of the cloth called kain bentabur, which is
satin, with threads of gold wire forming the pattern of
it.   These cloths cost about forty to fifty Spanish
dollars, 8*l*. to 10*l*. sterling.   They wear no head-dress,
and their hair, which is but loosely confined, without
the aid of combs or other contrivances, but the greater
part being doubled and passed under a few hairs
separated from the rest, hangs at the back of the head,
in a large and loose knot.

It is difficult to conceive how the women of the upper
class pass their time confined in the harems of the great :
the apartments allotted to them are small and dark, and
each wife or concubine has a number of slaves of her
own, with whom the other wives do not interfere ; their
cookery, and all their proceedings, appear to be carried
on entirely independent of each other.   The indolent,
enervated persons who now form the principal part of
the nobles of Bruni and Sambas, confine themselves to
the apartments of the women during the whole of the
day, what little business they transact being done about
ten or eleven at night, which is to them what the day
is to other people.   They are fond of playing at chess,
and those of them who are industrious, as were several

of the murdered pañgerans, employed themselves in the manufacture of krises, and the carving and polishing of their beautiful sheaths and handles; in this work they excelled all their subjects.   The education of the existing nobles of Bruni has been much neglected, and the greater part of the young nobles, with the sultan at their head, can neither read nor write; of such a state of things the middle classes of Sarawak would, as has been already observed, be ashamed.

The men amongst the Malays do not, as do the Javans, suffer their hair to become long, but have it always cut short, and their heads very frequently shaved; they do not wear beards, and are naturally without them. The greater part carefully shave off the few hairs they have upon their faces, but some encourage to a great length three or four straggling hairs on the upper lip, and evidently contemplate with satisfaction this contemptible approach to what is generally supposed a sign of manhood.

It may be useful to mention, that the only oil used by the women in the cultivation of their hair is that freshly expressed from the cocoa-nut: this is perfumed by allowing the flowers of the various plants, previously mentioned as being used in the adornment of their hair, to remain for some time in it, the fat oil of the nut extracting and retaining the essential oil of the fragrant flowers.   I have been told by Mr. Brooke that in Macassar, and on the coasts of Celebes, the rajahs' domestics prepare, with great care, an oil for the use of their women which is supposed to be of a highly invigorating quality, but it is probable that the luxuriance of the hair of the women of these countries is, in a great measure, constitutional; although it cannot be denied that they take the greatest possible care of it, and pride themselves on its profusion.   Should it be falling from weakness, many superstitious practices are resorted to for the purpose of preventing it: in these cases the fat extracted from venomous snakes and of crocodiles is foolishly considered very efficacious; for the feet to come in contact with the ground during the period when they use these, and similar remedies, is supposed to destroy their good effects; and even when the hair is in the finest condition, such parts of it as separate from the head during the operations of dressing it, are carefully preserved, never being thrown out, or burnt, or otherwise destroyed, as bad consequences are supposed to follow such treatment of any part of it to the remainder.   Perhaps the vendor of the next oil purporting to be that used by the natives of the Indian islands may profit by the above remarks, and recommend to the ladies of Europe the fat of snakes and crocodiles instead of bears and other animals; it may be remarked, however, that that which the old women who recommend its use to the young girls in Sarawak sell to them, is seldom the fat of those animals, but usually some vegetable oil, which is made to answer the purpose, snakes and alligators being more difficult to obtain.

As the women here are more scarce than the men, as in all countries where polygamy prevails, on marriage the bridegroom has to pay for his wife instead of receiving a dowry with her : this does not so much obtain amongst the higher ranks as in the middle classes of life ; so that for a man of the class abang-abang to marry is a very expensive and difficult affair ; he has, perhaps, to pay slaves, goods, and money, to the value of several hundred dollars for a girl whom he has never seen, and who, when he does see her, may, perhaps, soon give him cause to repent of his bargain ; but though, under the Mahometan law, divorces are easily obtained, they do not often proceed to this extremity, as were the wife to be divorced without her own consent, the husband being unable to prove against her adultery, or any other cause of equal weight, he would lose the whole of the money and property he had given for her, and which it had, perhaps, been difficult for him to collect ; so that they generally find it convenient to agree together,—the husband consoling himself sometimes, but not frequently, with taking another wife or concubine or two.

Polygamy, however, is very seldom practised by the people of the middle class, though tolerated by law ; the rajahs and nobles alone keeping large numbers of concubines. Many of the respectable people of Sarawak have frequently told me that one wife was quite as many as they could govern, and that in many instances they themselves were governed by that one. On account of the practise above detailed of paying for their wives, it frequently happens that free people of the poorer classes are unable to get married, unless they sell themselves into slavery, or become bound to serve for their wives. In former times their services never expired, but they are now limited, a certain reduction being made monthly for the services of the man ; if he has married a slave. The price paid amongst the poor people for their wives is generally about the same as that at which the woman would be valued if a slave. In consequence of this scarcity and demand for women, daughters are not, as in some other Eastern countries, considered a burthen, but are nourished and cherished with the same care as the sons, who are always well treated by their parents, the Malays being passionately fond of their children. Instances in which children are neglected or unkindly treated are very rare, while those in which an excess of fondness is injurious to their offspring are of frequent occurrence : the avaricious old Dattu Tumuñggong of Sarawak is the only instance which came under my notice of a father treating his son unkindly. This was caused by the notice taken by the Europeans of the youth, who is a highly respectable trader of the town. The old man fancied that his son envied his title, and wished to gain sufficient influence with the Europeans to induce the rajah to supersede him, and confer his rank upon the son, who was already, by successful trade, quite independent of the Dattu.

The peculiar feature of the Malayan character which, under circumstances of dejection of spirit, of fear, or of losses, causes their madness to assume that wild and destructive form known to the English as running a-muck, and by the natives themselves called meng-ámuk, has yet to be spoken of. One case which occurred during my stay at Sarawak arose from fear: the man had, however, been previously subject to fits of insanity. It was during a rumour of an attack on the settlement caused by the firing of some guns early in the morning before the inhabitants were stirring: the person in question seized a large and heavy sword in one hand, and a spear in the other, and rushing out of the house, struck at indiscriminately any one he met; nine persons being severely wounded by him before he reached the jungle whither he directed his course. Five of these people died of their wounds; the insane murderer was killed afterwards by the Dyaks, in an attack which he made on one of their villages some days after he had first fled into the jungle; during the interval, he was the terror of the inhabitants, who durst not venture into the forests about their ordinary avocations, while they were tenanted by so dangerous a character.

Another case happened without the least appearance of previous madness, but was unattended by serious consequences, except to the deranged person; and other instances were fortunately prevented before the afflicted person had been able to accomplish any serious injuries. This peculiar form of madness, which has been usually ascribed to the restless temperament of the Malays acting upon diseases of the brain, is not known to exist in other nations; and though madness amongst the Dyaks of Borneo is not of unfrequent occurrence, it never takes this destructive form. What has been previously said of the quiet and peaceful character of the people of Sarawak, would not interfere with the solution of the causes leading to it above referred to, as in all the cases above mentioned the afflicted individuals were foreigners; and that first described, and which was so much more than the others destructive of human life, was perpetrated by an Illanon, a native of one of the piratical states of Magindanau. The same term meng-āmuk is used by the Malays to designate furious fighting in battle.

In arts and manufactures the Malays of Borneo have not surpassed their neighbours on the peninsula and in Sumatra, and are certainly inferior to those of Java; in the construction of their houses they display no skill or taste, and their uncouth appearance makes them precisely resemble an English barn upon posts: the causes of the inferiority in neatness of construction, and also in durability of the materials of which they are built, are to be found in the insecurity of property consequent on the uncertain and oppressive government which has prevailed in the kingdom of Bruni during the past forty or fifty years

We have seen that during the visit of Pigafetta the town of Borneo was built of wood on strong and substantial posts; it is now constructed entirely on nibongs, which soon decay, and is thatched with the nipah-leaves, of which the sides also are composed: under a good government the natives would, however, soon improve in the construction of their houses, and the people of Sarawak are rapidly substituting houses of large dimensions and durable materials for the small and inconvenient huts they previously inhabited. The houses in all parts of Borneo are built upon posts generally about four or five feet from the ground, but sometimes more : the object of this originally was for the purposes of health, and as a means of preservation from noxious reptiles, and in some instances, hereafter to be described, as a protection against their enemies. The towns are always situated on the banks of rivers, and such low places are often chosen as are overflowed by the tide; perhaps these spots have been fixed upon that the water might cleanse the impurities which are frequently allowed to accumulate beneath their residences. Borneo and Kalekka are the only two towns which I have seen built entirely in the water, the whole of the houses, with the exception of that of the sultan and one or two of the nobles, being built upon posts fixed in the mud banks of the river. That such situations should have been chosen is the more strange, as at low water a stench, which cannot be of a healthy nature, arises from the mud, which to an European, or stranger not accustomed to it, is very offensive; the natives of the town affirm that this does not affect their health. The river at the place where the town is situated is very wide, and receives the waters of the Sungie Kadyan, a tributary stream; the main river forms the principal street of the town, and on it are situated the large houses of the nobles and princes.

The houses are disposed with more regularity than in most Malayan towns, being intersected by water-lanes at right angles from the main water-street, so that the whole town is divided into a number of solid squares of houses, each of which communicates with one of the streets of the town. The palace of the sultan is a large building of wood, situated on the neck of land formed by the Kadyan river, and a few hundred feet from its mouth : it is surrounded by a high pagar of split and flattened bamboo, neatly plaited into a close fence, so that nothing can be seen from the outside ; strangers are never admitted into the interior. Every thing about the palace had a much neater and cleaner appearance than the other parts of the town (May, 1845), and the landing-place to it was defended by six small brass guns on handsomely carved carriages ; both the general audience-hall and the private reception-room were situated outside the enclosure of the palace. On the low point of land, which was not occupied by the buildings of the sultan's residence, were lying several fine large brass guns without carriages, some of them fifty-six pounders, which had been cast in Borneo in earlier times, others were said to have been presented by the Kings of Spain to former Sultans of Bruni; the whole of these guns have been captured by the British since this account of Borneo was written. The palaces of the rajahs, which are ungainly looking, but very large wooden buildings, are the only ones of this construction, and most of these are in a dilapidated condition ; their mosques, of which there are several in the town, are in an equally ruinous state.

The public market in Bruni presented an unique

and interestingly novel appearance, being held upon the water by the women, who arrive every morning from the country with fruit, vegetables, and other articles for sale; the vendors are generally two or three in each boat, every one of them provided with a large hat made of palm-leaves, and of an umbrella shape, which serves to protect the whole person from either the sun or rain. They each have also a paddle, with which they manage their little canoes—which are almost level with the water's edge—with the greatest dexterity. Early in the morning the market boats assemble; first about the middle of the town; but floating up quietly with the sluggish tide, or down, if the water be ebbing; during the day, it is seen moving slowly in and out of the different streets with an occasional purchaser, who is making a bargain with a market woman separated from the rest, in the eagerness of trade having forgotten to direct her little boat in the same course as the others, but, the purchase completed, she soon joins the remainder, and is lost in the crowd. This fleet of market boats numbers generally from 150 to 200, and the whole business transacted in them is conducted by women. It has generally entirely dispersed by noon.

Houses built of stone are never seen in Borneo, but traces of images and Hindu sculpture, hereafter to be described, prove that during the prevalence of the Hindu-Javan power in the island, stone-work was known, though perhaps never practised by the natives of the country, the few images to be found having, perhaps, been brought

from Java. Even in working in wood, though not unskilful, the Malays have very bad and inadequate tools.
Their planks for house-building they generally purchase
of the Chinese carpenters and sawyers at Sarawak, as
they themselves do not use the large saw for cutting
up timber, their boat-planks being formed with great
labour and waste of wood with the biléong, a small
kind of adze, which is the only cutting instrument
employed also in making their fine posts of balean and
other hard woods. They are, from their great practice, very dexterous with this instrument, and the surface of the posts formed by them is as smooth as if the
plane had been used to them, and the square form is as
well preserved as if they had been cut out by the saw.

In boat-building they have attained much greater
perfection than in other carpenters' work, and
in this art they have lately very much improved, and
endeavour as much as possible to imitate the strength
and durability of English ships in the construction of
their large boats. Thus they now copy the ships of
Europe; and all the boats of Sarawak have sails of light
canvass, and cordage of excellent quality, instead of the
clumsy mats and inelegant rattans formerly in use.

The people of Sarawak and of the west coast of
Borneo, and indeed of the island generally, are far
behind the natives of Celebes and Java in the manufacture of cloths. They grow no cotton, and the cloths
they make are from cotton thread which they annually
import from Singapore. They have no variety of
patterns, all their cloths being variations of a red

tartan. The sarongs, or cloths worn round the waists of the men, and into which the kris is frequently stuck, manufactured on the coast, are, however, much preferred to any cloths the produce of Europe, or of Celebes or Java, on account of their great durability. The sarongs from Celebes, which, next to their own, are most esteemed, sell in the bazaar for two dollars each; the coarsest of those of the town sell for three, and the finest and those brought from Kalekka for four or five dollars. A much finer and dark-coloured kind, the produce of the looms of Soolu and Magindanau, are very highly esteemed. They cost on the west coast from eight to twenty dollars, and are rarely to be purchased; at Bruni, where they are more commonly used by the people of rank, their price is very little lower, though the supply is greater and more regular.

It is curious that the price of these cotton cloths should be more than that of silk of the same size, the produce of other countries where the art of weaving is in greater perfection. All the fabrication of cloths is carried on by the females, and a slave who is clever at this branch of industry is proportionately valued. Though silks are much worn by the women, they do not attempt themselves to manufacture them; they are all brought from Singapore, and those manufactured at the Anambas islands, particularly at Siantan, are generally used. They are of the same patterns as the other Malayan cloths, and cost in Sarawak about three to four Spanish dollars, or 12s. 6d. to 16s. 8d. sterling. Those brought from Palembang and Tringganu are of stronger quality and thicker texture, and of course are higher in price, sometimes reaching ten Spanish dollars.

The satins and silks of other patterns used are the manufacture of China. The kain benang mas and kain bentabur, or cloth of gold thread, are brought from Singapore, and are principally the manufacture of Sumatra. Most of the women practise embroidery with gold and silver thread, to adorn the ends of their square pillows or the corners of their beautiful mats of open work, which are brought from the Natunas islands ; but though this accomplishment occupies much of their time, they have not attained to any great perfection in it. Were they instructed in the art from Manilla or China, they would, as they have a natural taste for the employment, soon excel in it.

The mats mentioned in the preceding paragraph, though not produced on the island itself, are strictly to be counted amongst its manufactures, as the Natunas, where they are made, though not politically, are geographically a portion of it. I have not had opportunities of seeing this manufacture carried on, but understand that it occupies the time of the women of Sirhassen, as the produce of the silk cloths does those of Siantan. The mats are made of a beautifully soft and white rush, the larger ones having a broad border of open work of pretty patterns round the edges, and which is larger as the mats decrease in size, they being always made in sets, until the smallest one, which lies above, is formed entirely of the open work, through which the under mats are seen; but in fine and larger sets two or three of the upper ones are generally similar to the small ones above described: they are very expensive in Sarawak, but this is on account of their rarity, and I presume that a fine set in the islands would not be very costly. This manufacture seems to be carried on in no other part of the Archipelago, and the produce of these islands is generally seized by the Rajah of Lingin, in the Straits of Rhio, who, on the ground of his unjust title to the kingdom of Johore, claims the sovereignty of these islands. They export to Sarawak numbers of mats made of the same material as those above described, but without the open work; these are sold for about one rupee each.

It would have been reasonable to suppose that where gold is so plentiful and so highly valued, and much used as an ornament, that the natives themselves would have been at least as clever in the manufacture of it as the Sumatrans and Javanese, but it does not seem that they have ever even attempted themselves to form it into ornaments, but trust entirely to foreign nations for their supply of artisans in the precious metals. Some of the Borneans were workers in gold, but their masterpieces were of the coarsest description, seldom exceeding in beauty the productions of the Sea Dyaks. The Javanese carry on this profitable trade at Sarawak, but these do not equal the gold-smiths of Sumatra, and are ignorant of the manufacture of the beautiful filligree work of that island, so much valued in former times in England. The ornaments, for which purpose alone the gold is used, are the pieces or thin plates for the jackets of the women; these are of various forms, according to the taste of the wearers; the patterns are stamped upon them from the inside; they are worn, by such as can afford it, in three rows of nine plates each upon the breast, and two rows of smaller plates of the same number, in the shape of stars, are frequent in addition to the others.   About three bengkals (five ounces) of pure gold would be necessary to make the ornaments for the jacket of a dattu's daughter; besides these the ear ornaments and buttons for the wrists, with brace- lets for the younger girls, consume a great quantity. The ear ornaments are small and neat; they are not pendant, but generally of the shape of an eight-rayed star; they fasten by a nut which screws into the tube passing through the lobe of the ear, instead of a ring.   To all their gold they give the high rich colour so much admired amongst the Sumatran nations: this is termed sapoh, and is performed by a powder made of nitre, common salt, and alum, which is laid on the gold, being kept over a slow fire until it dis- colours, and becomes yellow or red, according to the time it remains in this situation, and the intensity of colour the gold is wished to retain.

Blacksmiths are more common among the natives than any other workers in metals.   The iron they use is all purchased from Singapore, the ore of the country not being smelted, though I have been told that the Chinese once smelted the ore of a richer quality in the neighbourhood of Tanjong Dattu.   The bellows used by the blacksmiths are formed of two wooden or bamboo cylinders, with pipes leading from the bottom of them into the fire ; the wind is forced through these pipes by two stout sticks, to which are attached large bunches of feathers. These are worked, alternately, by a boy seated high enough for the purpose, and throw a strong and constant stream of wind into the fire. Their fuel is charcoal ;—even where coal is found the natives never use it. The skill of the blacksmiths, which is considerable, is principally exhibited in making their instruments of carpenters' work and weapons, and a person skilful in the manufacture of the kris and spear can always obtain abundance of employment. The adze and axe of their own manufacture are preferred to those sent from England, which are frequently of a very inferior quality. None of the smiths have attained sufficient skill to be able to make a musket, though these, and large guns, have been made in former times in the capital. The Bugis people of Celebes prefer their own clumsy rifles, which are fitted with locks from Singapore, to the finer ones from Europe. These people practise rifle shooting much, and have generally been found in Singapore equal to Europeans who supposed themselves skilful in shooting at a mark at long distances.

Brass, though the manufacture of it was formerly extensively practised in Borneo, is now only worked, and to a very small extent, by a few artisans from Java. They make dishes, cooking-pots, and other utensils of it, but not in nearly sufficient quantities to supply the demand for these articles, large quantities being annually imported from Java. Copper is not used, but being mixed with gold, forms a beautiful compound metal, much valued by the Borneans for ornamenting the handles of their long krises.

In their apparatus for the capture of fish, they have attained greater perfection than in any of the mechanical arts, and the contrivances for the capture of this favourite article of food are very numerous. The principal are the inclosures of stakes, drag-nets, casting-nets, traps, placed so as to swing to each tide; and with hook and line: prawns, shrimps, and small fish are taken with hand-nets in the fine season. The quantity of fish taken by these various contrivances is enormous. They are salted and dried, as has been before stated, and sent into the interior parts of the country. The river fish in general are not so much esteemed as those taken at sea, though they also are frequently caught, principally by means of hooks and lines attached to the light wood called plye, already described. Pieces of the wood, cut into the shape of birds, may frequently be seen floating down with the tide, to each of which is attached at the neck a strong line supporting a baited hook. The proprietor is generally not far off, and, on the float bobbing under water, soon seizes it, and captures the fish which has taken the hook, but though large, cannot keep the light float under water. A fine fish called by the natives 'ikan malang,' is the one most frequently caught in this manner.

The Malays of Sarawak seldom apply themselves to gardening or agriculture, trusting entirely for their supplies of rice and fruits to the industrious Dyaks of the interior, and to the Chinese gardens in the town for the vegetables they require. Some of the chiefs and principal persons who have slaves about them from agricultural countries, generally employ them in making and taking care of farms and gardens at a distance from the town, to which they regularly bring the produce to their masters. Many of the traders have latterly expressed a desire to become planters, and it is probable that young and profitable plantations of the cocoa-nut, betel-nut, and fruit trees, will soon become common; at present they import the whole of the quantities now so largely consumed of these two former useful articles, and it is to be feared that the ease with which large profits are gained in trade, and in working the gold mines, will for a long time prevent any considerable progress in agriculture, and until competition shall have reduced the one to its proper standard, and taxes restrict the working of the other, we cannot expect to see any great improvement in the cultivation of the land, or in the mechanical arts, though perhaps the instructions of missionaries may assist in diffusing a desire to become greater proficients in these branches of industry amongst them.

In war, as far as the English have had opportunities of observing their behaviour, the people of Sarawak have not been found deficient in courage, though they seldom show that carelessness of life which makes other tribes altogether regardless of danger; the feats

M

of courage displayed by the late Patingi Ali, who
accompanied the forces under Captain Keppel against
the pirates of Sakarran, were of such distinguished
fearlessness as to call forth the voluntary acclamations
of the Europeans engaged.   The wars of Sarawak are
like those of most nations in a similar state of civilization, long, protracted, but very bloodless, and the
account of the manner of conducting the operations
against the rebels of Sarawak, detailed in Mr. Brooke's
Journal, published in Keppel's book, is the narrative
of all their bloodless campaigns.   The present forces
of Sarawak comprise all the male inhabitants capable
of bearing arms, who are obliged to attend their chiefs
on any expeditions which they may have decided as
necessary for the good of the state, government supplying them with food during their continuance.
There are now belonging to Sarawak, and which are
kept constantly ready for service, eight large war-boats,
which can each carry sixty men, and one six-pounder
gun ; most of them carry in addition to this two
lelahs, or long brass swivel guns, and small arms in
proportion, the whole of which, with the ammunition,
are provided by the government.   The weapons in
use amongst the natives are principally spears and
swords, the kris being not here so much in repute as
amongst the people of the north, whose krises are much
larger and more serviceable weapons than those used
by the Javans and Malays in the western part of the
Archipelago : the blades are also without the damasked
appearance which renders them valuable amongst

these latter people; the steel is better tempered, and being heavy and two-edged, they are used to cut as well as thrust. Bucklers made of a round form, small, and of rattans firmly plaited, which are serviceable to resist the stroke of a sword or the thrust of a spear, are in general use among them. The bow and arrow, if they ever used these weapons, have now entirely given way to the musket, which is in such general repute among the nations of the Archipelago as to be an article of greater traffic that almost any other commodity of European manufacture. It is by the dread the natives of the interior have of fire-arms that the Malays are suffered to occupy the coasts, and thus tyrannize over the people of the interior. The Dyaks of Sakarran and Sarebas have often told me, that were it not for the noise of two or three old muskets which they possess, they should never be able to stand against the Kyans, whom they own to be a more brave and dangerous enemy than any of the others they have to encounter.

At the marriages and other festivals, music is in high repute, but generally of the coarsest and most noisy description. Until the recent introduction of some of the Javanese musical instruments, those of the Sarawak people consisted only of the gongs of different descriptions, and the tom-toms, or drums, similar to those used by the natives of India. At these feasts dancing girls are never introduced, they not being known in the settlement, except to such as have seen them in Pontianak, Singapore, or Java.

In conversation I have learned from the chiefs that they consider dancing as an indecorous and unbecoming amusement. Singing and recounting romances are practised at all their festivities, and of these amusements they are very fond. The practice of the religion of the Prophet restrains the Sarawak people from drinking; but to all kinds of boisterous mirth they are naturally averse. They are not, however, averse to society, and are fond of associating with the Europeans; many of them used nightly to visit Mr. Brooke's house, where chairs were placed for the principal personages: they entered readily and sensibly into all conversations on subjects which were familiar to them, and always evinced a strong desire to be informed on such points as they were ignorant of, never, like the conceited Chinese, pretending to despise what they did not comprehend. The extent and importance of the English nation was a subject on which they perpetually were asking questions. The variety of our manufactures, and the application of steam-power to machinery, were subjects on which they exhausted us of information. There is no doubt that, should nothing interfere to prevent the carrying out the measures of the present ruler of Sarawak, it will ere long become a state of the greatest commercial importance: the facilities which the character of the people, and the richness of its productions, offer for the profitable employment of British capital and skill, will doubtless soon be made available in developing its valuable resources.

CHAPTER VI.

IN pursuance of the plan it is our intention to follow in describing the inhabitants of the island in the order in which they are best known to us, which will nearly correspond also with their relative political importance, the Dyaks next present themselves to our notice, sufficient we trust having been said to give the reader a general idea of the Malays of the coast of Borneo, and to leave on his mind a more favourable impression of the character of some of them than the nation generally has hitherto enjoyed.

The Dyaks appear to be divided by many customs and usages naturally into two classes, which have been called by Mr. Brooke, Land and Sea Dyaks; the latter appear to have been the more savage and powerful, the former the more quiet and easily managed. Amongst the sea Dyaks the practice of preserving the heads of their enemies, anciently instituted that they might be kept

as memorials of triumph, has degenerated, from its
originally sufficiently barbarous intention, into a passion
for the possession of these horrid trophies, no matter
how obtained. Amongst the land Dyaks the custom
still remains as it was probably at first instituted,
and no wish for the possession of a head would tempt
these people to take one unless it were that of their
enemy with whom they were avowedly at war. These
land Dyaks differ more decidedly in other particulars
from those who frequent the sea, all of which shall be
related in the chapter upon their customs and manners.

The sea Dyaks, or such as are in the constant habit
of frequenting the ocean for the purposes of carrying
off the heads of fishermen, or any other persons whom
they may find in a situation not capable of defence,
inhabit principally the countries lying in the interior
of the great rivers Sarebas and Sakarran, with their
numerous and large branches. Settlements of them,
which, however, appear to differ in some measure, are
also found on the Kenawit and the neighbouring
branches of the river Rejang, and one tribe also belonging to this division has its chief settlement at
Lundup, pronounced Lundoo in the Sarawak territory.
As it is from this tribe that the following remarks are
principally drawn, except where it is expressly stated to
the contrary, I think it right to give the reader a just
idea of its geographical position. This tribe, the name
of which is Sebooyoh, misprinted Sibnowan in Captain
Keppel's book, came originally from the country

situated about the sources of the western branch of the Batang Lupar river, in the direction of the lake Danau Malayu and the Pontianak river. They were expelled from thence by their enemies, and descending the Batang Lupar, established their villages on a small river named Sebooyoh, from which they are now designated. This river is situated a little to the westward of the mouth of the Batang Lupar, between it and the Sadong rivers. From this they carried on war with their old enemies of Sakarran with various success, but were finally compelled, about ten years before the new era of Sarawak, again to decamp farther westward, when they divided into three tribes, and settled in the villages they now occupy. That portion which followed the chief orang kaya of the tribe, and whose family has for many generations produced its chief, settled at Lundu, which has now become a beautiful fortified village, and from which the gallant old chief has frequently made successful expeditions against his hereditary enemies.

The river of Lundu is situated to the westward of the Santu-bong, or western entrance to the river of Sarawak : this river, which is not large, has its rise in the Sarawak territory and country occupied by the land Dyaks of Singhie. Another large village of the Sebooyoh Dyaks is established on a creek of the Sarawak river about a mile below the Malayan town ; the creek is called Peduñgan, and the Dyaks are often designated as orang or Dyak Peduñgan—the men or

Dyaks of Peduñgan.   The village established here is well built, and contains about sixty families; it is not fortified in any way, though the Dyaks possess some small brass guns.   The other divisions of the tribe, which are equally under the protection of the government of Sarawak, have villages on the Samarhand and Sadong rivers, but many little clusters of houses are to be found scattered about in the country near the mouths of the above-named streams, nominally belonging to the tribe, though not residing at any of the principal villages.   The Dyaks of Lundu have been a pet tribe of Mr. Brooke's, on account of the heroic gallantry displayed by them and their chief on many occasions of difficulty and danger.   The conduct of the orang kaya, and his assistance to Mr. Brooke in the Seni-awan war, are fully detailed in the Hon. Captain Keppel's work, whom they also accompanied in his expeditions against Sakarrau and Sarebas, which are their favourite places of attack, they being always anxious to revenge themselves on these people, who have caused them so much loss and trouble during their residence in their former villages.

The country occupied by the sea Dyaks on the great rivers is generally flat towards the sea, but more un-dulating in the interior.   It is covered in many parts with dense forests, and the soil is rich and productive, so that, when peaceably disposed, they are large ex-porters of rice, and all kinds of fruits are abundant and very cheap in their districts.   As far as is yet known of the products, gold is not one of them, nor have I seen specimens of any other metals which have been extracted from their soil. Small paths intersect the forests between the villages of all the Sakarran and Sarebas tribes, so that a constant communication is easily kept up, and as their practices and interests are identical, the good understanding which has long existed between these powerful tribes of savages is likely to be maintained, as they probably very well know that a quarrel between them would only end in the ruin of both, their enemies being so numerous, and anxious to revenge upon them the many injuries they have sustained at their hands.

Though the Dyaks generally build their villages near the river for the convenience of launching their boats, there are many of them situated so high towards the sources of the streams as to be unnavigable from the rapids; the people inhabiting such join the boats belonging to some village situated lower down, and are thus enabled to participate in their piratical practices. The villages of the sea Dyaks are formed upon one plan, the houses being, if the tribe be small—that is to say, of about sixty families—all collected under one roof. Each house has its separate door, which opens into a broad verandah covered in by a continuation of the pitch of the roof, and which answers all the purposes of a street, being floored with laths of bamboo or nibong, and on a level with the flooring of the houses. One terrace of such buildings is often 500 or 600 feet in length, and the houses being built on very strong posts with wooden sides, and covered with atap, they present frequently a neater and more comfortable appearance than the frequently ruinous houses of the Malays. Besides the door opening into the verandah, they have on each side of their dwellings, which consist only of one room, a door communicating with the residence of the next family, so that, if it were an advantage, a person could traverse the whole length of the terrace without appearing on the verandah at all. The windows of their houses are part of the roof, which, in the construction of the house, has been separated for that purpose ; it is raised and supported open by a notched bamboo or other stick, and when shut is undistinguishable from the rest of the roof. The ataps composing the thatch are not each tied to the rafters, but being bound into large sheets are secured only in a few places, so that in case of fire, by the few fastenings being cut, they are easily slid from the steep sloping roof, and prevented from adding fuel to the, without them, too inflammable dwellings.

The large covered shed or verandah above described is the place where all the in-door occupations of the men and women are carried on, and when not engaged in out-door occupations, they may be all seen here together pursuing their varied avocations ; the men in preparing weapons of the chase or war, or instruments of agriculture, the women in cleaning rice from the husk, making mats, baskets, &c. As the inhabitants of the different villages combine to repair or rebuild them all at the same time, their houses and terraces have always an uniform appearance, and are all of the same size. In the interior arrangements of their houses the fire-places, of which there are two, are placed on each side of the principal entrance; each is formed of a kind of shallow box, or framework, of strong pieces of wood filled with clay; this is supported on strong wooden posts reaching through the flooring to the ground, and extending to the top of the house. On the clay are four or five stones of a convenient size, which serve for sustaining the cooking pot over the fire, which is placed in the space left between them, and is always of wood, a large supply of which, split and ready, is always kept dry on another framework above the fire-place, and supported by the same posts. This it is the duty of the women constantly to replenish from the trees which have been felled in clearing the ground, and which are strewed abundantly all over their farms. As the roofs are high in the centre, and slope at a sharp angle, much room in the top of the house is rendered available by the Dyaks, who erect another flooring over the one they constantly use; thus they have a large and useful loft where they stow their baskets, mats, and implements of agriculture during the season they are not in use. As may be supposed, people in their state of barbarity have little need of furniture, which for the most part is used to administer to the purposes

of luxury. The Dyaks eat their food from the ground
for a table; each having taken a portion of rice
which he considers sufficient for him, this, if he be not
provided with a plate, which many of them are, is
placed upon a clean leaf of the Dillenia speciosa, and
he dips his hand into the common stock of salt which
is placed in the centre of the group. If they have
flesh to their repast it is partaken of in a similar manner to the salt. They never drink during their meal,
but on rising wash their hands and mouths, and afterwards take a draught of water from the bamboos,
which are always kept full near the fire-place. Though
they eat from the ground or floor of their houses, they
rarely sit cross-legged upon it like the Malays, but
have each a small block of wood about three inches in
thickness, which they use as a seat by day and a
pillow by night.

Around the walls of the apartment hang the
gongs and other musical instruments, and such portions of their dress as they do not happen to be
using, together with their spears, shields, and instruments of war. One side of the house always contains
a rack, in which are placed the naked swords of the
family, the sheaths hanging by their side. The doors
of their houses are protected on the inside by a bar,
but as pilfering is rare amongst these people, it is
perhaps more to prevent intrusion when they wish for
privacy, than as a protection against robbers. This is
rendered evident by the doors, which cannot be fas-

tened on the outside, being closed when they are at their farms by the mortar in which their rice is cleaned, and which always stands outside the door in the verandah, or some other heavy piece of wood being merely placed against it. The whole of their buildings, though of so substantial and good appearance, are formed and fastened together without the assistance of nails, their place being supplied by rattans and other cordage.

The language of the sea Dyaks, though altogether different in such parts as having not been adopted from the Malay, is merely a less refined dialect of the language spoken over all Polynesia, and its connexion with that of the other wild tribes, particularly those of Sumatra, is easily to be traced. It is not nearly so melodious in sound, or so copious in its extent, as the Malay, though the Dyaks do not scruple to extend it by adding foreign words whenever they find it neeessary, so that a great portion of the words of their vocabulary are from the Malay : the intercourse, which has been generally friendly, between the two nations has also encouraged this adoption of foreign terms. Specimens of their language are given in the work of Captain Keppel, from the vocabularies of Mr. Brooke, and as I can vouch for their correctness, it is not necessary to repeat them here. The different tribes into which the sea division of the Dyaks is again separated have each dialects, which differ in a trifling measure from that generally spoken, but as far as I

have been able to learn, not nearly so much so as
amongst the land Dyaks, and never so much but that
the tribes belonging to this division, situated most
distant from each other, are prevented from the most
free communication. This greater similarity of dialect
amongst these many villages, than prevails amongst
the land tribes, may easily be accounted for, by the
greater friendship and intercourse which has subsisted
perhaps from the time of their separating from each
other : as far as is known, at no period of their history
were they ever at war with each other, but were always
the foes of the Kyans and land Dyaks in their vicinity ;
the land tribes, on the contrary, appear always to have
been at war with all the tribes in their neighbourhood,
which, though perhaps they did not cause the yearly
average of a single death, effectually prevented all
friendly communication.

The religious observances of these people are very
little known, but in their state of civilization it cannot
be supposed to extend beyond a few superstitions
and belief in spirits of woods and mountains ; their
chief deity is called Batara, a pure Sanscrit term for
God, but this appears to be the only relic left them
of their former intercourse with the Javan Hindus,
who seem never to have possessed so much influence
over the sea Dyaks as over the land tribes, none of
the peculiar Hindu customs of these latter obtaining
among them. The doctor and priest of the village,
who is termed manang, is a very curious and mys-

terious character, and I have not been able to learn
that a similar functionary exists amongst the wild
tribes of the other islands, but as far as my inquiries
in Borneo are concerned, the curious practice of priest-
craft which follows is peculiar to the sea Dyak tribes.
The manang is a person of great consequence in the
village, all diseases being brought to him for cure; to
perform this, if the disease be internal, he calls together
all the friends of the sick person, and by making, with
the assistance of others playing on gongs and tomtoms, a deafening noise, sufficient to kill a person
in ordinary health. He pretends to converse with the
spirit which troubles the afflicted person. This method
of treating diseases is not very conducive to the restoration of health, but if the strength of the person is
sufficient to bear him through, it is well; but should he
die, no blame is attached to the manang, but it all
devolves upon the malignant spirit, who is certainly
not so black as, on these occasions, he is painted.

I have not been able to hear correctly whether the
pamali, or the taboo, hereafter to be described, is
practised on these occasions, but as it is an institution
anterior to the introduction of the Hindu religion on the
west coast, I should suppose it here to be practised
with the same rigour as amongst the land tribes.

But to return to the dress and habits of life of the
manang. He is generally old, and rich from the many
presents and payments made to him by those who
require his services : his dress precisely resembles

that of a woman, wearing no chawat, or waistcloth, as the men, but the bedang, or short dress of the other sex, hereafter to be described, together with the appropriate ornaments. Not satisfied with the assumption of the dress of the women, the manang, the more to resemble them, takes unto himself a husband, who is generally a widower having a family, and who, in expectation of inheriting the manang's property, is glad to comply with his caprices : he is treated in every respect as a woman, and does not go to war with the men; he sees little of his husband, and the fact of calling a person by this name appears only to be necessary to render his assumed character more complete.   I could never learn any thing of the history of this curious institution from the Dyaks themselves, they declaring they knew nothing of it, and merely saying that it was an old custom, and laughed with us at its absurdity : perhaps it originated in persons of natural imbecility, being compelled by the tribe to assume the garb and habits of women, and thus have become through time a custom followed by men who were apparently in every respect fitted for the ordinary intercourse of society.   I do not know whether they are brought up to this profession, but I rather think that they enter it after having attained a considerable age.   I never saw any one who had a wife or children of his own, though they might have perhaps been married while young; they are permitted to adopt the children of other people, and this they frequently do.

Perhaps they only become manangs after having proved themselves incapable of becoming the fathers of families, but I am not inclined to believe that such is the case.

In general appearance the sea Dyaks have the advantage of the Malays and land tribes, being of a higher, though still short, stature, well made, and with limbs of excellent proportions; a subdued and calm, but resolute air; an imposing carriage, walking with a light and graceful step, and peculiarly self-possessed bearing; these qualities impress the stranger more favourably than the smaller stature, less elegant figures, darker features, and more cunning expression of the countenance of the Malays.

The dress of the sea Dyaks is very simple, the principal article of it being the chawat, a long, narrow cloth, which passing several times round the waist, and being brought between the thighs, has its broader and ornamented ends hanging before and behind to the knees. The ends hanging thus have very much the appearance of broad tails at a distance, and when these are made of the inner bark of trees, as is frequent among the land Dyaks, might easily suggest the idea of tails; and we consequently find that a race of men with these appendages inhabiting the interior is a notion very prevalent along the coast. In ordinary weather, and when about their usual occupations, the chawat above described is their only clothing, but in wet or cold days they wear a coarse jacket of cotton,

N

coloured brown ; these jackets and chawats are manufactured by the Dyaks of Sakarran and Sarebas, as are
also the cotton bedangs of the women, and in times of
peace they form an article of export to all the tribes
of the neighbouring countries, the natives of none of
which manufacture them for themselves.

A war party, or individuals of the Dyaks of Sakarran
and Sarebas, are immediately recognised by the members
of the other tribes by the abundance of their brass ornaments, and particularly the number of rings in their
ears, the outer cartilage of that organ being pierced with
holes along its edges for its whole length for their reception : the hole in the lobe of the ear contains the
largest and greatest number of these ornaments, three or
four being frequently found in it, sometimes equal to three
inches in diameter. The whole number contained in
each ear of the Dyak varies from six or eight to fourteen, and in young men, occasionally to eighteen ;
these gradually decrease in size towards the top of
the ear, where they are very small. Other ornaments
of brass-wire are distributed in profusion about their
persons, particularly on their legs and arms ; these
latter are frequently covered with numerous rings of
very strong brass-wire about an eighth of an inch in
thickness, the elbow joint is the only part left bare,
and it is frequently adorned with a large white bracelet
made of the kima-shell ; occasionally these rings of
brass are flattened and stamped in various patterns,
but the more general taste is to leave them round and

plain, taking great care to keep them highly polished, One would think that the necessary weight of so much brass would be an inconvenient and cumbrous burden, but habit, and the taste for finery, soon reconcile this people to the load, and having been inured to it from their earliest infancy, they do not feel it so much as strangers would necessarily do. Large rings of this wire also adorn the legs of the young men from immediately below the knee to the middle of the calf of the leg, and on their necks strings of the teeth of their enemies, and of bears, panthers, and other wild animals, are their favourite ornaments.

In peace, their head-dress is a handkerchief, or a piece of the inner bark of a tree, dyed of a bright yellow, and is so disposed that its ends stand up from the forehead; their hair is cut in such a manner as to give to their features the most savage-looking appearance, being shaved from that part of the head near the temples in an arched form, so that the ends of the two arches meet in the middle of the forehead in a fine point: the hair is cut short in front, but left long and flowing behind. In war, they wear jackets of a thicker texture, which are also padded with cotton to such a thickness as to enable them to resist the blow from the point of a wooden spear. Their head-dress on these occasions is a kind of fillet, about two inches broad, made of red cloth ornamented with very small white cowrie shells, or beads, worked into different patterns; from these fillets rise feathers of different kinds of birds, but

the white tail feathers, each having a broad black band
across it, of the rhinoceros hornbill, are preferred;
they have no covering or protection for their thighs or
legs, but leave them as on ordinary occasions; their
parang, or large chopping knife, is suspended from
their left sides, and another string supports on the
opposite side the little basket which contains their
sirih leaves, betel-nut, and lime, for chewing;
these are placed in little cases of bamboo ornamented with brass or silver, and very much carved,
but after a very rude manner.   A similar bamboo
case, and which is generally also carried in this little
tambuk, or basket, contains their tinder, flint, and
steel; a long knife is generally attached to it.

The women of these tribes are, like their husbands
and brothers, short in stature, generally more stoutly
made than the Malay women, and with well-developed
figures; they are very much fairer than they, or even
than the men of their own tribes: while young many
of them would be thought very pretty, but soon, from
their hard duties and other causes, they become stout
and plain, and when old are frequently very ugly.
When brought up amongst the Malays they continue
much longer in their prime, and are generally thought
prettier than the women of that nation: their hair,
though naturally as good, from want of care and cultivation never attains such length and profusion amongst
those who reside in their own villages, though in circumstances which give them time for the adorn-

ment of their persons it attains equal length and luxuriance.

They are, like the men, fond of ornaments of brass or silver, and display them liberally on their persons; their principal article of dress is the bedang, a very short petticoat of their own cotton fabric of a coarse texture, and dyed of various patterns, but always of a brown or black colour. This scanty garment reaches from the hips to the knees, and is sustained in its position by being tucked in and fastened by a belt of fine brass chain-work, with a clasp, which encircles it; amongst those tribes that are richer than others, silver chain is often substituted for brass, and amongst the poorer ones, split rattans, coloured, or black, are frequently used: above and round this belt, and the upper part of the bedang, are innumerable folds of chain of brass, silver, and rattans, and when the wealth of the individuals will admit of it, strings of small silver coins are employed.

Their necks and breasts usually support numbers of folds of the same materials, with the occasional addition of beads; but these they do not so much esteem as the Dyaks of the hills: their arms are adorned with bracelets of silver very neatly made, being formed of thin plates of a broad and convex shape, so that they stand out from the arm; they have the patterns stamped upon them from the inside, and wear them from the wrist up the arm to the elbow, eight or nine in number; they do not, like the women of some other tribes, wear brass-wire above the elbow joint.   The women of the Sebooyoh and other tribes wear in their ears ornaments of gold or silver, which are of such an extent of surface as entirely to conceal that organ : like the bracelets, the pattern is stamped upon them from the back, and the thin plate is soldered to a small tube which passes through the hole pierced in the ear, and is fastened by a nut in the manner of the more elegant ear-ornaments of the Malayan women before described.   When about their household employments, these ornaments and this dress are generally worn by the females, but when they pursue their out-door duties a jacket similar to that of the men, but of a little finer texture, envelopes the upper part of their persons, and protects them from the thorns of the jungle.   In the house they wear no head-dress, but abroad a large hat, made of coloured rattans very finely woven, protects them from the weather : in size it approaches that of the market-women of Bruni, but is more peaked at the top, and of a much more elegant appearance.

From the little friendly intercourse between the town of Sarawak, and the Sarebas, and Sakarran Dyaks, I have not been able to collect such accurate details as I could have wished respecting the government established amongst the people of these rivers, which differs considerably from that of the hill tribes, and more nearly approaches that of the orang Kyan, to the eastward of them, in many of their institutions.

The sea Dyaks appear to form a connecting link between the land tribes and the Kyans, showing that they are all of the same family; and, perhaps, these three great and distinct divisions are but the descendants of three different emigrations at periods remote from each other, and when peculiar causes might have altered, as we now see them, the characters of each.   All the tribes of Sarebas, though each has its particular chief, acknowledge in war the authority of the orang kaya Pa-mancha; but it does not appear that, excepting when his orders and instructions agree with their own wishes, the petty chiefs, who command their own boats and the people of their own villages, pay particular attention to them, but still they always look up to this old man—who has distinguished himself by his bravery—with respect, and his opinion possesses great weight in their councils, more particularly, as, from his sanguinary nature, and the long practised custom of taking heads, his store of which he is always anxious to increase, the counsels of peace are seldom those he offers to the nation.

In Sakarran they have several chiefs of great authority; that part of the country which lies nearest to the sea is under the authority of one head chief, named Gasing: he is a man in the prime of life, a very sensible and fine-looking fellow; and is, I believe, anxious to be at peace with the English, but finds it impossible to control his followers, and the other chiefs of tribes, who are of a different opinion.   At a council, which met at the junction of the Sakarran

and Batang Lupar rivers, an embassy sent by Mr.
Brooke from Sarawak in the end of 1845, I heard
this man declare, before several chiefs and many
people, that he would with his own hand kill the first
who committed piracy on the ocean, or in any way
departed from the wishes of Mr. Brooke; several
other chiefs asserted the same, but we afterwards
heard that they were compelled ultimately to join the
war faction, by their people deserting to the villages
of the interior, whose chiefs were all of the opposite
party.

Gasing, in this part of the Sakarran country,
is acknowledged to have very considerable influence,
if he has not lost it by his advocacy of peaceable
measures. Under him is a chief named Bulan, or
the moon; he is called the war-chief, and directs all
the operations at the encounter of a hostile fleet or on
the attack of a village. He appeared to us a man
of but little intellect, who had attained his rank by
nothing but his bull-dog courage. During the council
above mentioned, he sat without taking the least notice
of the proceedings, and, as soon as it was over, came
to our boats to solicit cloths and handkerchiefs as
presents. This man once led an attack against Banting, the village of the Balow Dyaks, allies of Sarawak,
while his son and nephew were in our hands; so that
judging, as he must have done, that his son and
nephew would be put to death by the Europeans, he
must have made up his mind to sacrifice them to his
passion for heads.

His son and nephew had been sent to Singapore at Mr. Brooke's expense, and at their own request, during the short interval of quietness, which occurred after the peace above mentioned; they had received from Mr. Church, and other gentlemen of Singapore, much attention and many presents, and were about returning to Sarawak in the schooner, when their relation broke the peace by attacking our allies. They were very much afraid that we should revenge ourselves upon them, but, as may be supposed, they were sent back to Sakarran, with all their valuables, unharmed. Though the effect of this generosity, and of the general conduct of the government of Sarawak to these people has not yet been visible, it is doubtless working, and must soon appear; and, though such a savage as Bulan can, perhaps, never be affected, there is a strong party favourable to the English rising in their tribes.

Besides the two principal chiefs above named, they have one called Lingie, who is designated the trading chief, and who appears to have the regulation of the commerce of the river. This man has given several proofs, at the risk of his life, of his anxiety to prevent war between his river and the settlement of Sarawak: on one occasion he came, pulling night and day, in a small boat, at Gasing's request, to inform Mr. Brooke that a fleet of eighteen boats was going to descend the upper part of the river on a cruise: by his information they were all captured. The commander of the fleet heard that he had gone to give this intelligence, and followed him for about fifty miles; if he had been caught, his life, with that of his people, would have been sacrificed to his anxiety to maintain peace.

In several conversations I have had with Lingie he has painted, in striking colours, the benefits which would arise to this great agricultural country from the preservation of peace, and the miseries entailed upon them by being at war with Sarawak, which prevents them bringing their padi and bees'-wax, cloths, &c., to market, and supplying themselves with salt, which is almost as necessary as rice to the existence of a Dyak, and their supply of which, being all obtained from the coast, is easily, and generally, stopped on their rupture with the Malayan powers. This man related to me an anecdote of himself, which, notwithstanding the defence they made, proves the actual fear in which they held the force under Captain Keppel. Lingie was in his house cooking a pot of rice (his wife and family having been previously sent into the jungle for security, together with those of the other men inhabiting his village), and listening anxiously for information of the English force, which had attacked the town of Pa-mutus, and which Sereib Sahib, who defended it, had assured the Dyaks could never be taken by the orang putih, or white men, when a gun, discharged below his residence on the river, informed him that Pa-mutus was taken, and that the English were ascending the stream. Alarmed by the report, he seized his cooking pot and rushed out of the house, the door of which he reached in time to see his friends and followers scampering off to the jungle for protection; he lost no time in imitating their example, with his rice-pot in his hand; and so great was his haste that his chawat, or cloth, having become unfastened and fallen to the ground, he rejoined his companions in a state of perfect nudity, not daring to stop to pick up his fallen covering. He told me that he was not ashamed to confess himself afraid of the English, on account of their fire-arms, but that if swords and spears were their weapons he would not mind them so much.

Besides these three principal chiefs of the Sakarran Dyaks, each village has its head, who, in the general council of the nation, has an influence proportioned to the individual character of each one. Of these a fine young man named Mata-hari, or the sun, has already distinguished himself in their piratical expeditions, and is a general favourite with their tribes. No other chief is allowed to interfere in the government of these villages, their internal management being left entirely to a council of the old men, by whose advice the orang kaya generally guides his conduct.

As the interior of the countries of Sakarran and Sarebas has never been visited by Europeans, excepting on hostile occasions, we have no means of judging of the number of villages it contains; but according to the best native authorities, they are more numerous and thickly inhabited than the villages of the poor, and till recently oppressed, land Dyaks, many of whose women and children have been taken from their homes, and now swell the number of these tribes of their enemies. Having always preserved peace amongst themselves, these two powerful nations have been able to preserve their country from invasion, and to inspire terror wherever they carried their arms. The only exception to this appears to be the Kyans, who have always been able to repel the invasions of these, who, amongst the weaker tribes, have sustained, from their uniform success, the reputation of a courage which they suppose themselves to be incapable of withstanding.

The passion for head-hunting, which now characterizes these people, was not formerly so deeply rooted in their characters as it is at present, and many of the inhabitants of Sarawak have assured me that they well recollect the tribes first visiting the sea with that ostensible and avowed object. In a limited extent the custom is probably as ancient as their existence as a nation; but though other tribes appear to be equally addicted to the practice, there can be little doubt that it is a corruption of its first institution, unless, as Forrest says of the Idaan of the north of Borneo, they consider human sacrifice the most pleasing to the divinity, and lose no opportunity of presenting it; but having conversed with the Dyaks frequently respecting this practice, they gave no such reason for it, and merely accounted for it, in their usual method, by saying, that it was the adat ninik, or custom of their ancestors.

The Malays themselves, who now frequently feel its bad effects upon their persons and nation, have been in a great measure instrumental in encouraging this barbarous practice. During the prevalence of the Arab power in Sadong under the Sereibs Sahib, Muller, and their relations, and the misrule of the chiefs of Sarawak during the ten or twelve years previous to Mr. Brooke's arrival, these unprincipled chieftains found the practice of head-taking amongst the Sakarrans might be made serviceable to their interests. The poor hill Dyaks, who had been previously protected from the ravages of the fierce Sakarrans only by the Malays residing between them and their foes, and having been robbed of every thing calculated to excite the rapacity of their rulers, made an effort to save their wives and daughters from the slavery which threatened them, by concealing themselves in the jungle. The Sakarran Dyaks were then called in by the extortionate and foolish rulers, and, assisted by a party of Malays with firearms, generally found the hill Dyaks an easy prey. Thus an opportunity was presented to them of acquiring abundance of victims, whose heads the Malayan chieftains allowed them to retain, while they took all the plunder, and shared the slaves. In these expeditions, several of which occurred annually, the greater part of the Dyaks of Sarawak and Sadong were attacked, their men and women slain and decapitated under the most cruel circumstances, and the virgins and children were carried by their parents' destroyers into captivity. Those who, by concealment, had succeeded in escaping the sword of the oppressor, from their hiding-places beheld the flames consume their remnants of property and their villages. It can easily be imagined after this account of their sufferings, which might easily be swelled by an enumeration of horrors common to civilised, and many peculiar to barbarian warfare, with what pleasure they hailed the return of peace, which Mr. Brooke's arrival promised them; and the gratitude they now feel, and the affection with which they regard the man who saved their residue from starvation, slavery, and death, is equal to the sufferings from which his humanity delivered them; and the only fear which has hitherto, since the establishment of his government, alloyed their happiness is, that any accident should interrupt the protection they have hitherto received; but now they have gained so strong a hold upon the sympathy of the generous British nation, there is little prospect of this fear being ever realised.

By such encouragement the sea Dyaks have been confirmed in the practice of head-hunting, and taught to consider the divided and weaker tribes of the hills their natural prey. It is difficult to conceive how their rulers could have been so blind to their own interest, as so to oppress the people from whom they gained their revenues and subsistence, and for the sake of a trifle more at one time than they were in the custom of demanding, to destroy their only hope of a future supply. Perhaps the Arab Sereibs, whom Sir Stamford Raffles in describing truly says, " hold like robbers the offices they obtain as sycophants, and cover all with the veil of religious hypocrisy," thought that after they had destroyed the land tribes, they would subsist entirely by piracy on the part of the sea Dyaks, and by their piratical relations with the Soolu and other nations who frequented the coasts and bays of their territories. Pa-mutus in the Sakarran river was the scene of their overthrow, and though the Sereibs were not taken, the principal of them, Sereib Sahib, has since died, and the remainder, scattered about amongst the tribes of Sarebas and Sakarran, are in a great measure the cause of the bad conduct of these tribes. At the capture of the eighteen boats formerly mentioned, three of them were present, and fled in such haste to the jungle that their gold ornaments and fine clothing fell into the hands of the Balows.

As these Dyaks constantly retreat before a superior enemy into the jungles and fastnesses, it has been found almost impossible to bring their forces either on shore or at sea to a general action. Could their fleet be once caught in a bay, or other situation in which European sailors could teach them the fatal effects of grape and canister, they would be careful in venturing again to disturb the peaceful navigation of the sea. From the lightness of their

construction, their swiftness, and their light draft of
water, they are always able to evade the boats of our
cruisers; but should it be found advisable on the
establishment of Labuh-an, to reduce these people,
who are now—no less than the Lanuns and Soolus,
though in a narrower sphere—the terror of the coast,
they can be easily and effectually blockaded, and thus
soon reduced to quietness. At present, though they
have seen the gallant Captain Keppel in their river,
and at their own doors, they have no adequate idea
of our power, and fancy, as they have frequently
committed piracies since they were last visited, with
impunity, that no further notice will be taken of
them. It is to be wished that they may soon find this
an erroneous notion, and learn, though circumstances
may for a time prevent their punishment, that the
trade and interests of civilised nations cannot be
interrupted with impunity.

So difficult is it at present to induce them to leave
off, as a body, their piratical habits, that though the
first act of Mr. Brooke in the country, even before he
assumed the government of Sarawak, was to turn
back a fleet of ninety boats which had been invited
by the rajah to attack a land tribe, they have frequently since had the ignorance or impertinence to request his permission to destroy towns and villages under
his protection. Their first act of piracy since the expedition of the 'Dido' was to send out the fleet of
eighteen boats, previously mentioned as having been
captured by our allies, the Balow Dyaks. This

occurred in October, 1845. In November the late
Mr. Williamson, then Mr. Brooke's secretary, was
sent to them accompanied by a considerable force,
and having with him the Balow chiefs. They were
met at the Malay village, at the junction of the Sakarran and Batang Lupar, by Gasing, Lingi, Rantap,
Bulan, and other chiefs of Sakarran, and a treaty of
peace was agreed upon, a pig being killed, as is their
custom. This, however, was not long observed. In
March, 1846, a large fleet, led by Bulan, the war-
chief of Sakarran, attacked the village of the Balow
Dyaks, and killed thirty-five persons, though they had
some Malays in the place, and one or two small guns,
which were taken. The success which attended this
expedition was on account of their having surprised
the village when the men were all absent at the farms.
During the past season, the Sambas and Sakarran
Dyaks attacked one of the kampongs of Kalkeka, the
next considerable river eastward from Sarebas, and in
the government of the Dattu Patengi Abdulraham, of
Serekei, who, however, assisted by a force of the Kyans
who inhabit the interior of his country, so amply
retaliated, that upwards of fifty of the people of Sarebas were killed or taken captive.

On another recent occasion the son of the old Orang
Kaya Pa Mancha, the principal chief of Sarebas, was
slain by our Dyaks, who accompanied a fleet in search
of these pirates, and this has given them another
opportunity of swearing to possess themselves of the

head of the Rajah of Sarawak, and annihilating his settlement. A stage for drying the much coveted head has been accordingly erected, and one of their rare and much valued jars has been prepared for its reception.

At the attack on the Balow village, in the height of their excitement, Bulan is reported, with others, to have called out to the assailed, that his only wish was that a steam-ship, of which in reality they have the greatest possible dread, might heave in sight, as he would then have the pleasure of showing the Balow people how he would treat their friends, the English, previously to taking their own heads. A similar cry, taunting the Princes of Borneo with their relations to the English, was raised at their unfortunate massacre, and the arrival of British ships was in the same manner spoken of in derision; but on Admiral Cochrane's appearance in the river they quickly retired from their forts. It has been before stated, that while the taunting expressions above recited were used by Bulan, the son and nephew of this thoughtless savage were in the hands of the English: he is reported to have said, when reminded of this circumstance, that his sons were clever in the jungle, and that he trusted to their making their escape as soon as the news reached Sarawak.

Though from their friendly intercourse with the Malays they have adopted some of the customs, and have borrowed considerably from the language of that people, they have not introduced polygamy, or, with the exception of slavery, any other of their reprehensible practices. The ceremony of marriage, as far as I have learnt, is very simple, and consists merely in the persons, who have previously agreed upon the point, living together, and a feast being made on the occasion to which all who choose may repair. Their marriage feasts, like all the others, usually end in the whole of the persons assembled becoming intoxicated with a fermented beverage which they make from rice, and which they affirm they were taught by the Chinese. The state of morality amongst the Sakarran and Sambas Dyaks is strangely more lax than in any of the other tribes. It is affirmed, and they themselves have frequently told me, that it is the common custom for the unmarried women to have amongst the similarly situated of the other sex, lovers to whom they are liberal of their favours: this proceeds with the knowledge and consent of the parents for some time, but if the girl should prove pregnant, the father of the child must take the mother for his wife; but if the connexion should long continue without the attainment of this desired result, the acquaintance is discontinued, and they each seek new sharers of their loves. Should they not be constant to each other during this stage of their intimacy, the offence, though public, never becomes an occasion of scandal to either person concerned, and nothing is said of it except, perhaps, by the one who has been deceived.

Though virtue before marriage is thus little respected, faithlessness after the marriage feast has taken place is a grave and serious offence in which the whole village is concerned. I believe it is punished by fine, but the offence is of such rare occurrence that no person to my knowledge ever incurred the penalty. The license granted to the young women appears amongst these people only to extend to their own nation, but it is probable, and in fact certain, in some tribes, that their favours are liberally extended to the Malays, should any happen to reside in their vicinity. This laxity of manners has been carried so far, that I have been assured that should a chief, or distinguished warrior of another tribe, travelling through the country, rest for a night at a village, it is a necessary part of their hospitality to provide a girl for his companion; but my information on this particular is derived from the Malays. I, however, think it correct, as a similar custom is always followed by the Kyans.

The promiscuous intercourse between the unmarried of the two sexes above described is a curious institution, and not known to the hill tribes. From the father of a child being compelled to marry its mother, and from their never being known to have any reluctance to do so, it would appear to have been originally practised as a precautionary measure arising from their fear of not becoming the fathers of families, which the Dyak would consider the greatest possible misfortune, though, from the facility with which they can separate, but which they seldom avail themselves of, such a practice would not seem necessary. All the Dyaks are exceedingly fond of their children, and proud of their families in proportion to the number of them. The curious practice of sinking their own name on the birth of the first child, and being afterwards denominated by its name with the prefix of the particle Pa, is strongly illustrative of their family pride. The Pa placed before the name of the child is a contraction of the word bapa, and gives a stranger immediately to understand that Pa Such-an-one is the father of children. Thus the chief of the land Dyaks, who is, or was, named Nimūk, is called . Pa Jaguen, Jaguen being the name of his eldest child. This curious custom is also mentioned by Mr. Marsden as being prevalent among the inland tribes of Sumatra. The term Ma, a contraction of the word ama, is mother, and is also occasionally used as a polite method of designating the mother of a family; but they are always called in the village by their own names. It may be observed of this custom, that, should the eldest child be dead, or lost, having become a slave to the enemies of the tribe, the parent is called after the next surviving one, or the next in seniority which remains with him. Thus Pa Jaguen was called Pa Belal until his daughter Jaguen was restored to him from Sakarran slavery by the assistance of the Rajah of Sarawak. I have had frequent proofs of the love they bear their children, and the longing with which they desire the return of such as have been carried into slavery. Mr. Brooke has been the means of restoring many of those objects of their solicitude by his negociations with the Sakarran and Sarebas Dyaks, although this has not been accomplished without a large pecuniary sacrifice: the gratitude they show for the happiness he has conferred upon them has amply repaid him for his liberality. The girls are equally the objects of the tender care of their parents with the boys; and though, in their prayers, the Dyaks always ask for male children, the females, who are nearly equally useful to them, are not treated with less kindness, and are never neglected. Amongst the sea Dyaks are no houses erected, as of the hill tribes, to be hereafter described, for the reception of the unmarried men; but though they are supposed generally to sleep in the verandah of the village, the interior of the houses is not denied to them.

The duties of the women are various and numerous; though the whole care of the house devolves upon them, they are not exempted from participation in the labours of the field. They always rise before day-break, and, if it be the season, accompany their husbands to the farm, carrying with them their breakfast of rice which has been previously cooked; but as they generally have a hut at the farm, they often cook their rice there. Their labours of husbandry consist in clearing away the brushwood, while the men fell the larger trees, in sowing their padi seed, and weeding the plants after they have sprung up, and in collecting the harvest when the crop is ripe; this, as the padi seldom all ripens together, is a tedious and laborious occupation, as they have to cut off each ear, or head of the padi, separately. They generally return to their houses half an hour before the men, who arrive at dark, so that they may have their plain and simple food prepared for them; this seldom consists of any thing but rice and salt, except when their traps are successful in procuring them better fare. Though they have numbers of fowls, pigs, and goats, about their houses, they seldom kill them excepting on occasions of general festivity. When they can afford to purchase salt fish from the Malays, they much prefer it to animal food.

Nor after the harvest has been gathered, and the labours of the farm have for a time ceased, are the women allowed to be idle; they have constant employment in making cloth of the cotton, as already noticed; fine mats of rattans worked into pretty patterns; baskets for the next season, made of split and coloured rattans, which they carry on their backs, suspended by a band which crosses the forehead; clearing padi from the husk, so that it may be brought to market as rice, or preparing it for their own use; these, together with their household duties, attending to their children, and carrying wood and water for their families, fully occupy their time, and the cheerful alacrity with which these are all undertaken by them, is alike

pleasing and instructive to the beholder. But while
so many employments and labours fall to the lot of
the women, the men, unlike those described as the
inhabitants of the South Sea, and other more eastern
islands of Polynesia, do not dissipate their time in
debauchery or indolence, but are equally active and
industrious with their weaker helpmates. The heaviest
labours of the farm, the management of their trade
with the Malays, building and repairing their houses
and boats, making their implements of husbandry and
war, employ all the time remaining from their expeditions of hunting and piracy. It is very probable
that, from the number of slaves in their possession,
the sea-Dyaks, particularly those of the Sarebas and
Sakarran tribes, do not personally labour so heavily as
those of the hills ; this may account for their finer appearance, which has been constantly observed by the
residents at Sarawak. Not being stunted by hard
work, and frequent scarcity of food, their limbs more
freely develope themselves than those of the poor and
hitherto oppressed hill-Dyaks, who, having lost their
only assistants by their children being carried into
captivity, where they perform for their enemies those
services which had otherwise assisted them, are compelled themselves to toil from day to day for the
subsistence of such as remain, and to endeavour
to procure money to purchase back the absent. The
slaves of the sea-Dyaks do not in general appear
to be hardly treated, as in their wars only such as

are young are taken captive; these, after living with their captors for some years, lose the remembrance of their families, or, perhaps, only recollect that they were destroyed, and consequently fall into the customs and practices of the people amongst whom they live, and from whose power they soon lose all hope of deliverance. In many instances children, who have been taken from the land-Dyaks, become so endeared to their conquerors, that these latter adopt them as their own, and they are then admitted to all the privileges of the free-born of the tribe, and inter-marry with the sons and daughters of the other inhabitants of the village. Instances are not uncommon when children thus treated have forgotten their parents, and expressed, when the opportunity of returning to their tribe has presented itself to them, an unwillingness to avail themselves of it, thus causing to the parents who had so tenderly cherished the remembrance of them, infinite agony; but, when they have once arrived at their native village, and experienced all the kindness of parental affection, these impressions soon wear away, and they are alway finally glad that they had been restored. In the villages the slaves are not distinguishable from their masters and mistresses, as they live all together, and fare precisely the same, eating from the same dish, and of the same food; this, as has been before observed, is principally of a vegetable nature, though no superstitious observance prevents them from partaking of the flesh of animals, as amongst the inland tribes. Nearly all the beasts of the forest are eaten by these people, even monkeys, alligators (if small), snakes and other reptiles are esteemed. Like the French, they regard frogs as a delicate dish, and bestow considerable pains in procuring them: their rice is cooked in brass or earthen pots, called priuks, which they purchase from the Malays; and plates of English manufacture have recently become very general among them. They eat from the plates with their right hand, compressing the rice (which is not cooked dry as that of the Malays) into a ball of convenient size. They know no way of cooking flesh but by boiling it, which they do in bamboos, having previously cut the whole animal into small pieces.

I once saw some Dyaks roasting a monkey, but did not stay to observe whether they did not boil it afterwards, as they generally partially roast these animals to free them from the hair. They have very little idea of flavouring their food except with salt, though they sometimes employ chilis, or small capsicums, turmeric, and ginger for that purpose. The Sebooyohs, who have lived more intimately with the Malays than the other tribes, have very much improved upon their cooking, the methods having been copied from their Mahometan neighbours. As they have no occasion for fire except for the purposes of cooking, their houses have no chimney, and the little smoke which is created finds its way through the crevices of the roof; and, as they rarely, with the exception of the Sebooyohs, who affect Malayan habits, indulge in the luxury of mosquito curtains, the smoke is rather beneficial than otherwise, as it protects them in some measure from the attacks of these tormenting insects, which, though not numerous in the interior, are, with sand-flies, very abundant on the sea-shore. They generally carry with them in their tambuk a flint and steel, for the purpose of making fire; but should these not be with them, but little difficulty is experienced in obtaining it from two pieces of bamboo, or by friction of a hard and soft stick, the latter of which soon takes fire.

The whole of the sea tribes dispose of their dead by burial, which, together with their not abstaining from the flesh of animals, induces me to suppose that the Hindu religion never influenced them, as it evidently has the land tribes; or that, if they knew any thing of its institutions, the impressions having been less strong have been by time altogether removed. A person having died, the manang, or doctor, who has been in attendance during the sickness, has also the superintendence of the interment, and the grave being prepared, the body of the deceased, dressed in his finest apparel, is placed in it, together with his sword, spear, gongs, and other property : if the family has been rich, the ornaments of gold and silver are added, and frequently a sum of money, amounting to forty or fifty dollars, in addition, and the earth covers the whole.

No ceremony attends the interment at the grave, but a pig is killed in the village, and the rite is terminated much in the manner of an Irish wake. This practice of burying property was practised by the Indians of North America, and probably by those of the southern division of that continent, and must have originated in a belief in the future existence of the deceased person, and that he would require these things in another state ; but at present, as far as I could learn, these people have no idea of the sublime belief of the soul's immortality ; and though some of them have asserted that the spirits of deceased persons wander amongst the mountains, the more frequent answer was, that they knew nothing of their fate.   The memory of a person, and the respect paid to him, is not supposed to be obliterated at the festival on the day of his burial, but, at long and uncertain intervals, other feasts are made, when some of the relics of the deceased, as a portion of his clothes or weapons, are treated with a place of ceremony at the banquet, and looked upon with great respect. The whole of these and their other festivals end in the same manner.   On account of the ignorant custom of burying such valuable property as above described with the bodies of their deceased relations, it frequently happens that a father, unfortunate in his family, is, by the death of his children, reduced to poverty.

On one occasion, the Europeans of Sarawak having been invited to be present at one of these wakes of the last son of the chief of the Pedungan village, the old man lamented that, having with each of his children, who had all died successively, buried a considerable portion of his property, he was now not only childless but penniless. Of this he did not complain, but that having deprived himself of his wealth, in accordance with a sacred custom of the Dyaks, the repose of his children had been violated, and the sacrilegious Malays had opened the graves, for the purpose of abstracting the treasures which had been placed there. Mr. Brooke, to whom the complaint was made, very properly consoled the old man by telling him that, if by any means the perpetrators of this act could be brought to justice, they should be severely punished; and, turning to the Malayan chiefs in attendance on him, requested them to assist in discovering the offenders. This was comfort to the Dyak chief, as during the government of the Malayan rajahs he durst not have complained of such an offence, it being no transgression to defile the grave of the infidel.

CHAPTER VII.

LIKE the whole of the aboriginal inhabitants of Borneo,
the sea-Dyaks hold periodical feasts, which usually end
in scenes of debauchery and drunkenness. Many occasions give rise to these, particularly the planting and
harvesting of the padi, and the capture of the heads
of their enemies : the latter is a disgusting ceremony
to an European, though the Dyaks view it only with
sentiments of satisfaction and delight. The fleet,
returning from a successful cruise, on approaching the
village, announce to its inhabitants their fortunes by a
horrid yell, which is soon imitated and prolonged by
the men, women, and children, who have stayed at
home. The head is brought on shore with much
ceremony, wrapped up in the curiously folded and
plaited leaves of the nipah palm, and frequently
emitting the disgusting odour peculiar to decaying

mortality ; this, the Dyaks have frequently told me, is particularly grateful to their senses, and surpasses the odorous durian, their favourite fruit.   On shore and in the village, the head, for months after its arrival, is treated with the greatest consideration, and all the names and terms of endearment of which their language is capable are abundantly lavished on it : the most dainty morsels, culled from their abundant though inelegant repast, is thrust into its mouth, and it is instructed to hate its former friends, and that, having been now adopted into the tribe of its captors, its spirit must be always with them : sirih leaves and betel-nut are given to it,—and finally, a cigar is frequently placed between its ghastly and pallid lips. None of this disgusting mockery is performed with the intention of ridicule, but all to propitiate the spirit by kindness, and to procure its good wishes for the tribe, of whom it is now supposed to have become a member.

The head having been thus cared for, the whole of the tribe partake of the pigs, rice, fish, and other food, which have been provided in the greatest profusion for the joyous occasion.   These pigs, taken always from the largest and fattest in the village, have been previously valued by the old men, and their owner is paid for them by rice, which is raised by contributions from the whole tribe, the proprietor of the pig remitting his share of its cost.   After having eaten sufficiently, the tobacco is produced, and they

chew betel and smoke cigars, drinking at the same
time large quantities of the liquor of the fermented
rice before mentioned, or of the toddy of various palms
provided for the occasion : during the drinking the
dancing generally commences ; this is performed with
the recently-acquired heads suspended from the
persons of the actors, who move up and down the
verandah with a slow step, and corresponding movements of their out-stretched arms, uttering occasionally
a yell, which rises fierce and shrill above the discordant
noises of the gongs, chanangs, and tortewaks, to which
the dancers move.   Another amusement at these festivals is carried on by two persons standing or walking
with a theatrical air and peculiar step, and with canes
in their hands, reciting to each other in a rude ex-
tempore verse, the heroic deeds of their fathers and
their ancestors, to which, if they live under a Malayan
government, and the prince has any share in their
affections, they add his memorable achievements and
exploits. I heard them once, in this interesting manner,
recount the whole of the events of the Seniawan war,
the arrival of Mr. Brooke, &c.

The " harvest home," and other feasts of a more
pacific character than that above described, like it,
consist in eating, drinking, and dancing, but in these
the heads are not introduced, and the women take
part.   Games are also practised at them, some of
which astonished us by their similarity to those
practised by the peasantry of Europe, particularly

that of climbing up a large pole, the being able to do which is also a necessary qualification of a pânglimà, or fighting chief,) previously greased to render the achievement difficult of performance, and to the top of which a piece of pork is attached. This meat is the reward of the person whose agility renders him the first to attain this eminence, and the frequent failures in the attempts call forth from the gazing crowd bursts of laughter, as loud and long continued as from those who gaze at the similar spectacle at an English country fair.

In the useful arts, excepting such as their habits render absolutely necessary, the Dyaks have made but little progress, though more than many of the similarly situated neighbouring tribes. It has been before remarked that they make the 'chawats,' jackets, and 'bedangs' in general use amongst their own and the more western tribes ; but as this manufacture is carried on only by the Dyaks of Sakarran and Sarebas, I have no means of describing the method of its workmanship. Iron being necessary in the formation of their weapons of war, they have studied, and brought to greater perfection its workmanship than others of the mechanical arts. It is probable that before the introduction of European bar-iron into the country, the natives fused and wrought the ore of the island, as many of the Kyan and other tribes, who have little intercourse with the coast, do to the present day. The blacksmith, with the exception of the 'manang,' or

P

doctor, is the only person in the village whose time is solely occupied by a profession or trade. If the black-smith of a village be celebrated for the goodness of his work, he is not only employed in the manufacture of the arms and instruments necessary for his tribe, but those made by him sell for higher prices than those of his neighbours, and he is sure of plenty of employ-ment and considerable profit. The smith's shop is always a little apart from the houses of the village, to prevent accidents from the fire; the bellows precisely resemble those of the Malays, the two bamboos, or hollow trees, before described; a stone is generally the anvil, but when a heavy piece of iron can be obtained it is preferred. His instruments are all of his own making, and rude in their construction; the vessel in which the water for cooling his work is held is a block of wood hollowed out. The 'parangs,' or chopping-knives, and 'pedangs,' or swords, of which there are several denominations, spear-heads and fish spears, are the principal articles of their manufacture. The chopping-knife, which the Dyak always carries by his side, is a rough and awkward looking instrument, though the Dyaks use it with facility: the blade, which is broadest towards the end, and small and square towards the base, is generally from twenty-four to thirty inches in breadth, the hilt being bent from the blade backwards, which makes it appear clumsy; the axe fits into a wooden handle, and the blade, which is round or square at the end, is preserved by a sheath made of two pieces of wood bound neatly together with plaited rattans, and bands of brass or silver.

The sword amongst the sea-Dyaks, though often precisely similar to the 'parang,' is frequently, amongst the Sebooyoh Dyaks, of a curved shape, the broadest part of the blade being at the point of its curvature, but not having the backward bend of the handle. It is altogether a more serviceable weapon, the hilt being generally made of deer's horn, very rudely carved. An ornament projecting from the lower part of the weapon, near the handle, serves as a guard for the hand; the handle of the weapon is generally ornamented with brass and silver; the sheath with a large bundle of the fine feathers of the argus pheasant, from which the quill has been pared, which, by its rigidity, would prevent the wind causing the feathers to wave about.

The spears of the sea-Dyaks are made of several forms, but those most used are the broad, double-edged blades, which are about one foot or more in length; these are attached to handles about six to eight feet long, as are also the sagittate blades, which are next in esteem. They are frequently made in pairs, so that their blades fit into a double case; they are then carried as one weapon. The 'sumpitan,' which is a tube of eight to ten feet in length, through which arrows or darts of nine to twelve inches are blown, the points of which are generally poisoned with the upas, are sometimes used by those Dyaks in the vicinity of the Kyans, from whom they have perhaps borrowed the practice; neither bows nor arrows are known in the islands.

In action, the left hand of the Dyak supports a
large wooden shield, which covers the greater part
of his body. It is made of the light wood of the plye
or jelutong, about three feet long, and twenty inches
broad, convex towards the centre, and of the same
breadth throughout, but cut off angularly from each
side at the ends, so that its greatest length is the
middle. The 'badju tilam,' or padded jacket, has been
before noticed. The spears used for throwing at the
enemy, and with which an engagement is usually commenced, are about three feet long, made of durable
wood, which is further hardened by fire : they seldom
do much injury to the enemy if he be prepared to
receive them: they are thrown with great force but
little skill, as they never practise during peace the use
of the weapons of war.

The wars of the sea-Dyaks are very frequent, and
much more bloody than those of the Malays or the
land tribes. Many of the feuds in which the Dyaks
of Sarebas and Sakarran are now engaged, are quarrels which arose in the times of their ancestors ; and
the ostensible object in carrying on of which now is,
that their balance of heads may be settled ; for these
people keep a regular account of the numbers slain on
each side on every occasion: these memorandums have
now, perhaps, become confused amongst the sea-tribes,
but amongst those of the hills, where fewer people are
killed, and fighting is less frequent, the number to
which each tribe is indebted to the other is regularly
preserved. A hill chief once told me that he durst

not travel into another country, which he wished to visit, as their people were the enemies of his tribe; when I asked him in surprise, having supposed that he was at peace with every one except the people of Sakarran, he told me that in the time of his grandfather the people of the other tribe had killed four of his, and that in retaliation his tribe had killed three of the other, so that there was a balance of one in his favour, which had never been settled, nor had any hostilities been carried on for many years, yet all intercourse between the tribes had ceased, and they could only meet in a hostile character. It is by these, and similar causes, that the hill Dyaks, unable to unite to form any combined plan of defence, so easily fall, one by one, before the league of Sakarran and Sarebas. Should peace be brought about, it may be done by the tribe, which, in balancing accounts, is found to have taken most heads, paying for the difference to the other tribe in goods; in this computation the value of males is estimated at about twenty-five dollars, 5*l*. 4*s*. 2*d*., and females from fifteen to twenty dollars each; when the difference is thus adjusted the two contracting tribes feast and dance together, and are friends until some new occasion of quarrel happens, and disturbs their amity. The sea-Dyaks, however, rarely adjust their differences with the other tribes, they having gone on so long, and their debt being so large to so many tribes, that were they to attempt the payment, they would find themselves bankrupts immediately; and I suppose that were they to give themselves in exchange for the slain, they would not, with their wives and children, be sufficient in number to compensate for them.

The heads of their enemies are, amongst the sea-tribes, preserved with the flesh and hair still adhering to the skull, and these trophies are not, as amongst the land-tribes, the general property of the village, but the personal property of the individuals who capture them, though the honour of the tribe is augmented by their being in the village. The skull being freed from the brain, which is extracted by the occiputal hole, the head is dried over a slow and smoking fire until all the animal juices have evaporated : they are preserved with the greatest care, and baskets full of them may be seen at any house in the villages of the sea-tribes, and the family is of distinction according to the number of these disgusting and barbarous trophies in its possession ; they are handed down from father to son as the most valuable property, and an accident which destroys them is considered the most lamentable calamity. An old and grey-headed chief was regretting to me one day the loss he had sustained in the destruction by fire of the heads collected by his ancestors. As I heard nothing of his property, which had been very considerable, I supposed that he had succeeded in saving it, until, on making inquiries, he told me that it had been all destroyed, but he would not have regretted it so much if he could have saved the trophies of the prowess of his fathers. It is said that the practice of head-hunting, for which purpose alone their piratical expeditions are now undertaken, has been carried so far, that a Dyak cannot marry until he has at least once obtained a head. The chief of the Lundu village told me that such was the custom, but that in his tribe it had been dispensed with, as the difficulty of getting heads was so great under Mr. Brooke's government, the wars being unfrequent, and cruising parties not being allowed to go out. The old gentleman seemed to think it a pity that a custom so calculated to inspire the men with courage should be set aside from motives of humanity, and is decidedly of opinion that "none but the brave deserve the fair."

On one occasion Lingir, a chief of one of the Sarebas tribes, appeared at Sarawak with his head shaved, and in his most desolate and ragged attire, but attended by thirty-three boats, to request permission of the rajah to attack the Dyaks of Lundu or Samarhand; he gave as a reason for the strange request, that his brother had died, and that he could not celebrate his funeral until he had somewhere obtained a head. This resembles the custom of those nations who sacrificed their slaves on the funeral pile of their deceased masters; and it is said that in the countries of the Kyans, which bounds that of the Sarebas Dyaks on the south and east, this custom of sacrificing slaves is still prevalent on the death of a chief. From

the above anecdote of Lingir, it would appear necessary
before a man can marry, or bury a deceased relative,
that he embrue his hands in human blood! and thus,
how many victims must be sacrificed to this sanguinary
and ferocious custom.   Lingir, of course, was unsuccessful in his application to Sarawak, and being
desired immediately to return with his fleet, he captured the heads of four unfortunate fishermen, with
whom he fell in, on his return.

Boats being so necessary to the sea-Dyaks for their
cruises, they have attained to greater perfection in
building them than in most other arts, and have succeeded in getting them of so light and fast a construction, that they surpass in this respect the canoes of
Siam and some other more civilized and powerful
states.   They appear long since to have left the simple
canoe, or boat formed of a single tree; and at present;
though these are the only ones of the land-Dyaks, the
smallest boats for river purposes are not formed on
this principle.   Their war-boats, which are called
' bankongs,' are generally of great length, frequently
as much as seventy feet.   They are built very high
abaft, and high forward, so that, when they have not
their crews on board, they appear merely to touch the
water in the middle; when laden, though high fore
and aft, they are not above one plank from the water
in the middle, and being built without a sharp keel,
are very crank; but, as they carry no sail, they are not
afraid of capsizing.   They are built from a flat keel

without timbers of any sort, the planks being mercly sewn one to the other, or rather tied by rattans, through holes about eighteen inches apart, and, thus supporting each other, they are caulked with the soft bark of a tree of the tribe Myrtaceæ, and payed with the preparation of dammar and oils, as used by the Malays for their trading prows. They are fancifully painted, and sometimes decorated with a dragon, or some other monstrous figure-head; and painted on a board at the stern are frequently human figures in indelicate positions.

They are steered sometimes with a rudder, but more frequently by paddles, and from the assistance the men paddling are enabled to give, they turn as on a pivot, and consequently lose so little time in this evolution, that before an English boat could accomplish it, they would be far a-head, being considerable gainers by the manœuvre. Formerly they had no protection for the men paddling the boat excepting from the weather, which was afforded them by mats, called 'kajangs,' made of the unexpanded leaves of the nipah palm sewn together and dried in the sun. These were of sufficient length to reach across the boat, and were so light that they were of no inconvenience, but having recently feared to meet the war-boats of Sarawak, and the gun-boats of the English cruisers, they have added two heavy planks of wood along the side of each boat above the heads of the rowers, which they suppose to be grape-proof.

These encumbrances must take much from the lightness of the boat, and consequently from its speed, probably without much assisting the security of those
whom it necessarily delays.

When going into action, the boat is cleared by its
' kajangs' being all thrown towards the stern, where the
steersman sits. The pânglimàs and warriors rise to their
feet in the centre of the boat, a sufficient number to
paddle being left sitting down on the bamboo laths
which form the platform, or open deck. By the side of
each warrior is a large bundle of the wooden spears formerly described, with which the action commences at
the distance of fifteen or twenty yards, and when the
boats have approached closer, it is carried on with the
iron-pointed spears, which, being too valuable to throw
away, are kept for close quarters. As their naval
engagements for the most part occur near the shore,
one party generally jumps overboard, and with a
yell of triumph the victors decapitate the slain ; and
if they think themselves of sufficient strength, or are
not satisfied with the heads already captured, they pursue the fugitives into the jungle, where they generally
get a few more heads. These boat engagements seldom happen, it being the universal practice of Dyak
warfare never to attempt by force, an object which they
can accomplish by stratagem ; so that we constantly
see that their successful expeditions are always directed
with the view of surprising their enemies, their object
not being to acquire glory or military renown, but

being actuated solely by the desire of procuring heads without exposure to themselves.

Their history would show us but few examples of that personal courage and distinguished bravery which dazzle the imagination of politer nations; there are, however, many examples in which individual gallantry has distinguished the Dyak character, and these abound as much in the land as the sea division. The chief of the Sow (hill) tribe, the orang Kaya, Pa-Mancha of Sarebas, and the chief of Lundu, have on several occasions thus distinguished themselves.

The latter, on one occasion returning from a cruise against his old enemies of Sakarran, and being at anchor with two 'bankongs' in the mouth of the Batang Lupar river waiting for the ebb tide, found himself surrounded by a large returning fleet of these people. It was in the dawn of morning, while the mist lay upon the water, and their approach had been made known to him by the quick and regular stroke of the paddles. His force being so inferior, he would not have ventured to attack them, but they perceived him, and, imagining they should obtain an easy victory, attacked him at once on all sides; but the discharge from several lelahs and muskets in their faces, at the distance of but a few paces, made the bravest of them recoil. They, with frantic yells, returned to the charge again and again, but were each time repulsed with a severe loss, and their attacks were less spirited than at first. Meantime, the old chief seeing this, and fearing the exhaustion of his stock of ammunition, which alone gave him any chance with his numerous foes, had weighed, and during the latter part of the action was paddling towards home with all hands that could be spared from his lelahs (brass swivel-guns carrying half-pound shot), followed by his occasionally attacking enemies, who did not leave him, so much would they have valued the head of this their oldest and most formidable foe, until he had gained his own river; at which, when he arrived after a whole day's pulling, his ammunition was exhausted, as well as the strength and courage of his men. Though several of his people were wounded, he had the satisfaction of knowing that he had fought for hours against a large fleet of his enemies, of whom many were slain; but he had not the only pleasure for which he then longed—the opportunity of bringing away their heads in triumph. Both the Sakarran and Sarebas Dyaks have frequently attacked this chief in his stronghold, the beautiful village of Lundu, but have always been repulsed by the guns supplied to him from Sarawak, in which his safety alone consists, and which enable him to defeat ten times his numerical strength. He delights in avenging the many ills his tribe has suffered from the people of Sakarran, and is always anxious to be let loose against them. Excepting on this difficult to be eradicated custom of barbarism, he is the most respectable and well-behaved of the Dyak chiefs tributary to Sarawak, and is truly the father of the people under his charge, on all occasions sacrificing his own interest to the good of the settlement of Lundu, which, though under the government of a Dyak, is also a Malayan Town.

In defensive warfare the Dyaks surround their village with a high palisading of palm or other trees, and about all the woods in the neighbourhood are planted 'ranjows,' or small sharp-pointed bamboos, which, on account of the mass of decaying vegetables, are with difficulty detected, and are in consequence, together with pit-falls and other contrivances, of great annoyance to a bare-legged invader. As the sea-Dyaks only go on cruises in the fine season, or from April to October, their boats are taken to pieces during the bad monsoon, by cutting the rattans adrift which hold the planks together.

Forrest notices an instance in which a fleet of the orang Tedong, a piratical people of the east coast of Borneo, and who very much resemble the sea-Dyaks, being shut up in a bay by a Spanish cruiser, which probably hoped they would surrender, they evaded their enemy by cutting the rattans of their boats, which are of similar construction, and carrying away the planks through the jungle; this can very easily be done by the crews of the boats. The sea-Dyaks, during the wet season, lay up the planks of their boats in sheds until the returning fine monsoon invites them again to venture on the ocean. As these planks cost the Dyaks, who are unacquainted with the use of the saw, or any other instrument for forming them but the 'biliong' or adze of the Malays (which can also be used as a chopper,

the blade being turned in the haft, which is adapted
to it either way), their preservation is an object of
no small importance, two only being obtained from a
large tree with infinite labour, it being very necessary
that the planks of the boat, on account of her construction, should all be of the same length as the
' bankong.'   These boats, according to their size, carry
crews of from thirty to ninety men, and it is computed that, without making any extraordinary exertion, the rivers of Sarebas and the Sakarran branch of
the Batang Lupar could send to sea 200 of them,
averaging fifty men each.   From the nature of these
boats, and the slightness of their build, it may easily
be imagined that they are not manageable in a sea-
way, their length causing them to open at the seams :
on such occasions, should they not be near enough to
the land to run into smooth water, the crew all jump
overboard, and hang by the side of the boat : this I
have been assured they have done for many succes-
sive hours when the squalls, which are usually short
in these tranquil seas, have been prolonged, so as to
render it necessary.   In this situation they take it by
turns for one or two to enter the boat, and cook and
eat their rice, until the squall is past.

The Dyaks, on their cruises, are capable of enduring
great fatigue, and, if they meet with reverses, have frequently to contend with the pangs of hunger.   It is no
uncommon thing for the Dyaks to pull for eighteen
hours, with only short intervals of rest sufficient to boil
and cook their rice, and this, from the beautiful regu-

larity of their strokes, and their being long accustomed to the practice, does not appear much to fag them; in smooth water, and, without tides, at their regular stroke, they pull about six miles an hour, but when exerting themselves fully can double that rate of speed.

The 'tambangs,' or sharp built sampan boats of Singapore, which are so renowned throughout the East for their speed, are soon lost sight of by the Dyak 'bankongs,' and I should think it probable that no boats in the world could equal them for speed. Each tribe of the Dyaks has peculiar strokes in which it delights, so that in the dark a Sarebas or Sakarran boat could tell whether an approaching one was of Lundu, of the Balows, or a Malay. The Malays also have many methods of paddling, in which the Borneans, or natives of the town of Bruni, excel the inhabitants of the other villages on the coast. On their cruises the Dyaks, who are not, in their sober moments, friends of boisterous mirth, never make use of the cheering and inspiriting songs of the Malayan boatmen : the noise made by each paddle beating time on the gunwale of the boat is to them sufficiently enlivening, and they want no other encouragement to exertion when it is necessary.

When they have met with reverses on an expedition—such as when they lose their boats and are forced to find their way through the jungle, without food, to their homes, perhaps at a great distance—famine is very oppressive to them, though some parts of the woods produce ferns and other edible roots in abundance ; but these generally grow on the river's banks, and in open places where the fear of the enemy prevents the fugitive Dyak from searching for them : on those occasions he has recourse to the bark and leaves of trees ; and sometimes, to still the cravings of hunger, an oily earth, which is found in some places, is eaten.

On one occasion the men from a fleet of Sakarran Dyaks having been driven ashore, they were twelve days in reaching their homes, having lost five persons by famine, and many by their unrelenting enemies. The difficulties they had to encounter in walking through forests belonging to the enemy, and which were unknown to them, in crossing rivers, and eluding pursuit, were innumerable. Two poor fellows of this party were discovered crossing, on a log of wood, one of the numerous creeks ; and another party, which had taken possession of a deserted house, were found in it by their enemies, who had no pity upon their miserable condition.

About this time (1845) Gila Beranhi, one of the chiefs of Sakarran—who had been one of the most relentless pirates—before his death, which occurred after only two days illness, is reported to have called his tribe about him, and exhorted them to leave off piracy, as the failure of the expedition just recorded, and his own approaching death, were all brought about by the supernatural power of the Rajah of Sarawak, whom he said it was impossible to withstand ; so that we see the first slight check to the conquests of these hitherto invincible tribes, leads their ignorant minds immediately to attribute to superhuman influence, the results which the most common prudence must foresee will attend their opposing the regular force of a civilized enemy. The cognomen of this chief, Gila Beranhi, may be literally translated, " the madly brave," in allusion to the ferocious courage displayed in his wars with the enemies of his tribe.

Though agriculture is so generally practised by the Dyaks, they have not made in it so much progress as, from its necessity to their existence, might have been expected. The cause of their never having attained to greater perfection in this art is probably to be found in the immense productiveness of the soil they cultivate, which, with little care beyond the planting of the seed, yields such heavy crops, that the most moderate skill and attention are repaid so amply, that the inducements to improvement, which excite more civilized, but less favoured nations, have no existence here.

In July and August the Dyak, having previously fixed upon a spot convenient for a farm, begins the labour of felling the forests ; in this he is assisted by the females of his family, who clear away the brushwood; slaves and male children fell the larger trees. The extent cultivated by each head of a family depends upon his industry, and the wants of his household : an industrious person always prepares more than will be necessary for the supply of his household, so that, with the surplus, he

Q

may be enabled to buy little luxuries for himself, and brass wire, &c., for his daughters and children, from the Malays, who always come to the villages to trade when the harvest has been gathered in. Having felled as much forest as he thinks sufficient for his purpose, which—considering the only instrument they employ is the ' biliong,' or small chopper of theMalays—-is accomplished with astonishing quickness, the fallen giants of the jungle are allowed to remain prostrate, until a succession of dry days has so parched them, that, being set on fire in several places on the windward side of the field when a fresh breeze is blowing, the whole is, in a few hours, consumed with a flame, and smoke, and crackling noise, which, at a distance, is awfully beautiful, and the sublime appearance of which, when many farms are thus burning together, can scarcely be conceived: the heavy dark cloud which hangs over the country, caused by the smoke, for many miles previously to the ascent of the flames, has frequently been mistaken for one of the thunder clouds which are seen to gather, of this solid and black appearance, only in tropical countries. So great is the resemblance, that persons accustomed to the appearance have frequently remained undeceived, until a gust of wind carried the bright flames high above the intervening jungle, and displayed to the spectator a scene of the most majestic beauty, which certainly equals, and probably surpasses, the burning of the grass on the plains of North America.

When the fire has exhausted itself, and the ground is again cool, which, from the frequency of rain, is soon the case, the Dyaks collect, from the black and charred trunks of the trees, the smaller ones suited to the purpose, and commence making their ' pagar,' or fence, for the protection of the future crop against the inroads of the deer and wild hogs, which would soon injure and destroy it. The method generally used in constructing this fence, is by raising one pole above another, horizontally, and sustaining them in this position by stakes driven into the ground, at an angle, and opposite to each other, so that the bar rests upon the crutch formed by their crossing each other. The pagars, or fences, are about six feet high, and the bars about fifteen inches one above the other; they are strong enough to resist the encroachments of wild animals for one season : for more they are not required, being then split up, and used in the houses for fire-wood.

In parts of the country more populous than others, it frequently happens that the Dyaks have not, in their territory, old jungle; or it is at such a distance from their houses, that the labour of carrying the produce to them would be very oppressive in a country where the services of no domestic animal are available for this purpose. Such situations are not so laborious to prepare, but being destitute of that rich layer of vegetable mould, and the fertilizing properties of the burnt wood, are not nearly so productive. The pagars of these farms, in which bamboo always abounds, are frequently made of this light and easily worked material, the ends being stuck into the ground, and supported by cross bars, which run along the whole length of the fence, and to which the perpendicular stakes are attached by lashings óf rattan, or other súitable substance. The burning being finished, and the pagar made, though this latter operation is frequently delayed until the seed has sprung up, no other preparation of the ground is deemed necessary. The plough, and other instruments for turning up the soil, the inventions of nations more advanced in the art, are to them unknown; but if the former were introduced, it would be useless in many places, as the sides of steep hills are frequently chosen for the farm.; and, in all cases, it would be unavailable while the natives continued to leave their fields after but one year's cultivation, as the labour of removing the trunks of the large trees, which are now allowed to decay in the field, fertilizing it as they crumble into earth, would not be compensated by the produce of the ground they occupy, if the field were not cultivated for a succession of seasons.

The padi seed, which is saved with the greatest care from the choicest of the preceding season, is planted in holes, made by a blunt-pointed stick, at the distance of from fifteen to eighteen inches apart every way. Three or four seeds are dropped into each hole by the women and children, who cover them by scraping a little earth or ashes over them with their feet. ‘Jagong,’ or

Indian corn, or maize, as it is frequently called in Europe, is planted sparingly at the same time; and as it is ripe and off the ground in three months from the time of sowing, it does not injure the padi, amongst the rows of which it is sown; and as it comes in at a season when the rice is getting exhausted, and the second crop not ready, it is of great use to the Dyaks, though not so much esteemed as rice as an article of food. On the larger collections of ashes they also sow the seeds of gourds, pumpkins, a kind of melon without flavour, and cucumbers, of which they are very fond. These trail along the ground amongst the stems of the padi, to which they appear to do no injury, and continne bearing for some time after the rice crop has been gathered in.

After the field has been all planted, the Dyak and his family occupy themselves in building a hut on some elevated position in the field, for the convenience of being able to reside at it constantly during the periods when it most requires their care, and for storing the harvest when ripe from the rain, until they can carry it to their granaries, which are generally near, but apart from the houses of the village. The 'dañgau,' as this hut is called, is always upon posts, and with a raised but not covered platform before it, for the convenience of drying the padi before it is placed in the baskets in which it is to be conveyed to the granary. During its growth the field is always weeded twice: this, as they are assisted by no tools, with the exception of their parang, is a very toilsome occupation, which is always carefully accomplished by the industry of the Dyak, as the rapid growth of the weeds would soon spoil his crop, and render unavailing all the labour his farm had previously cost him.

About March or April, or from six to seven months after the period of its sowing, the padi puts on the beautiful appearance which informs the delighted husbandman of the approach of the reward of his labours. At this season the field of the Dyak presents a more lovely picture to the eye than the farms of Europe. The yellow padi is everywhere relieved by the gaudy flowers of the bayam, a kind of vegetable, which resembles the Amaranthus, or prince's feather of our gardens, and its large tufts of orange and crimson enhance the beauty of the pleasing scene. As the heads of padi seldom all ripen together, or so regularly as the ears of other grain in England, no sickle is used in reaping, nor are the stalks bound into bundles. Every person in the family of the Dyak, armed with his or her basket and knife, is employed in going regularly over the field, and taking off all the ripe heads, with but a few inches of the straw, the bulk of which is left standing on the ground, where it decays, and nourishes the earth which produced it. Each person, when the basket is full, carries it to the dañgau, where it is rubbed from the ear, frequently by the hands; but this irksome method is, by those who have large farms, avoided by a sieve which they erect outside the hut, with split rattans fastened into a frame-work, and supported by four posts, over which also the roof is extended : a mat is placed under the sieve, and the heads of padi, being put into it above, are worked backwards and forwards over the fine rattans of the sieve with a wooden instrument which they have for the purpose, until the padi, being freed from the stalks, falls into the receptacle below, whence it is taken, and being well dried in the sun, is finally conveyed to the granary of the family, until wanted for the purposes of trade and of home consumption.

Every year the series of operations above detailed is repeated; the soil, perhaps, being exhausted by the enormous crop it sometimes produces in favourable seasons. Last year was one of those, and I saw hundreds of acres of padi which had fallen to the ground for want of hands to gather it; the crop having been so much larger than the Dyaks, who generally calculate these matters very shrewdly, and plant no more than their own family can conveniently manage, had anticipated. The Dyaks themselves, however, do not suppose that the soil is in any way incapable of bearing further culture; but give always as a reason for deserting their farms, that the weeds and grass which immediately spring up after the padi has been gathered, are less easily eradicated, than ground occupied by old jungle is prepared. They never return to the same spot until after a period of seven years has elapsed, which they say was the custom of their ancestors; and then they find that the trees, which have, during that time, covered the ground, to the destruction of the deleterious lalang grass and other weeds, are easily felled, and the ground prepared; though, as has been before noticed, the crops from such land are not so abundant as those from the 'utan tuah,' or old forest, which in consequence is, notwithstanding the greater proportionate amount of labour requisite to bring it under cultivation, always, when procurable, preferred.

It will be seen from the above statement that the farms of the Dyaks are prepared towards the end of the dry season, so that they have the wet monsoon to bring the padi to maturity, and the beginning of the following fine weather, April and May, to ripen the grain. Some tribes have a succession of farms coming in a few weeks later than each other, but never more than three. The hill Dyaks seldom plant their farms till a month or two later than the sea tribes, who consequently have the first of the market; new rice always selling for a higher price than the old, the former being esteemed' sweeter and more nourishing by the Malays, who are the purchasers.

From the mode of pounding the padi in mortars, to free it from the husk, adopted by the Dyaks and Malays, none of the rice, the produce of the island, can be kept for any length of time: the grains being broken, and the enamel which protects them from the wevil being destroyed, that insect soon takes advantage of the circumstance to attack and destroy it; in the husk, or padi state, it may be kept for years without injury, and is in this respect supposed to be equal to the production of India or America.

Besides the farms above described, the Dyaks have small gardens, usually the property of women, in which they plant vegetables of different kinds, principally the 'trong,' brenjal of the East, and egg-plant of Europe, sugar-cane, plantains, yams, sweet potatoes, chilies, &c. A few plants of tobacco are generally found in their farms, the leaves of which they prepare by drying for their own use. Sisawi, a kind of mustard, and a species of millet, are also planted amongst the padi in small quantities. The sugar-cane, which grows very freely, is only esteemed for its saccharine juice, which they extract like the Malays, by chewing. Of the plantains they have several fine varieties; that most esteemed is the 'pisang amas,' or golden plantain; its fruit is small and not angular, the bunch is, however, uncommonly large—it is of a rich golden yellow colour, and much finer flavour than most of the other kinds. The 'pisang merah,' or red plantain, called 'pisang udang,' or prawn plantain, by the Malays, and 'pisang baddat,' are the next in esteem, and resemble each other, except in colour, which in the former is red, in the latter yellow, with green ends; many others are very fine, but as the varieties are so numerous it is unnecessary to particularize them : the 'pisang tandok,' or horn plantain, bears fruit of from twelve to eighteen inches in length, and is a well-flavoured variety.   Pine-apples are seldom cultivated by the Dyaks, though they are found apparently in a wild state about most of their villages ; in such situations the fruit is small and of little flavour, and it is remarkable that the Dyaks, who delight in the cultivated ones from the Chinese gardens at Sarawak, should take no care of their own.

The ancestors of the Dyaks having for many centuries occupied the countries these people now inhabit, fruit trees are scattered in abundance all over its surface, particularly near the banks of rivers, and all jungles abound with them.   The most esteemed kinds surround their villages, and these, with other in easily accessible places, are individual property; but those of the jungles are not owned, and the fruit of them generally becomes the property of the squirrels, monkeys, and birds, which frequent the forests containing them, unless the destructive Malay should see them, who, ever thoughtless of the future, immediately cuts down with his hatchet a tree which has taken many years to attain its fruiting state, and for the purpose of gathering a few for himself, destroys what might at some future time be of service to the Dyaks or others, who might, for the purposes of mining or agriculture, be compelled to reside in the vicinity.

As the woods of the country of the sea-Dyaks abound in pigs and deer, and the tribes are not prevented by any superstitious prejudice from eating the flesh of either of these animals, various contrivances are in use for their capture. The most common for the purpose of catching the larger game is called by them 'peti:' it is a strong spear of bamboo, laid in a horizontal direction above the ground, about the height of the body of a pig or deer. A sapling, bent for the purpose, forms the spring by being held back; a string crosses the path of the animal, the least touch on which pulls the trigger by which the sapling is retained, and which, springing forward, forces the bamboo in a straight line across the path, and consequently through the body of any animal that may happen to be passing. As these traps are so placed as to be with difficulty discovered in the jungle, the traveller has to be careful, as to be trans-fixed with one of these spears set for deer, would occasion death. The Dyaks themselves, though very careful, have frequently met with such accidents.

A few weeks before leaving the country one of my men, who was bringing to the hut where we were stay-ing, with his companions, a deer which had been shot for our dinner, missed the path in the dark, and struck his foot against a trap of this nature, which had been set for pigs; the spear transfixed his thigh, making a large and ragged wound, from which, however, he fortu-nately recovered; had it been a deer-trap instead of a pig-trap, the spear would have passed through his waist, and have certainly killed him. Pigs are also caught in pit-falls; ranjows, or sharp bamboos, being placed at the bottom, on which they fall. Ranjows are also planted on the steep sides of mountains, so that

the pigs, in hurrying down the declivity, often receive
them in the breast, and being thus staked, soon bleed
to death, and are discovered by the Dyaks. The
smaller kinds of game, such as porcupines, palandok,
or mouse-deer, small pigs, pheasants, and partridges,
are caught in springes, and by those alone a clever
woodsman can daily supply his family with this kind
of food in abundance, the cord made use of for the
springes is of their own manufacture, very fine and
strong; it is made from the inner bark of several
kinds of trees. They have also cage-traps, into which
the squirrels and mouse-deer are attracted by choice
food, and which fall upon and detain them. Pigeons
and other birds are caught with springes and bird-
lime placed in the trees which they frequent for food,
particularly the different species of 'kayu ara' (Ficus),
which are very abundant, and on which the many
species of these birds delight to feed.

A practice of fishing, used by the Dyaks of all descriptions, and which has been observed also of the
natives of South America, with whom these people
have many things in common, deserves particular
notice. It is called fishing with tuba, and is thus
carried on: large quantities of the tuba being collected, which is the root of a climbing plant (Meni-
spermum), though the same effect is produced by the
fruit of a tree grown extensively for that purpose,
the tribe intending to fish proceed in their boats to
the mouth of a small river, or creek, which has a bar

of sand at its entrance, so that, at low water, it has little or no communication with the sea; and having distributed the bundles of tuba in equal proportions to all the boats present, the persons in them proceed to beat up the roots on the thwarts of the canoes, frequently pouring water on them, until the whole of the narcotic principle is extracted and collected in the bottom of the boat, in the water which, during the process of beating, has been poured over the roots, and which has now become of a white milky colour. At low water, and at a signal given by the chief, all the boats simultaneously commence baling out the water charged with the narcotic into the river, and this, spreading through the waters in every way, stupefies the fish. The smaller ones, being most readily affected, first float upon the surface, and are taken with the light and sharp-pointed spears of the Dyaks. Soon the larger ones, beginning to feel its influence, also come to the top; then it is that the best of the sport commences : fishes of the largest size, together with small alligators, appear for an instant struggling to free themselves from the lethargy occasioned by the infected waters. The Dyaks, who are ever on the alert, paddle instantly towards them, and three or four of the barbed spears are immediately thrust into their scaly bodies by the different boats, which arrive together at the scene of their struggles : occasionally a large fish, in his dying agony, is too powerful for his assailants, one or two of whom are sometimes dragged into the water, where, if the place be shallow, they dispatch their prey with their parangs or knives. Many other ludicrous accidents occur, which, when large crowds are assembled (as is the case when the tuba is collected at the expense of and for the amusement of the Europeans, and on which occasions the whole country is invited to be present, and those who wish to share in the sport), afford merriment to those who are merely spectators. From the first appearance of the fish the sport lasts about two hours, when the influx of water from the rising tide dissipates the narcotic, and such fish as remain recover from its effects. Other kinds of fishing are not much practised by the Dyaks, who trust almost solely to the Malays for their supply.

CHAPTER VIII.

THE HILL DYAKS—THEIR CHARACTER—THEIR RELIGION AND SUPER-
STITIONS—THEIR DEITIES—INVOCATION OF THEM—PROPITIATION
OF THEM AND OF THE RAJAH—CEREMONY PERFORMED BY MR. BROOKE
—THE PAMALI, OR "TABOO"—A DYAK FUNERAL—A PECULIAR
SUPERSTITION OF THE DYAKS—THEIR ABSTINENCE FROM ANIMAL
FOOD—ANCIENT DYAK MONUMENTS AND DRAGON-JARS—THEIR
VENERATION FOR CERTAIN PLANTS—SUPERSTITION OF THE DYAKS
OF SARAWAK—SPECULATIONS AS TO THE ORIGIN OF THE DYAKS.

THE Hill Dyaks, or as they call themselves, " Orang
Gunong," or Men of the Hills, differ in many peculiarities from the Dyaks of the Sea tribes. The
principal tribes of the Dyaks of the country of Sarawak
are of this division, and they are consequently the
people whose miserable and oppressed condition has
recently called forth so much of the attention and
sympathy of our country. This division of the Dyak
race occupies the most western portions of the island.
The tribes of the Malayan states of Pontianak, of Sambas,
of Sarawak, and of Sadong, all belong to it, and the
hilly interior of these countries is peopled entirely by
them. In personal appearance, the Dyaks of the Hills
very much resemble those of the other tribes already
described; but they have a more grave and quiet expression of countenance, which gives to their features a
melancholy and thoughtful air. It is very probable,

that their many miseries may have much increased this
appearance, though it is natural to them, being observable, in a less degree, in all the tribes of both divisions. Their countenance is an index to the character
of their mind, for they are of peculiarly quiet and mild
dispositions, not easily roused to anger, or the exhi-
bitiou of any other passion or emotion, and rarely
excited to noisy mirth, unless during their periodical
festivals. Their dress, when they have property sufficient to obtain one, is the long cloth, or " chawat," the
manufacture of the Sakarran Dyaks ; but poverty more
frequently compels them to supply its place with a
rough substance made of the bark of several trees,
particularly that of the genus *Artocarpus*, which
produces the bread-fruit. Their head-dress is of the
same material, being a strip of the bark dyed yellow, and
twisted into folds, after which it is bound round the
head. For ornaments, they wear bracelets of the red
wood of the heart of the Tapang tree, which, after
exposure to the air, becomes black as ebony, and being
without its brittle qualities, is more durable ; and broad
armlets, which are made of the shell (Kima) from the
coast of Celebes, and which, when polished by length of
use among the Dyaks, resembles ivory, but never acquires
its yellow tinge, always remaining of the purest white
colour.

The young men, who affect gallantry, wear innumerable strings of beads around their necks, and
also cover the upper portion of the arm with rings of

the black iju, or horsehair-like substance formerly described, plaited very neatly. This, to the eye of an European, is the most becoming of all their adornments, the dark black of the material contrasting agreeably, but not too decidedly, with the brown colour of their skins. They, also, like the Sakarran Dyaks, wear their sword, or parang, on the left side, and the little basket (tambuck) in which are their sirih leaves, and to which the knife is attached, on the right, and these, together with a single ring in their ears, usually of broad flattened wire, but frequently of the very smallest dimensions, together with a jacket of Sakarran manufacture, in wet weather, complete their clothing, ornaments and accoutrements for ordinary occasions.

The women, in appearance, differ but little from those previously noticed. Being, however, used to harder labour, they have not so much time to spend upon their toilette, and their hair is consequently coarser and less luxuriant. Some of them are fond of ornaments of opaque and very small beads, which by the Semproh, Sebongoh, and other tribes on the southern branch of the Sarawak river, are worked into very pretty head-dresses. This ornament is made of the strung beads of various colours, disposed in broad transverse bands: they are about four or five inches in breadth, and open at the top, so that they resemble a broad fillet.

The young girls of these tribes, also, like the men, wear beads on their necks, and their arms are covered with brass wire, excepting such parts as are reserved for the displaying of the valued shell bracelets already mentioned, of which two on each arm are the favourite numbers. Their dress is the " bedang" of the Sakarrans, with the rattans and appropriate ornaments, as among the women of the Sea tribes. Silver or gold is, however, never seen amongst them, their poverty effectually preventing any display of this kind.

Amongst the tribes on the western branch of the Sarawak river, the dress of the women is in- creased by the addition of an article, called by them " Saladan:" it is made of a bamboo, split, flat- tened, pared thin, and dyed black : being thus pre- pared, it is fitted to the body, and secured in its form and position by brass wires passing across its breadth, which also serve for the purposes of ornament : they are placed at the distance of about one inch apart from each other. Girls begin to wear it at the age of five or six years, and as it is too small to be taken off and on, being made on the body, it is only removed by destroying it, when the condition of the wearer renders a larger one necessary.

This curious article of dress is confined to the tribes of Sarawak, called Singhie, Sow, Serambo, Bombuck, and Peninjow, who in their dress also differ from the other tribes of the Hills in this, that their women wear no beads for ornament, and the men only those of two colours—black and white. Transparent beads are not esteemed by any of the tribes I have visited ; small and opaque ones alone being valued by them. The colours, most in demand, are the two above mentioned ; but yellow and red are also much sought after. The girls of the tribes on the western branch of the Sarawak river never wear the brass-wire above the elbow-joint of the arm, nor have I seen them use the white bracelets, so common in the others of the southern river, the use of which amongst these tribes is apparently confined to the men.

In travelling amongst the Dyaks, it is well to be provided with a stock of brass-wire and small beads, together with Java tobacco, with which to requite their services; but as, since confidence has been restored among them, they are in the habit of visiting Sarawak, and making their own purchases, in those tribes where the use of money is understood, it is always preferred as payment for their labour.

The Hill Dyaks are a more amiable people than the Sea tribes, previously treated of: their morality is of a higher standard, their gratitude is undoubted, and their hospitality to strangers well ascertained. It has been previously mentioned, that the Malays, who spend amongst the Dyaks, for the purposes of trade, that portion of their time which, during the prevalence of the boisterous monsoon, they are prevented from navigating the ocean, never think of carrying with them, on leaving their houses, more than sufficient provisions to last them till they reach the first village at which they intend to begin their barter, the Dyaks always freely supplying them with such as they have.

During the two years which I spent for the most part amongst their tribes, I always found them obliging, and anxious to perform for me any service in their power, and on leaving a village, they wished to load me with rice, fowls, and fruits, which I was always obliged to insist upon their retaining, as they were useless to me.

On many occasions, I have known that, towards the end of the season, before the new rice was ripe—which is generally a time of scarcity with them—and when there was very little to eat in the village, these people have brought it out to present to me; but at this season I never taxed their liberality, but always brought with me a supply from the town sufficient for my wants, and was frequently able to return, in their necessity, that with which they had so freely parted, earlier in the year. In travelling also, I found them willing, on all occasions, to furnish me as many men as I might require for the transport of my luggage, which was usually, on a long journey, from twenty to thirty; by these means, my traps followed me from village to village, all over the country, without any person with them, every thing being left to the care and known honesty of the Dyaks; and though many of my things were the articles they would most have valued for dress or ornament, an instance of the slightest pilfering never occurred, though it might have been constantly committed, without the slightest danger of immediate detection.

On leaving a village, my property, which had been in use, was left strewed about the house in which I had been staying, my Malays rarely troubling themselves to see anything properly packed; but the scrupulous carefulness of the Dyaks prevented the loss of anything, and I have been followed by them with articles which had been thrown away, but which they feared might be of service. Having intimated to the chief the village to which I was going, I generally found that my baggage was there nearly as soon as myself. It is difficult, however, to engage them to assist the adventurous traveller in the ascent of mountains, from the superstitious dread they have of the spirits with which the summits of the higher hills are supposed to be peopled: everything upon them is sacred to the spirit of the place, and having got them to the top, it was difficult to teach them to be of any service. They would by no means be instrumental in destroying a stick, or shrub, to make us a tent or fire, until they had seen that no harm occurred to the Malays, who had no scruples of the kind; and had any one of my attendants unfortunately died, or had an accident of any serious nature happened to them after any of these excursions, I should probably have never been able to obtain another to accompany me.

Their whole lives being spent in the jungle, these Dyaks are of the greatest possible assistance to Europeans, whose pursuits lead them into its gloom. When overtaken by night, in the forests, or on the mountains, their burdens being placed on the ground, they distribute themselves around, and soon return with sticks and palm leaves, of which excellent tents are speedily formed, in which to pass the night; the floors of these are always raised above the ground, to preserve the inmates from the attacks of the leeches which abound amongst the dead leaves on the ground, and which are a great annoyance to the traveller in these wilds. The roof of such a tent is impervious to the weather, and the whole time employed in the construction does not exceed half-an-hour: fires are lighted in them, and the traveller having changed his wet and disorderly apparel for a clean and dry suit, may proceed to cook his provisions. The nearest bamboo bush will furnish him with an excellent candlestick, and the rattan will answer all the purposes of a corkscrew, if the benighted wayfarer be fortunate enough to have occasion for its services.

Gratitude, which is too frequently found a rare and transitory virtue, eminently adorns the character of these simple people, and the smallest benefit conferred upon them, calls forth its vigorous and continued exercise. It cannot, then, be wondered at, that this amiable quality should lead them, in their simplicity, to consider with a reverence bordering on adoration, the great benefits they have received from European influence in their country. When we consider the oppression of which they were the objects, and the state of misery to which the tyranny of their former rulers had reduced them, and from which the kindness and power of an individual of a race, distinct from any of which they had previously heard—differing not only in features and complexion so remarkably, but also in the feelings with which he regarded their poor, distressed and destitute condition—we can scarcely blame them, that in the excess of their thankfulness, they should have considered as supernatural, the person who relieved them from their wretchedness, and by whose cherishing care and protecting kindness, they once more enjoyed the lives and liberties with which the great Creator had endowed them. We accordingly find that several of their tribes have ascribed to Mr. Brooke the attri-

butes and powers of a superior being ; and believe that
he can, by his word, shed an influence over their
persons or property, which will be beneficial to them.
In all their prayers, he is named with the gods of their
superstitions, and no feast is made at which his name
is not invoked. This misdirected gratitude shows the
force with which that virtue influences their minds, and
promises, when the Missionaries shall have arrived at the
scene of their holy labours, to be a feature of their
character which will be of the greatest advantage and
assistance to them, if properly directed.

The amiability of the Dyaks of the Hill tribes is
of a superior character to that of those before
described; the licentious intercourse between the
sexes is not here permitted ; and so strict are these
people in encouraging virtue amongst their children,
that the young and unmarried men are not permitted to
sleep in the houses of their parents, after having attained
the age of puberty, but occupy a large house, of peculiar
construction, which is set apart for their use in the
village, and will be hereafter noticed. Neither has
the passion for taking the heads of their fellow creatures,
for the mere purpose of complying with a brutal
custom, and satisfying a barbarous appetite, ever
entered their civil institutions, though to preserve the
skulls of their enemies, as memorials of their triumph,
has prevailed. The practice of slavery does not disgrace
their usages, nor is piracy practised by their tribes.
Crime is so rare amongst them, that its punishments
are only known from tradition ; and they live at present

in a state of happiness and contentment, which, perhaps, is at this time enjoyed in so high a degree, by no other people upon earth.

The language used by the tribes of Land Dyaks, though differing very much from that of the Sea tribes, has very great affinity with it; but like the dialects of the natives of America, all the little tribes differ considerably from each other, though it generally happens that a cluster of these, whose villages are not far apart, and the origin of which can generally be traced to one which is the most ancient, and parent of the others, do not differ in dialect so considerably as to prevent oral communication : thus the tribes on the southern branch of the Sarawak river all understand the language of the Suntah and Sempoo people, two nations to which they owe their existence.

Amongst these people, nothing is more difficult, and requires more study and a better acquaintance with their manners and habits, than to procure anything like accurate information respecting their religious belief and superstitious observances. My residence in the country was too short, and my knowledge of the language too imperfect, to allow me to inquire so much concerning them, and to understand so well as I could have wished, and hope at a future period to be able to do. In their superstitions appear to be strangely blended the observances of the Hindus and the rites of the natives of Eastern Polynesia; the existence of the "taboo" of the latter people proving that the influence of the religion of the Brahmins was never strong enough, altogether to abolish the more ancient superstition of these tribes. At the present time, they believe in a number of divinities, or different orders of spirits, the chief of which, though they vary in many villages, is the god called "Tuppa" by most of the tribes; though amongst some, a deity named Jerroang, has the precedence.

To a stranger asking them the name of their God, they universally answer "Juwata;" but on closely questioning them, they call this deity Juwata Laut; meaning that they have received the knowledge of him from the Malays, and that his divinity has no proper place in their mythology. Few people will hesitate in pronouncing Juwata to be a corruption of the Sanscrit word "Dewata," which has been adopted into the Malayan language, and is a term for an order of celestial beings in the Hindu mythology. In the belief of the Dyaks, Tuppa and Jerroang are supposed to be eminently powerful and beneficent beings, controlling, not only the actions of men, but those of the spirits of an inferior order. They delight in doing good to the human race, and have been the bestowers of all the most sacred gifts to the Dyaks, who say that in ancient times they received the Padi from the former: other, but less powerful spirits, are the Perchaah, the Jim, the Kamang, and the Trin, all of which are generic terms for classes of beings. The Perchaah appear to be the ministers of the two powerful divinities (or classes of divinities), Tuppa and Jerroang. "Jim," is, perhaps, a corruption of the term "Jin," evil spririts

of the Arabians; and this is the more likely, from
their being considered of the same nature by these people,
and inimical to mankind. They are thought to be
inhabitants of the lower regions of the air, but not
to ascend to the loftier residences of the good and
beneficent gods. The Triu and the Kamang are
spirits of the woods and mountains; and the martial
genii of these people—the Trin—are inhabitants of the
forests and lofty hills, who constantly descend from
them to visit and bless the houses of their votaries,
whom they also accompany in their expeditions against
their enemies. In person, they are supposed to
resemble the Dyaks themselves, whom they delight in
benefitting.

Far different from this mild and benevolent character, is that of the genii of the hideous and savage
Kamang, whose joy is in the misery of mankind,
and who delight in war and bloodshed, and all the
other afflictions of the human race. They mix personally in the battles of their votaries, not from any
wish to assist them—though they may be, in some
measure, propitiated by feasts in their honour—but that
the carnage may be increased, for they are said to
inspire desperate valour. In person, they are as dis-
gustingly ugly as they are barbarous and cruel in their
dispositions: their bodies are covered, like those of the
Oran-utan, with long and shaggy red hair: they are
mis-shapen and contorted, and their favourite food
is the blood of the human race. They, like the spirits
called Trin, of whom they are supposed to be the enemies,

and to whom their power is reported to be equal, reside on the earth, in the woods and mountains. Such is all the information I am able to offer respecting the spirits and divinities, in the existence of which these tribes believe. I am perfectly aware that there are many others whose names I have not recorded; but that these are the only ones supplicated on ordinary occasions I am sure, having made repeated inquiries, and been present at many invocations of them, some of which will be described in the course of the work.

Tuppa or Jerroang is always invoked at their agricultural and other peaceful feasts, and, together with the sun, moon and stars, and the Sultan of Bruni, and their own Rajah, are requested to shed their beneficent influence over the seed Padi, and to render the season propitious to its growth. They regulate their agricultural seasons by the motions of the heavenly bodies, particularly the Pleiades, which they call ' Sakara,'* and to the several stars, on which they bestow the attributes of gods. On all occasions of great festivities, such as the planting the seed, or gathering in of the harvest, a stage of bamboo is erected in front of the door of the village chief, on which the offerings to the gods are placed, consisting of the choicest morsels from the plentiful feast which is always provided on these occasions. From this food, the gods are supposed to extract the essence, and the remnants are eaten by the Dyaks as sacred morsels at the conclusion of the festival. The Triu and Kamang spirits of war are only invited to

* Is this the Batara Sakra of the Hindu Javan mythology, to whose particular care the earth was confided?

the feasts connected with, or occasioned by blood-shed.

These fierce spirits are invoked in a manner peculiar and different from the more powerful divinities. The person who is deputed to call them, and who is generally the chief of the tribe, having prepared a sirih leaf with lime, betel-nut and tobacco, places it in his mouth, and, having chewed it for some time, commences the prayer, speaking in a very fast manner, and occasionally blowing towards the top of the moun-tains the betel and sirih he has been masticating. The invocation ends in a loud, long-continued and most ludicrous squeak, during which I had the greatest difficulty to keep the Malays, who accompanied me, from interrupting the ceremony by their noisy laughter. This invocation is carried on in the Dyak language—at least such of the words as I could catch were of it—though the missionaries of Banjar assert that the Kyans of that part of the country have a language peculiar and sacred for this purpose: some specimens of it are published in the Journal of the 'Halle Missionary Society,' from the pen of the Rev. C. Hupé.

On being questioned, the Dyaks have told me that they have not a distinct language for their religious purposes; and I think that amongst those of Sarawak, the apparent difference is to be accounted for in the peculiar intonation they give to the syllables when using them in their prayers. Some of the Dyaks, whom I had an opportunity of examining on this point, spoke Malay well, having lived while children in the Malayan villages; so that I think there could be no mistake, unless they willingly misled me, of which I do not think them capable. Nevertheless, some remnants of the ancient language of Java may be found amongst the people of Banjar, as from the more frequent occurrence of Hindu remains in the southern parts of the island, that religion has evidently been more prevalent there than in other places ; but if the language is still preserved, it is curious that the customs have so entirely disappeared, for, so far as I have been able to learn, no indications of their former existence are to be found amongst the southern tribes; and I am inclined to think that the ancient religion of Java was confined, in the southern parts of the island of Borneo, to the colonists from that country, and never had any considerable influence on the customs or habits of the aboriginal tribes.

Though the Dyaks, excepting on festival occasions, pay but little reverence to their divinities ; in situations in which they consider themselves particularly exposed to their power, they are much in dread of the malignant spirits. Their fear of disturbing the repose of these on the tops of mountains has been previously alluded to; and in such situations we seldom slept until they had recounted many stories concerning them. On the ' Gunong Matang,' a mountain about eight miles from the town of Sarawak, was a path beaten, probably by wild animals, to the very peak of the hill, which had never been previously ascended by the Dyaks : they pointed this out to me as the road leading to the residence of the Kamang, and which they used in their ascent of the hill; nor was I fortunate enough to find the tracks of animals, to undeceive them on this point.

On all feasts which have connection with war, the Trin and Kamang are invoked to be present, and a portion of the food is set apart for them, as on other occasions for the god, Tuppa, who is supposed not to attend with the Kamang and Trin, since his more pure and beneficent nature looks upon war with horror and disgust. The offerings to the Kamang and Triu remain exposed four days and nights, after which they are eaten, in a decaying state, by the Dyaks, who by doing this, suppose they perform a sacred duty.

At their feasts on less warlike occasions, their more powerful and good spirits are petitioned by prayer and supplication to be present; but as these festivals are intimately connected with their religious observances, I will in this place describe one which was made on my arrival at the village of the Sebongoh Hill Dyaks, in August, 1845, in honour of the first European visit to them. After having consented to remain while the chief collected the tribe, I sat down in the verandah of the house, which had been prepared for my reception by being covered with fine white Sirhassan mats: similar ones were also strewed from my boat to the houses, which are built on the banks of the river, so that I might not soil my feet in the ascent to them. Soon after I was seated, the Orang Kaya (chief of a village) requested me to give them a little piece of cloth, and a small silver coin—they wishing to cut off the string of a pillowcase for the first, but I gave them a grass-cloth handkerchief, which very much delighted them : the old chief brought out his wife to receive it, and the lady told me that it was to be hung up in the house as a memorial of my visit, and to preserve the village from evil influence.

When the feast was about to begin—or rather the preparations for it—I was desired by the Orang Kaya to accompany him to the stage before the verandah, which is used by the Dyaks for drying their Padi (Indian-corn), Jagong (maize), &c. Having determined, for the purpose of seeing the ceremony, to be quite passive in their hands, I accordingly rose, and went with him. The old man held in his left hand a small saucer, filled with rice, which had been made yellow by a mixture with Kunyit, or Turmeric, and other herbs. He then uttered a prayer in Malay, which he had previously requested me to repeat after him. It was addressed to Tuppa, the sun and moon, and the Rajah of Sarawak, to request that the next Padi harvest might be abundant, that their families might be increased with male children, and that their pigs and fowls might be very prolific: it was, in fact, a prayer for general prosperity to the country and tribe. During its continuance, we threw towards heaven small portions of the rice from the saucer at frequent intervals, and at the commencement of every fresh paragraph of the supplicatory address. After this had been finished, the chief repeated the prayer in the Dyak language by himself, throwing the rice towards the sky, as before; which, when he had finished, we returned together into the verandah, and the Orang Kaya tied a little hawk-bell round my wrist, requesting me at the same time to tie another, with which he furnished me for the purpose, round the same joint of his right hand. After this, the noisy gongs and tomtoms began to play, being suspended from the rafters at one end of the verandah, and the chief tied another of the little bells round my wrist: his example was this time followed by all the old men present, each addressing a few words to me, or rather mumbling them to themselves, of which I did not understand the purport.

Every person who now came in, brought with him several bamboos of cooked rice; and each, as he arrived, added one to the number of my bells, so that they had now become inconveniently numerous, and I requested, as a favour, that the remainder might be tied upon my left wrist, if it made no difference to the ceremony. Those who followed, accordingly did as I had begged of them in this particular. Soon after, a spotted fowl was brought in, having its legs tied together: it was held out to an old man, who also tied its wings, and the person who had brought it then made it fast to one of the posts of the door. Immediately after, a white one was brought, which was secured in the same manner. In half-an-hour the spotted one was again produced, and its legs being loosened, it was given into the hands of the Orang Kaya, who swinging it backwards and forwards over the heads of the seated people, repeated the same invocation as that previously used by the chief and myself outside. Having finished, the white one was given to me, and walking up and down the place, I went through the same ceremony. After this, the white one was presented for my acceptance, and another was given to my servant and people. The spotted one was then held by the Orang Kaya over the saucer containing the remainder of the rice we had not used outside : another man cut off its head with a sharp piece of bamboo; and the bloody rice was then carried out by the chief and myself, who went through the praying ceremony again. This finished, the gongs and tomtoms again began to play, the boys being the performers. The pig, which forms the principal part of the festival, was then killed with a spear, and being first partially roasted over a fire, was cut up into small pieces, put into green bamboos, and boiled on the spot; all the persons present assisting at this, to them, pleasing labour. After it was put upon the fires, the people all dispersed for about an hour: when they returned, everything was ready to be eaten.

I was now getting very tired of the proceedings, and should have been glad to get away; but retreat, without giving offence, was impossible. Everything being ready, and the feast served to the seated people, the fish, fowls and pig, of which it consisted, were soon made to disappear, together with a very large quantity of rice. They drank the palm toddy, and finished what wine I had with me. By the time this was accomplished it had become quite dark, so that I requested to be allowed to eat my own dinner, not having the slightest wish to taste the many things which the Dyaks had placed before me, and which they doubtlessly considered the most delicate parts of the entertainment. Having finished my meal, and lighted my cigar, the dancing was commenced by the old men of the tribe, who were tottering under all the fine clothes the village could produce. This uninteresting performance consisted in placing and sustaining their bodies in the most contorted positions, and moving up and down the verandah with the slow and shuffling step, and shrill scream of the Sea Dyak dances, which, excepting in the exhibition of heads, this performance much resembled. The actors were occasionally cheered by the spectators, on having performed dexterously some more difficult and inelegant contortion than ordinary; but as I did not sufficiently appreciate its beauties, I was unable to echo them. My Malays, however, who were living at the expense of the Dyaks, were liberal in their commendations. No drunkenness, or other indecent behaviour, was exhibited at this festival.

On taking my departure on the following day, I made presents to the principal people of the battik handkerchiefs, beads, and other trinkets they so much value. Had I permitted them, they would have laden my boat with rice and fowls, which, when I descended from the houses, I found waiting at the landing-place. At the feast above described, women did not dance,

as they were too bashful to perform before a stranger ;
but I have had opportunities of witnessing them on
other occasions, and am enabled to say that the
performance differs in no respect from that of the
men : like them, they dress in all the fine clothes
they can find, not in the least caring whether or not
they are elegant in appearance.

In other particulars, though they differ in some
trifling matters, the feasts of the other Land tribes
precisely resemble this of the Sebongoh people.   When
Mr. Brooke visits their residences, instead of suppli-
cating him, they each bring a portion of the Padi-seed
they intend to sow next season, and with the necklaces
of the women, which are given to him for that purpose, and which, having been dipped into a mixture
previously prepared, are by him shaken over the
little basins which contain the seed, by which process
he is supposed to render them very productive.   Other
tribes, whom from their distance he cannot visit, send
down to him for a small piece of white cloth, and a
little gold or silver, which they bury in the earth
of their farms, to attain the same result.   On his
entering a village, the women also wash and bathe
his feet, first with water, and then with the milk
of a young cocoa-nut, and afterwards with water again :
all this water, which has touched his person, is preserved
for the purpose of being distributed on their farms,
being supposed to render an abundant harvest certain.

On one occasion, having remarked that the crops of
rice of the Samban tribe were thin, the chief imme-

diately observed that they could not be otherwise, as they had never been visited by the Rajah, and he begged of me to try and induce Mr. Brooke to visit them, to remove the causes which had rendered their crop a small one.

The Pamali is a curious practice, resembling the " taboo" of the South Sea Islands, and is intimately connected with their festivals, and other religious or superstitious observances. The Pamali is of different kinds, and used on several occasions; but to describe the three principal ones, will be sufficient in a small work of this nature. These are the " Pamali Mati," or " taboo," for the dead; the " Pamali Peniakit" or that for sickness; and the " Pamali Omar" or that for the Padi farms.

The first, Pamali Mati, is on a house, and on every thing in it for twelve days after the decease of any person belonging to it: during this time, no one, who is not an inhabitant of the dwelling can enter it, nor are the persons usually residing in it allowed to speak to such, nor can any thing, on any pretence whatever, be removed from it, until the twelve days of the prohibition be expired: its conclusion is marked by the death of a fowl or pig, according to the circumstances of the family.

The Pamali Peniakit is undertaken by a whole village during any sickness which prevails generally amongst the members of the tribe; it is marked by a pig slain, and a feast being made in order to propitiate the divinity who has sent the malady among them; in its severest form, it is of eight days' continuance, and during this period every thing in the village is at a stand still, the inhabitants shutting themselves up from all intercourse with strangers. This form of Pamali prevented my personally visiting the Brâng and Sipanjang tribes, as they were under the taboo when I was in their vicinity, for a kind of dysentery which was prevalent among them.

The Pamali Peniakit is also undertaken by individuals when any member of the family is sick ; thus, parents often put themselves under its regulations, fondly hoping that by denying themselves for a time the pleasures of intercourse with their fellow creatures, they will prevail upon the malignant spirit, which is supposed to have shed its withering influence over their offspring, to restore it to its wonted health and strength. Bye Ringate, the chief of the Sennah Dyaks, was dying from a severe dysentery ; his children told me, sorrowing, when I visited their village, that pigs had been killed, and the great Pamali had been tried in vain, and that a person who had come from a distant tribe had also failed to effect a cure, and as a last resource, they wished to have some medicine from the Europeans. On returning, I sent some pills to him which Dr. Treacher, the clever surgeon at Sarawak, had given me for the purpose ; and though, when he found himself get better from their effects, he took more of them than he should have done, we had the satisfaction of hearing that he had perfectly recovered. I never visited the tribe after this occurrence ; but should suppose that it must have shaken their belief in the Pamali, and established the reputation of the European doctor in its place.

The Pamali Omar, or taboo on the farms, occurs immediately after the whole of the seed is sown: it lasts four days, and during that period, no person of the tribe enters any of the plantations on any account; a pig and feast are, according to their practice, also necessary. The proper observance of these various forms of Pamali is probably amongst the most ancient of their customs, and was practised by their tribes previously to the introduction of the Hindu religion.

The Land Dyaks have not among their tribes any of the peculiar functionaries described as " Manangs " in the preceding chapters; at least, none who assume their effeminate character and ridiculous habits; and they consider it a very strange custom in their neighbours. The only person who appears amongst them to be professionally connected with their religious observances, is the " Balean," who prepares the piles for the burning of the dead, as these Dyaks do not dispose of their dead relations by burial.

These piles are generally erected at the foot of the hill on which the village is built, and the body is conveyed to the place as soon as it has been prepared. It is borne by the male relations of the deceased, and followed from the brow of the hill, where the female relatives station themselves; by their cries and lamentations, though these are not of that kind which are intended merely to attract the sympathy of passers-by, but are such as are caused alone by heartfelt and genuine sorrow. The body, being surrounded and covered with wood, is altogether consumed by the flames, the ascent of which, and of the smoke, are carefully watched by their assistant relations, who draw from its perpendicular direction, an augury favourable and satisfactory to them. Should, however, the smoke ascend, from wind or other causes, in a slanting manner, they depart, assured that the Antu, or spirit, is not yet satisfied; and that soon, one or another of them will become his prey. This, however, gives them but little uneasiness; as death, to their ignorant and unenlightened minds, displays no terror; and though they shun it with that instinctive fear which is common both to animals and men, they have by no means the dread of the King of Terror common to more enlightened nations.

Though a knowledge of a future state has evidently been, at some time, prevalent amongst these people, many of them, at the present time, have no idea of the immortality of the soul; though some have a slight and confused conception of it. These say that the spirit of a deceased person haunts the house and village it had formerly inhabited during the twelve days of the Pamali; but the Dyaks of the western branch of the Sarawak, who do not practice the Pamali so rigorously as those of the southern river, say that it departs, at the burying of the body, to the woods or mountains, or goes they know not where. One instance came to my knowledge inferring a partial belief in the transmigration of the soul; but as it is a solitary example, I merely give the anecdote without any comment

It occurred in October, last year, as I was on the road to the Gunong Pennerissen, which I intended to ascend in search of plants, and which is situated on the confines of the Sangow and Sarawak territories. Walking through a jungle between the villages of Sennah and Sudoish, a large snake crossed our path; and when I inquired of the Sennah Dyak, Pa-Benang, who was walking before me, his reason for not killing it—his parang having been drawn, and his arm arrested when raised to strike—he told me that the bamboo bush opposite to which we were then standing, had been a man, and one of his relations, who, dying about ten years previously, had appeared in a dream to his widow, and informed her that he had become the bamboo tree we then saw, and the ground in its immediate neighbourhood, and everything on it, was sacred on this account. Pa-Benang told me, that in spite of the warning given to the woman in the vision, that the Dyaks should respect this tree, a man had once had the hardihood to cut a branch from it, in consequence of which he soon after died; his death being considered by the tribe as a punishment for his sacrilegious act. A small bamboo altar was erected before the bush, on which were the remnants of offerings which had been, but not recently, presented to the spirit of the tree.

Besides the trace of the Hindu religion, which we have recorded, in the disposal of their dead by fire, other relics are to be discovered in their customs, particularly in that which induces them to abstain from the use of animal food of several kinds. This practice—as indeed all those which have any connection with Hinduism—is observed more strictly amongst the Singhie, Sow, and other tribes of the western branch of the Sarawak, than amongst those of the Southern stream, where the old Polynesian customs are more venerated.   Thus it is that the Pamali is less practised amongst the former than amongst the latter tribes; and from this we are led to infer that this country was, most likely, the boundary of the spread of the religion of the Brahmins, and that its influence had not extended to the eastward, as the Dyaks of Sadong retain but few traces of its existence, and those of Sakarran and Sarebas none at all.   Some of the tribes of the Sadong River, situated farthest to the eastward, are said to bury their dead, as do all the Dyak tribes beyond them.

The ox, the buffalo, the deer, the goat, fowls and some kinds of vegetables, are forbidden food 'to some or other of these tribes.   Of these animals, those which are held most sacred are the bull and cow, and nothing would induce a Dyak of any of the tribes of Sarawak, to eat anything into the composition or cooking of which either the flesh of the animal, or any part of its productions has entered; so that, if offered any of the food which has been prepared for an European, they immediately ask if it has been cooked with butter or ghee; in which case they will not partake of it.   So strongly is this superstitious prejudice rooted in their minds, that Dyaks, who have become Mahomedans at the age of five to seven years, and who since that period had resided among Malays, still adhered to the practice; and at the feasts of these latter people, and when on other occasions they have opportunities, never partake of such food.   The prohibition against the flesh of deer is much less strictly practised, and in many tribes totally disregarded. As usual with the relics of the religion of the Brahmins, it is less prevalent on the southern than on the western branch of the river of Sarawak, many of the tribes of the former having totally set aside the custom. In the large tribe of Singhie, it is observed in its fullest extent, and is even carried so far, that they will not allow strangers to bring a deer into their houses, or to be cooked by their fires. The men of the tribe will not touch the animal, and none but the women or boys, who have not been on a war expedition, which admits them to the privileges of manhood, are allowed to assist the European sportsman in bringing home his bag.

It is amongst this, the Sow, and other tribes on the same branch of the river, that goats, fowls, and the fine kind of fern (paku), which forms an excellent vegetable, are also forbidden food to the men, though the women and boys are allowed to partake of them, as they are also of the deer's flesh amongst the Singhie Dyaks. The tribe of Sow, whose villages are not far from the houses of Singhie, does not so rigorously observe the practice. Old men, women, and boys may eat of its flesh ; the middle-aged and unmarried young men only being prohibited from partaking of it. I think, however, that the practice of using the flesh of the animal in question is one of recent introduction, and probably first used by them in the scarcity of food, in the time of the native Rajahs of Sarawak, by whom, more than any of the others, this tribe was oppressed. I am induced to entertain this opinion, from having observed several of the men deny themselves its use, and from the abundance of the herds in their district of country. In those places where the tribes have had, for a long time, no scruple regarding the use of its flesh, the animal is never plentiful, on account of their ingenuity in catching or destroying it.

Their not using the milk or butter of the cow, in which the Hindus delight, has been accounted for on the supposition that, at the first introduction of the animal into Java, from whence it came to Borneo, this was a precautionary measure to encourage the breed, by not depriving the calves of their natural sustenance. None of these animals are now to be found in Sarawak, with the exception of the few belonging to the Europeans, and introduced by them from the northern parts of the island, where large herds of the descendants of some brought thither by the Spaniards about two hundred years ago are found. They are reported to have been kept in considerable numbers by the natives of Sarawak, until the disturbances, when they were all destroyed. The Malays make no use of the milk of the animal, nor do the inhabitants of Java.

From the prevalence of the indications of the influence of the Hindu religion, observed in their customs above detailed, we might suppose that the traces of its monuments in the arts of building and sculpture, so common in some parts of Java, might be also found here; but, as has been previously observed, it is

probable that this and the neighbouring river of Samarhand, were the most eastern confines of its sway,
and that the people were neither sufficiently numerous,
nor zealous enough in the exercise of its precepts,
to render it advisable to incur the necessary expense
of bringing these things from Java, or of importing
Hindu artists from thence.   One positive monument
of these people has, however, been found in Sarawak,
though in a much mutilated state.   It is the image of
a bull, carved in stone, and in a crouching position,
similar to one sketched in Sir Stamford Raffles's History
of Java, fig. 5, in the plate from subjects in stone, found
near Singa-Sari, in the district of Maling, in Java.

The Borneo specimen is too much disfigured to
ascertain whether its trappings had been the same.
This relic was much venerated by the Dyaks, who
protested against its being removed, declaring that the
country would be deluged by rain, and that other
supernatural events would occur, if it were allowed to
go out of the province.   They were finally prevailed
upon to permit its removal to Sarawak, by the argu-
ment, that an object of such veneration should not
be permitted to be exposed in the jungle, and that
it should be placed under a shed in the town, where
it now accordingly stands.

Two other objects, the workmanship of a people who
had attained to some degree of skill in the art of working
stone, have been discovered; the one at a point of the river,
about six miles above the town of Sarawak, called Battu
Kawa ; the other on the Samarhand river, near Ledah

Tanah, and called by the Malays, Battu Berala, or the Idol Stone. The best idea of the shape of this last will be given by the accompanying engraving.*

The Battu Kawa is not in any way reverenced by any of these people, and from the square hole in the centre, and its being situated in a place where Mohammedans are known to have been buried, I have thought that with a post, which may have decayed, placed in the hole of the stone, it may have served to commemorate the interment of a saint, or some other distinguished person of that religion. But the Malays deny all knowledge of its uses, or the period of its construction, and none of them are now capable of producing anything like it in stone.

The Battu Berala, on the contrary, is highly venerated by the surrounding Dyaks, who suppose the slight elevation on which it is placed, to be the resi-

---

* Dimensions of the Battu Berala :—2 feet 7 inches across the upper surface. Diameter of the round hole, 12 inches ; diameter of the square hole, on the lower surface, 7 inches. Thickness of the whole stone, 6 inches ; thickness of the upper edge, 4 inches.

dence of some great spirit, in whose honour, once a year, the Dyaks are said, at this spot, to hold a great feast, bringing the pigs and provisions from their village for this purpose. I exceedingly regret that during the time I visited the stone, it was impossible to proceed further up the river, which becomes small at this distance from the sea, to learn from these Dyaks themselves the whole of the particulars concerning it. Such information as I was able to obtain respecting it, is derived entirely from the Malays who are well acquainted with the customs of the Dyaks of the river, and many of whom speak their language with facility. None of the Dyaks will cut down the trees or make their farms near this place, as they fear to draw upon themselves the anger of the divinity residing in it. Other stones lay about the Battu Berala, one of which appeared to have formed part of the shaft of a column, but they were so broken, that nothing certain, as to their original shape or uses, could be gathered from these fragments.

Though these stones are few in number, the image of the bull alone, and the veneration in which it and the Battu Berala are held, are sufficient evidences that the religion which introduced and used them, has had some influence in this part of the island. In the southern provinces, and those of the south-west, where the colonies of Javanese were larger, and their communication with the parent country more frequent and regular, images of brass and stone are abundant; and even small temples are said, by the Dutch, to have been found in the vicinity of Sukadana and Banjar. Some jars and other earthenware, similar to that used in India in the present day, have been dug up close to the town of Sarawak, in the garden of Mr. Hentig, an European gentleman residing there. In one of the earthen jars, which resembled the chatty, used for cooking by the Hindus, were discovered the golden ornaments of the face, which are common amongst the people of Hindustan : this jar had, perhaps, contained the ashes of a person whose body had been burned.

Amongst the Dyaks are found jars, held by them in high veneration, the manufacturers of which are forgotten ; the smaller ones, amongst the Land and Sea Dyaks, but particularly with the latter, are common. They are called Nagas, from the Naga or dragon, which is rudely traced upon them. They are glazed on the outside, and the current value of them is forty dollars ; but those which are found amongst the Kyan tribes, and those of South Borneo and amongst the Kadyans, and other tribes of the north, are valued so highly as to be altogether beyond the means of ordinary persons, and are the property of the Malayan Rajahs, or of the chiefs of native tribes.

I have never had an opportunity of seeing one of these valued relics of antiquity, but am told that, like the Nagas, they are glazed, but larger. They have small handles round them, called ears by the natives, and figures of dragons are traced upon their surface: their value is about two thousand dollars.

In the houses of their owners, to whom they are a source of great profit, they are kept with pious care, being covered with beautiful cloths. Water is kept in them, which is sold to the tribe, and valued on account of the virtues it is supposed to possess, and which it derives from the jar which has contained it.

By what people these relics were made, and by what means they have been thus distributed, and the veneration for them so widely spread, cannot be at this time determined. Some of the jars were sent from Banjar Massin to China, by the Dutch, who hoped to make a profitable speculation by their credulity; but the artists of that country could not, though famed for their imitative powers, copy these with sufficient exactness to deceive the Dyaks, who immediately discovered that they were not those they esteemed; and, consequently, set no value upon them. From their price, it is presumed that these jars are very rare.

I think that I have now mentioned all the relics of a former superstition—but more recent than those proper to the Polynesian character—which are known to exist in the western and north-western provinces of the island. The veneration for certain plants, now to be described, seems to be more ancient than the introduction of the Brahminical religion, excepting in two instances, those of the Dracœna and the yellow bamboo —which, from their being natives of India, may have come with it.

The Dracœna resembles the species known to Botanists as "*Dracœna terminalis,*" and is not a native of the island. It is planted near their houses and around the "bulu gading," or ivory bamboo, which is held in great reverence. This beautiful cane, one or more tufts of which are found near every village, grows to the height of the largest of the genus: its stems are of a bright yellow colour, with a smooth and ivory-like appearance. Beneath its shade, and amongst plants of the crimson and pink-leaved Dracœna, is generally erected a little bamboo altar, covered in winter from the rain with a roof, but more frequently open. When protected, a ladder is usually placed for facilitating the ascent of the spirit to the offerings upon the stage, which are placed there on all their festival occasions: when the altar is roofed, it in general resembles a Dyak house, and thus becomes a little temple. No worship is paid to the tree, but the place on which it stands is considered sacred; and a plant is always procured and tended with care in every village, until it becomes a large and handsome bush. Its gracefully beautiful stems and foliage probably first attracted the attention of these people, and induced them to suppose plants, which were to them of so pleasing an appearance, equally the favourites of the gods.

The Bunga Si-kudip, as it is called by the Dyaks of the southern branch of the Sarawak river, and amongst whom it is held in the greatest esteem, though known, I believe to all the tribes, is the plant described by botanists as the *Pancratium Amboinense* or *Eurycles coronata*, a native of the Moluccas and other islands to the east-

ward; but as far as is at present known, a stranger to
the flora of Borneo, in the western parts of which, the
order *Amaryllideæ,* to which it belongs, is only represented by one species of *Crinum,* which is found on the
muddy banks of the river. By the Si-booyoh Sea
Dyaks, this plant is called Si-kenyang. By the Dyaks
of the southern river, the roots of this bulbous plant are
preserved with jealous care, being always taken up when
the Padi is ripe, and preserved amongst it in the granaries, to be planted again with the seed-padi in the
following season. It bears a beautiful crown of white
and fragrant flowers, which rise about a foot above the
bulb; the only plant which I saw in a flowering state
was at Sennah, and no consideration would induce the
owner to part with it.

These and other Dyaks assert that the Padi will
not grow unless a plant of the Si-kudip be in the
field, and on being asked respecting its origin they
answered, that Tuppa gave it to mankind with the Padi,
and requested them to take care of it, which they now
do. The plant I saw in flower at Sennah, had a
bamboo altar erected over it, on which were several
offerings, consisting of food, water, &c.

I think there can be little doubt that the plant has
been brought with the Dyaks from the country whence
they first emigrated to Borneo, and as it is not at
present known to be an inhabitant of any country west
of the island, it would follow that the people came from
the eastward, perhaps from the opposite island of
Celebes; but conclusions of this nature cannot be drawn

until the habitat of the plant be better ascertained. Should it be found to be held in the same veneration amongst the Kyan tribes, and the wild inhabitants of Celebes and the Arafouras of the different islands to the eastward become better known, the fact of this plant having been carried westward may be of considerable importance, in setting at rest the long agitated question regarding the direction in which the tide of population in the eastern islands flowed. That this island was peopled originally from the eastward, is, I think, to be deduced from the relative positions of the tribes :—the Kyans, the most strong and powerful, occupying the eastern coast, having driven the Sea Dyaks, the descendants of former emigrants, to the westward, who had previously forced the Land Dyaks, the first immigrants to the island, to retreat before them in the same manner.

Connected with the subject of their religious and superstitious observances, must be mentioned the faith they place in omens, which are principally drawn from the noises of insects ; they are esteemed favourable, or otherwise, according as they are in particular directions from the person wishing to consult them : they have also omens of other kinds, but I am not sufficiently acquainted with the subject to detail them. I may add, from my own observation, that they will never start on any journey, however short, until they ascertain from these practices, whether it will end favourably ; and should the omens not be at first as they wish them, they seldom have to wait long before a promising one is heard, as, from the number of insects which supply them, this necessarily cannot be long before it occurs. A seat is made at the approach to every village, at which all persons leaving their houses wait the wished-for signal, which shall announce a happy termination to the labours of the day, or other business on which they may be departing.

I have not observed amongst the Dyaks of Sarawak, that they hold in superstitious dread any species of birds, though such may be the case in some parts of the country, as it is mentioned by one or two writers, though by none from personal observation. I have shot all kinds of birds in their presence, and they never showed the least wish to prevent me, but were always amused at seeing them fall, and ready to eat such as I did not want for the purpose of preserving their skins.

From the foregoing very imperfect account of the customs of these people, connected with a religious pro-fession, it will be seen that several of the customs and observances of the Hindus have been grafted on the original and more ancient superstitions general among the inhabitants of Polynesia. All writers on the East have uniformly declared that, with the exception of the Papuas, or black race, inhabiting some of the more eastern of the islands, all the various tribes of the Archipelago have originated from one people, which Mr. Crawfurd considers a distinct race, and peculiar to those islands. I am not capable of giving an opinion on a matter so weighty ; but certainly think with the high authority above quoted, that they are not of the Tartar race, as had been formerly supposed; though the Javanese, who are the most distinct from the other races of the island, bear considerable resemblance to that division of the human family.

The natives of the continent of South America are little known, and I have met with no vocabulary of the languages of the central tribes of that continent. Usages cannot be depended on, as the same circumstances would produce similar habits among people who had no communication; but the use of the Sumpit-an, which prevails among the South Americans, is also common in Borneo, and is known to some more eastern islands. The Taboo, or Pamali, assimilates the Dyaks with the islanders of New Zealand and the Pacific Ocean; and, should the inquiry be properly carried out by persons residing on the spot, and who may have leisure and opportunity to pursue an investigation so interesting, we may hope, in time, to connect the inhabitants of all the islands closely one with another; and, finally, annex them to the continent of South America, or establish them— which is, perhaps, more probable—as a distinct race from any of those of Asia or the Western World. It will be my study, if opportunities occur, during a contemplated residence, which I hope may be long continued, on the island of Labuh-an, to prosecute these inquiries; and I hope that others, with similar advantages, will assist in the elucidation of the confused but interesting history of these nations.

CHAPTER IX.

THE nature of the relations which, until recently, existed amongst the tribes of the Land Dyaks, rendered it of paramount importance that the situation of each village should be such as was easily capable of defence. We accordingly find all the hills of the interior of the western portion of the island, on which springs of water are found, to be occupied by one or other of their communities; and one or two of these, which were possessed by numerous tribes, have been considered sufficiently strong to resist the Sakarran Dyaks, and have, accordingly, been unmolested by these ruthless spoilers, excepting in some instances, where small parties were discovered at a distance from their villages, or living at their farm-houses, and who were generally cut off; but in other cases, the difficulties of ascent have been overcome by the invaders, and the tribes massacred and destroyed. This, however, the Sakarran Dyaks could not themselves have accomplished, had they been unassisted by the fire-arms of the Malays.

In appearance, the villages of the Hill tribes differ considerably from the houses of the Sea Dyaks previously described: though they are built much upon the same principles Though these are by no means so well carried out, the same terrace-like arrangement is adhered to, where the nature of the ground will admit of it, but this arrangement is never seen in such perfection as amongst the Sea tribes, on account of the inequalities of the surface, and the rocky nature of the sides of mountains, chosen for their position.

For these reasons, a row of houses seldom contains more than from six to ten residences, and these rows are scattered in all directions, no regularity of position being attempted in the arrangement of the village, but each terrace being placed as near as possible to the others, for the purposes of defence and mutual protection. The houses, like those of the Sea Dyaks, are raised upon posts of Balean, or some other hard wood, though the latter are by no means so stout and large: more of them, consequently, are necessary to support the building. Their houses, individually, are generally much smaller and less commodious, particularly among the poorer tribes. But I have observed that those who have most felt the cherishing influence of the European government, have built houses equally commodious and substantial with those of the other divisions. This is

observable to a great degree in the Sow, Sennah, and
Sempro tribes. In the interior, these houses differ from
those formerly noticed, only in having at the end of
the house, farthest from the door, a raised platform,
about two feet higher than the floor of the apartment.
This serves as a seat for the family by day, and is set
apart for the use of the unmarried females of the house
by night. The roofs of these houses are lower, generally, among the poorer tribes ; and, amongst all, are
formed from a different palm from the Nipah, with
which those of the Sea Dyaks are composed. The
palms they use are of several kinds; and though not
gathered with such facility, on account of their greater
scarcity, they are reported to last much longer than the
other.·

The furniture of the houses differs in no respect from
that of those already described; and the flooring on
which the married people, with their younger children,
sleep, is of the same construction. One or more
cradles, formed of the hollow stem of the Sago-palm,
or a block of wood, in which a cavity has been made,
slung from the beams of the house by ropes attached to
both ends of it, adorn the room ; and a notched pole
serves them as a ladder to ascend to the loft of the
house.

In the villages of all the tribes of Land Dyaks are
found one, and sometimes more houses of an octagonal
form, with their roofs ending in a point at the top.
They always stand apart from the others ; and
instead of having a door at the side, these, which are

never built with verandahs, are entered by a trap-door at
the bottom, in the flooring. These houses vary in size,
according to the wants of the hamlet by which they are
built; but are generally much larger than ordinary
domiciles. The term by which they are distinguished

is " Pangah," " Ramin," being the Dyak word for an
ordinary house. The Pangah is built by the united
efforts of the boys and unmarried men of the tribe,
who, after having attained the age of puberty, are
obliged to leave the houses of the village; and do not
generally frequent them after they have attained the age
of eight or nine years. A large fire-place, of similar
construction to those of the ordinary residences, is placed
in the centre of this hall, and around its sides are plat-

forms similar to those used by the women in the other
dwellings of the village.

The Pangah, being generally the best house in the
place, is set apart for the use of strangers visiting
the tribe ; and in it all the councils of the old men
are held, and all business connected with the welfare
of the people is transacted. A large drum, formed
of the skin of some animal, stretched upon the end
of a hollow tree, is placed above the heads of the
persons on the floor, for the purpose of apprising the
village of any approaching danger. From the timbers
which cross the house and support the slight flooring of
the loft, where the young men keep their sleeping-mats
and other things by day, usually depend the skulls
collected during ages, by the tribe. But on account of
the bloodless nature of their wars, these are seldom
numerous ; and frequently would not equal in number
the heads in the possession of a single family of the Sea
Dyaks.

The villages of the Hill tribes are always, where the
situation has been long the residence of a tribe,
surrounded, to a great extent of country, by orchards
of the delicious fruits of these climes ; and on approaching their houses during the season when these are in
blossom, or loaded with their delicate fruits, the
perfume exhaled by them is most grateful to the
traveller, who is generally not long in seating himself
under the dense foliage of the beautiful mangusteen,
or the lofty and more spreading branches of the
durian ; in which position the Dyaks attending, soon

supply him with abundance of the choicest fruits of the earth.

Any one accustomed only to eat the fruits of the Malayan bazaars, cannot imagine the superior delicacy of flavour in those fresh plucked. In this state, the durian, which, after it has been gathered for a day or two sends forth a most offensive smell, is one of the most delightful of fruits, and its odour neither strong nor unpleasant. No one who has been used to this fruit in perfection, would never think of touching those of the bazaars; one taste of the garlic-like flavour —which if the offensive odour has not been sufficient— usually prevents the European from enjoying this fine fruit. To have it in perfection, it must be eaten immediately on its falling from the tree; those which are plucked, and ripen afterwards, being equally useless with those which have been two or three days from the orchard.

The Dyaks are passionately fond of this fruit, and distinguish it by the name " dien," which signifies " the fruit," *par excellence;* " dien," being the term for fruit in general, as well as for this species in particular. Its seeds, which are large, are roasted, when they resemble chesnuts, and are carefully preserved by the people, to be eaten when the season of fruits is past. To keep up the succession of these forests of fruit-trees, no care on the part of the Dyaks is necessary, so that they never think of planting young trees, but trust to Nature, which is here so prodigal of its care for a continuance of the supply, that a constant succession of young plants is kept up by the fallen fruits, precisely

in the same manner as the ordinary trees of the
jungle. The fruit seasons are, however, very pre-
carious, from the inattention with which the owners
regard their trees. The brushwood is allowed to grow
beneath them, and parasites and *Epiphytes*, both
injurious, but' the former particularly so, as they sap
the fluids of the tree which supports them, are allowed
frequently to cover the branches.

It is proved in the gardens of Europeans, in the
Straits of Malacca, that all the fruits of the Archipelago
will produce regularly, with ordinary care and culture,
a large and a small crop annually ; but here the trees
bear three, and sometimes four crops, in immediate
succession and in the greatest profusion, and are then
barren for two or three years, appearing to have
exhausted themselves in their unnatural efforts, so that
were it not for a few trees which are always unproductive
when the others bear, and *vice versâ*, the Dyaks
would frequently be without fruit for many seasons in
succession.

Near the houses are always planted the cocoa-nut
and betel-nut trees of the tribe; but so far inland,
and at any considerable elevation, they are long before
they come to a fruit-bearing state ; and then their
productions are small, and not to be compared to
those grown in the vicinity of the sea. They add,
however, much to the beautiful appearance of the
Dyak villages, over the houses of which they hang
above the surrounding fruit-trees, from the branches
of which their ripe productions may often be gathered
by merely reaching out of the skylight-shaped windows,

which open all round the roof of the Pangah, or "Head-House," as it has been injudiciously translated by the Europeans.

The fortifications of the villages consist principally of a strong palisading of bamboo stakes, or sometimes of hard wood, which are strengthened and fastened together by split bamboos being woven amongst the perpendicular posts, the ends of which, sharpened to points, project outwards in all directions, presenting an impassable barrier of spikes, like chevaux-de-frize, to the invader. This pagar or fence, is about six feet high, and surrounds all the village, in accessible positions: two gates are made in it, over each of which the worked spikes are carried, and when the entrance is shut, it presents an uniform appearance with the remainder of the fence. To complete their defences, Ranjows, and other means of annoyance to the enemy are resorted to, as by the Sea Dyaks, which have been mentioned in the chapter devoted to the description of their tribes. If the Dyaks, in a fortified village, such as that above described, are enabled to resist their invaders for one or two days, they generally escape, but should these be assisted by fire-arms, they have little chance, as they are so terrified at the report of them, that they generally desert their houses, and seek protection in the depths of the forests and the caves of the mountains.

The hilly country occupied by the Land Dyaks, is everywhere traversed by paths, which connect the different villages; these are carried over hills and swamps, without much attention to the nature of the ground, the Dyaks always endeavouring to keep their road as nearly as possible in a straight line. The object of the paths, until recently, has seldom been to connect the villages, and render communication between them easy, but this has generally been fortuitously brought about by the paths leading to the farms of the neighbouring tribes meeting each other.

All the paths of the Land Dyaks are formed of the stems of trees, raised two feet above the ground, on supports placed under them. Sometimes larger trees are employed for this purpose, but the usual size is about three inches in diameter: the bark from the upper surface, as they lie in their horizontal position, together with a portion of the wood, is cut off, so as to leave a flat rough surface for the foot of the wayfarer: in good roads, and where bamboos are abundant, these canes are employed; two large ones, laid parallel with each other, forming the breadth of the path; but as bamboos more readily decay than the wood of which the more common paths is made, these, though much preferable when new, and in dry weather, are more troublesome when old and decaying, or from the slippery surface of the bamboo on rainy days.

Should a river, or torrent, obstruct the way, the difficulty is soon removed by the Dyaks, who having previously sought and found two large trees opposite each other, which, as much as possible, overhang the river, carry the road up to a suspension bridge formed of bamboo, and hung by large rattans fastened above to the strong branches of the trees: the breadth of the path of the bridge, is never more than that of one bamboo, and a rail of the same material is carried along

its length, to afford a more apparent than real protection to the timid that may pass that way. The rail
slopes away from the footpath of the bridge at so considerable an angle, that the two sides cannot be reached
at the same time by stretching both the arms, and
they are so fragile, that it is dangerous to trust one's
weight upon them, so that Europeans find considerable
difficulty in crossing them, more particularly in such
of them as are agitated by the least motion of the
passengers, or of the wind. The Dyaks cross over them
with heavy burdens on their heads, without requiring
the assistance of the parapet, and merely balancing
themselves with a light cane held in their hands.

The great height above the water, frequently sixty
feet, and the foaming and boiling torrent dashing
amongst the rocks below them, have no effect upon their
practised nerves, but are obstacles which nothing but
necessity would induce the European to face. The
Dyaks, in this species of tight-rope dancing, have a
great advantage over the nations of Europe, in the
prehensile nature of their feet, their toes being as
useful to them as the fingers of their hands; and they
may frequently be seen seated with a knife between
their toes, with the back of its blade towards them,
cutting, by drawing the object they wish to sever towards
them, across the blade: flesh is always cut in this way.

For travelling on roads of this nature, shoes, with
soles of the least possible thickness, are preferable to
any others, as with them the feet are of considerable
service, and after six months' experience, the traveller will
be astonished at the proficiency he has attained in using

these curious paths ; and when, by chance, he meets
a muddy and much worn one, he will soon wish that
he were again in the vicinity of one such as we have
been describing. Such paths as are most constantly in
use, and those which are near the villages, are all put
into repair before the feast, 'Makan Taun,' which
resembles the harvest-home of the English, and at this
necessary preliminary to the festival, all the men of the
tribe assist.

The government of the Hill Dyaks, excepting in the
chiefs, which rule over several tribes of the Sakarrans,
resembles that of these latter people, and is of the most
patriarchal character. The Orang Kaya, or chief, is
elected by the people, though amongst tribes, tributary to the Malays, the Pañgeran, or Datta, to whom
the tribe pays revenue, is always required, or arrogate
to himself the right of confirming or rejecting the
appointment. In large tribes, two Orang Kayas are
frequently found : but the elder one has usually a slight
pre-eminence. Others of the principal inhabitants of
the village, are called " Panglimas," " Pangarahs," or
fighting chiefs, and these are raised to their position on
account of the courage and ability in war which they
are supposed to possess.

The Orang Kaya does not appear to possess the
slightest arbitrary power : the office is not hereditary,
and the person filling it, is generally chosen on account
of the wisdom and ability he displays in the councils
of the tribe, and which appear to fit him for the duties
of their representative in all their relations with their
Malayan masters, or with the neighbouring villages.

The only real advantage which accrues to the chief of a tribe, besides the standing and consideration his title gives him amongst his people, is the assistance he receives in his agricultural operations, the whole people combining to construct and take care of one large farm yearly for his benefit, the produce of which he receives. But in many tribes, this institution is neglected, and has dwindled into occasional assistance, when the chief chooses to demand it, on the land cultivated by his family.

All affairs connected with the prosperity or welfare of the village, are discussed by a council of the men of the tribe, which is always held in the " pangah," and at which every male of the hamlet may be present, though seldom any but the opinions of the old men are advanced—the younger people paying great respect to the advice of the elders at this council. If the chief be a man of known and reputed ability, his opinion, which is generally given in a long and forcible oration, while the speaker is seated, and without much gesticulation, excepting the waving of the head, is of very great weight, and his arguments most frequently convince the assembly, unless some other opinion be advanced and supported with equal ability, when the approvers of each, in succession, address the members of this little parliament—a fair and impartial hearing being given to all—though the discussions are often protracted till near morning from the preceding dusk, when one party either yields its opinion to the other, or the minority is compelled to give way—

U

these assemblies are never riotous, but always conducted in a quiet, grave, and business-like manner.

As has been previously remarked, these Dyaks, in their
different tribes, do not acknowledge the authority of one
chief, who has rule or influence over several of them;
though when a tribe is divided into several large villages,
each having an Orang Kaya of its own, respect is nominally
paid to the chief of the original stock; and when the
history of the Sakarrans shall be known better, perhaps
it may be found that such chiefs as Gasing, and the
Orang Kaya Pamancha, of Sarebas, derive their
authority from the circumstance of their tribes being
the most ancient, and the parents of the others. But
at present I am more inclined to believe that they are
chosen from the chiefs of tribes in the same manner as
the village chief is chosen from the wiser of the people,
solely on account of the reputation they have acquired
for discretion and valour.

It is difficult to ascertain the number of persons
composing the many tribes of the Hill Dyaks, but the
number in the territory of Sarawak may be approxi-
mated. They are divided into twenty-one tribes, which
are settled in twenty-nine villages, containing 1,500
families, or rather houses, which at the average of seven
persons to a house, not a large one, as two families
frequently occupy one residence, gives a total Hill Dyak
population of Sarawak of 10,500 persons; to which,
if 110 families of Sebooyah Sea Dyaks be added at the
same average, we have the total result of the Dyak
population of this territory, 11,270 persons. Of these

tribes, six have their villages on the western branch of the Sarawak, the remainder on the southern stream.

The Orang Gumbang are situated on the con fines of the Sarawak and Sambas territories; though as they, to use their own expression, eat the waters of the Sarawak (makan ayer Sarawak), which means, that the lands producing their vegetables are watered or drained by this river—they belong to its territory. They are divided into two villages, the one at Teringush, on a mountain of that name; the other on a well watered hill, called Gunong Api, or the fire mountain; though I have not been able to learn why this name, usually that of a volcano, should be applied to this quiet and peaceful-looking hill. Both Gunong Api and Teringush abound in springs, which form the sources of the western branch of the river of Sarawak, and meandering amongst the undulating land at their base, unite at the landing place of the village of Gunong Api, Teringush being situated about six miles from the latter hill in a southerly direction.

The two villages contain, each about sixty families, or doors, as the term "lawang," more properly is translated. On descending the stream, which, after leaving the position above named, becomes clear and tranquil, flowing over beds of sand and gravel, you pass first the village of Klokong, situated on the high left-hand bank, and near which several fine bridges, in excellent repair, cross the stream. It contains twenty-five families: in two hours more we pass the mouth of the Sungei Jaguoi, which has its rise on a hill, about six miles inland of the left-hand bank of the Sarawak river : on it is a village containing sixty doors, and immediately below the mouth of the stream, and on the right-hand bank, is the small village of Pasir Bruang, containing fifteen houses.

Following the stream, we pass successively the Battu Bidi, a limestone hill, in which antimony of the richest quality is procured by the Malays, and the great cave, called Lubong Angin, or the wind hole, in which a few swallows' nests are procured. These are both on the same bank of the river with the village last named. The next Dyak houses are placed on the high left bank, near Bow, where the greatest gold works are carried on, and which are situated on the opposite side of the river from that occupied by the Dyaks.

This village, at which is an excellent bridge, is called Subah, and contains forty houses : the four last-named villages all belong to the Sow tribe of Dyaks, whose principal station is on a hill called Rât, at the base of which flows the Sungei, or Ayer Tubah, a tributary of the Sarawak, which discharges itself on the left-hand side about four miles below the landing-place to the Bow gold mines. The village at Rât contains sixty houses, and has been the most oppressed, or amongst the most oppressed, of the Hill Dyaks of this country. They succeeded in defeating the Sakarran Dyaks, who, with a party of Malays, headed by Sereib Jaffir, were shamefully vanquished; but on a second attempt, were more successful, as they surprised the Sow village, which was then on a mountain of the same name, opposite to that they now occupy, while the men were absent at their ordinary avocations, and the women and children alone were in the place. They killed many of the occupants, and carried upwards of 200 women and children into slavery.

It is this division of the Sow tribe, which on Mr. Brooke's arrival, was found to be almost entirely without women; but many have since been restored to them, though numbers still remain in captivity. On account of the destitute state in which he found it, this tribe has been the peculiar care of Mr. Brooke, and under his fostering kindness, the village has been built on Rât, a much stronger position than that they formerly occupied, and the houses are now amongst the most comfortable and well-built of any belonging to the tribes of Sarawak:—the people also are prosperous, and their families increasing.

Next in order, following the downward course of the stream, we observe, after passing Tundong, on the right, the principal station of the Chinese, employed in the produce of vegetables for the use of their country-men working in the neighbouring gold and antimony mines; and about two miles inland, on the left-hand bank of the river, the Mountain of Singhie, which is occupied by the Dyaks of the same name, whose houses are about one hundred and forty in number, under the care of two Orang Kayas.

This tribe has the character of being the least cultivated of those of Sarawak; they have always been able to preserve their villages from the ravages of the Sakarran tribes, though many of their people were cut off at their farms in the low lands, at the base of the hill. Some years since, Mr. Brooke had occasion to demand, for the purposes of justice, two of their chiefs, who had been convicted of frequent murders for the purpose of obtaining heads, against his repeated warnings and authority. After some demur, they were given up, and since that time they have been a peaceable and contented tribe.

On the several occasions when I visited them, they were uniformly hospitable, but great beggars; they ask for every thing they see, but are as scrupulously honest as the other Land tribes, never thinking of helping themselves to any thing. The penkallan, or landing-place, of this tribe is about twenty-eight miles, by the river, above the Malay town of Sarawak, the residence of the Rajah, and capital of the province.

About eight miles lower down the stream, and half a mile inland from the right-hand bank, is situated the pretty mountain of Serambo, on which three friendly tribes have been long settled, and are probably but divisions of one. The porphyry sides of this hill are steep and rugged, and the path to the top is very fatiguing. The hill is covered with fruit trees, the property of the Dyaks; and the three villages are situated in beautiful groves of the cocoa-nut and betel-nut trees, which, by their graceful foliage, mark the situation of the houses from the river.

Bombuck and Serambo, containing respectively fifty and sixty houses, are placed about two-thirds of the way up the mountain; on the shoulder of which, near the top, is the village of " Peninjow," a collection of forty houses. From this village, a beautiful view of the whole of the country of Sarawak, towards the sea, is obtained; and from this height (900 feet,) the Mountains of Sadong, of Lingah, and the mouth of the Batang Lupar are easily discernible. At the foot of the hill, is situated the now decaying village of Seniawan, the seat of the war which ravaged the country on Mr. Brooke's arrival, the particulars of which may be found in Captain Keppel's work. The few Chinese who now reside here, subsist by the cultivation of vegetables, which they sell to the Malays, who pass the place on their way to the Dyaks' villages for the purposes of trade. Seven miles below Seniawan, the western branch of the river is joined at Ledah-tanah, or the tongue of land by that from the southward; and, together, they form the fine stream on which the town is built, about fourteen miles below their confluence

The southern branch of the Sarawak river has its sources in the Gunong Penerissen : the highest land in this part of the island. Penerissen, or Besuah, as it is sometimes called, is a table-topped mountain, about 4,700 feet in height, situated between sixty and seventy miles from the coast in a direct line. One of the tributary streams of the great Sangow River, which itself is but a branch of the still larger Pontianak, flows past its southern base; where also the Dyak tribe, S'Impio, who belong to the Pañgeran, at Karang-an-Amas, a Malay village, two days' down the stream. The Pañgeran is a vassal of the Rajah of Sangow, himself a tributary to the Sultan of Pontianak, and, consequently, of the Dutch, whose creation this potentate is. But neither the Sultan nor his allies are respected by this rich and powerful vassal, except when it suits his own convenience.

On the same waters, but higher up towards the river's source, are found the Dyak villages of Goon and Si-panjang, containing each sixty families : those of Goon, in two villages ; that of the same name with the tribe, and a smaller one, called Bétah. Near them, but to the northward, and in the Sarawak territory, are the tribes of Baddat, of sixty, and the Tabiah, of fifty families. These, with a large independent tribe, called Secong, on a mountain of that name, all frequent the Penkallan Ampat, for the purposes of trade with the Malays of Sarawak, who bring their goods thither.

On the Sarawak, or northern side of the mountain, about four or five miles from its base, is situated, amongst the most beautiful groves of fruit trees, and on either bank of a quiet and crystal stream, the well-built houses of the Sennah Dyaks. They have also another village, called Sudoish, to the eastward of this, which is composed of about thirty families.

This, however, is their principal village, and the residence of the Orang Kaya Bye Ringate, a chief respected and referred to by all the surrounding people. The Sennah village contains about sixty houses. These people succeeded in saving their property when attacked by the Sakarran Dyaks, having had notice of their intention ; but about sixty of the tribe were killed, and many taken prisoners. This village, situated on the level banks of the river, is not capable of any defence.

Near it, but inland, towards the east and north-east, and towards the Sadong river, are situated the houses of the Dyaks of Tumma and Sinang-kan, the former containing about fifty, the latter about sixty families, many of them refugees from the extinct tribe of Crow and others, sold into slavery by Serieb Sahib. Descending the stream from Sennah, about two hours in a fast boat brings us to the Penkallan Ampat, on the left-hand bank of the river, at a point of land formed by the junction of a smaller and more turbulent stream: it is called the Penkallan Ampat, from the four tribes, for the use of which it was first established, viz. Goon, Tabiah, Baddat, and Sipangjang; though, as has been previously stated, the Sicong and other tribes also make use of it for the purposes of trade.

The Sicong tribe contains three hundred houses, and has never been attacked by the people of Sakarran.

Below Penkallan Ampat, about half a mile, is the dangerous rapid called the Rheum Ledong, which has proved fatal to many Chinamen and others unskilful in the use of their paddles and management of their boats. About an hour after passing it, by following the downward course of the stream, we reach the landing-place of the Brang Dyaks, a poor tribe, much destroyed by the Sakarran people. The village, situated on a limestone, rocky and precipitous hill, a little way in-shore, contains about forty houses.

Another hour in a fast boat brings us to the junction of the Samban river, which flows from Gunong Scroung, a mountain 2,627 feet high, situated to the south-west, on which live the Dyaks, bearing the same name as the stream. Though the hill is very steep, the Sakarran Dyaks succeeded in destroying the houses, cutting down the fruit trees, and desolating the place. The village contains about fifty houses, and these Dyaks are the most poor and ignorant I ever visited. Passing the mouth of the Samban, we soon reach the fine village of Sebongoh, the well-built houses of which are seen peeping out from a forest of fruit trees on both banks of the stream, to the number of sixty. These people, though also attacked by the Sakarran Dyaks, appear now to be in a flourishing and happy state. Here I saw a woman whose body was monstrously swelled by dropsy. The Dyaks said that she was " bunting naga," or, pregnant with a dragon.

The next tribe is situated about two hours' fast pulling lower down; one rapid, but not a dangerous one, intervening. The houses of the Sempro Dyaks occupy both banks of the river, at the foot of the precipices Se-bayet and Gigi. The scenes of country, and the beauty of the banks of the river above this village are not to be surpassed. The limestone mountains rise suddenly from the plain in the most curious forms and rugged precipices; and the river runs quietly, smoothly, and brightly through this rock, the waters having worn it away, so that it overhangs them on each side, forming sections of deep natural arches, under which large boats take shelter from the passing showers.

The Sempro tribe numbers sixty families, and is one of the most happy and prosperous of them all.   A little below the village are two large and dangerous rapids. Near to the higher one, the waters of the small river Segou disembogue. It flows from the eastward, and on its banks are three small and impoverished tribes, that of Segou containing thirty, that of Staang twenty, and one other of twenty families. No other tribes are met with descending the river, until we come to the mouth of the Suntah stream. On the right-hand side, the inhabitants of a small village of Sempro Dyaks cultivate the land up this river, where diamonds are found in the greatest abundance. Suntah is an hour and a half fast pulling with the stream below Se-bayet ; and Ledah Tanah is about eight miles below the mouth of the Suntah river.

To the eastward of the river Segou is the ancient tribe of Suntah, situated on the Quap mountain. From three hundred these people have been reduced to sixty families, by the Arab pirate, Sereib Sahib   Their landing-place is on the Quap river, which discharges itself into the Sarawak, about eight miles below the town. The situation and numbers of the different divisions of the Sebooyah villages and tribes have been noticed in the preceding pages, which will give the reader, we trust, a more correct idea of the territory of Sarawak, and of its inhabitants, than the public are at present possessed of.

Besides the tribes now inhabiting the country of Sarawak, many more are anxious to be admitted from the territory of Sambas, and the countries of native princes ; but, wishing to live on friendly terms with all its neighbours, as far as possible, this immigra-

tion has been discouraged by the Government of
Sarawak, in all cases where it could by its influence
ensure their protection, without changing the site
of their villages   Much good has been thus done
in Sadong, the Dattu of which place, a weak and
easily swayed person, would, ere this, had the Sarawak
Government not interfered, have sold the whole of
his tribes of Dyaks into slavery; excepting such as,
to escape this fate, would have fled to Sarawak for
protection.

The chastity of the women of these tribes has been
previously incidentally mentioned, and the reader has
seen the care with which the young men are separated
from the girls.   They may marry at an early age,
and the girls are frequently married very young.   I have
never observed that they have any particular ceremony on
entering the marriage state, more than that of killing a pig,
or fowl, according to the circumstances of the persons;
though I must confess that my inquiries have been lax
on this point.   Adultery is a crime unknown, and no
Dyak ever recollected an instance of its occurrence.

They marry but one wife, though I have seen two
or three instances where a chief had two : the Chief
of Tabiah is one of these, and in consequence of breaking through the custom of the tribe, had lost all his
influence with its members.   Incest is held in abhorrence, and even the marriage of cousins is not allowed.
During my visit to Betah, a village of the " Goon"
tribe, in 1846, the Baddat Dyaks came with presents
of fowls and rice, their village being about ten miles
distant.   They had also a serious · complaint to make

against one of the chiefs of their tribe, for having disturbed the peace and prosperity of their village by marrying his own grand-daughter!—his wife and the girl's mother, his own child, being still alive. The chiefs who visited me, said, that since the occurrence of the above event, no bright day had blessed their territory; but that rain and darkness alone prevailed, and that unless the plague-spot were removed, the tribe would soon be ruined.

I told them that I had no power to interfere, but that I would lay their complaint before their Rajah, and in the meantime advised them to follow their own customs in the punishment and degradation of the offending chief; knowing that it was not Mr. Brooke's wish to interfere in the internal disputes of the tribes, when their own established usages were sufficient to restore order. They accordingly fined him heavily, and degraded him from the rank of Orang Kaya; but I do not know whether the girl was separated from him, although I believe not. They described the ludicrous scenes between the young wife—who was said to be about thirteen years of age—and the old one, as of very frequent occurrence; and that the whole village was disturbed by their altercations; as the young one wished her grandmother, on all occasions, to do the heavy work, to which the old lady would by no means quietly assent.

Though slavery, in its degrading form of trading in the liberties of our fellow creatures, is not practised by them, the system of slave-debtors is carried on, though to a very small extent. In scarce seasons, poor families are compelled to borrow of the rich, and it sometimes happens, that being unable to repay the debt, they live in the houses of their creditors, and work on their farms. They are just as happy, however, in this state, as if perfectly free, enjoying all the liberty of their masters, who never think of ill-using them. Since the security of property, consequent on the prevalence of European influence in the country, no persons have become slave-debtors; as, with industry, every individual can raise sufficient, and more than sufficient, to provide himself with food, and to pay the few demands upon him.

One curious custom of the Dyaks of the Hills, which was doubtless intended, in its original institution, to prevent the prevalence of indolence, is, that no Dyak can, under any circumstances, eat of new rice, until his own be ripe; and this is so strictly observed amongst the Sow and Singhie tribes that, when their own supply was finished, a few days before their harvest was ripe, though they had not eaten rice for four days, I could not induce them to partake of that I had brought with me from the town, because it was of the produce of that year's harvest, having been grown by the Sea Dyaks, who always make their farms earlier than the Hill tribes. Could they eat of new rice, many of them would, perhaps, from idleness, delay the preparing of their farms, hoping to borrow, and thus become indebted to their more industrious neighbours; but with this curious, but useful practice before them, they all plant at one time, and are, cousesequently, not burdensome to each other, and can only become indebted towards the end of the season ; when, even those who have had the greatest supply, have none to spare, as they generally run themselves so short, by selling their Padi to the Malays, as to be very frequently reduced to roots and sago for the month preceding the ripening of the coming crop.

The custom of head-taking, it has been before noticed, is not so deeply rooted in the habits of these people, as to prevent our hope of its being easily eradicated; though amongst the Sea Dyaks, it will probably be long before this desirable result be attained. A person afflicted with madness, and who had destroyed several others by running-a-muck, was killed by the Peninjow Dyaks, in an attempt upon some farm-houses and their occupants belonging to that tribe. The un-doubted custom was, that they should have the head; but some of the most civilized of the Dyak tribes, and who constantly frequent Sarawak for the pur-poses of trade, replied that they might bury it with the man, as they did not care about it : this shows with what facility they may be brought, by proper care and instruction, to the practice of better habits of life than they formerly led, and holds out an encouraging prospect to the Missionaries of their speedy conversion to the doctrines and practices of our Holy Church.

The heads of the enemies of these tribes are not preserved with the flesh and hair adhering to them, as are those of the Sakarran Dyaks ; the skull only is retained, the lower jaw being taken away, and a piece of wood substituted for it. These ghastly objects are hung up in the Pangah, which Capt. Keppel facetiously calls the " skullery," and are often painted with lines of white or red all over them, they are occasionally blackened with antimony, and have cowrie shells placed in the apertures of the eyes, with the flat, or white side outwards ; which, in some measure, resembles the closed eye, the little furrows appearing like eyelashes.

To have been on a war-party, is necessary before boys can be initiated into the privileges of manhood ; but at none of their ceremonies is the shedding of human blood practised, and such a thing would be thought of amongst them with horror and disgust. So much have these people been maligned, when called cannibals, that if told such a race of people do exist, they cannot credit it, and do not believe such enormities possible. When two or more tribes of Land Dyaks combine to attack another tribe, and one head only is obtained, it is divided, so that each may have a part ; in honour of this moiety, all the same ceremonies are observed, as if they had a whole head. I notice in Forrest's Voyages, and other works, that amongst the people of New Guinea, and other of the eastern islands, the bachelors of the tribes sleep apart, in houses appropriated to their use ; but as no particular description is given of them, it is presumed that they do not differ in their construction, from the ordinary dwellings of the villagers.

The diseases which are most common among them are those incident to their exposed manner of life. Agues and diarrhœas are the most prevalent, though opthalmia, in various forms, is very frequent, and sometimes occasions the loss of sight, from cataract, though a weakening discharge is the most common appearance. The skin diseases, common to the nations of the other islands, are also prevalent here. They are not infectious, and appear to be caused by bad and insufficient food. Several persons having been affected with them, on entering the service of the Europeans have soon lost the disease, though the marks and the discolouration of the skin remain.

At Sennah, I observed a small hut erected in a Rhambut-an tree, far above the ordinary houses of the village, and though in sight of, at some distance from them. I was told that it contained two persons afflicted with a loathsome disease, which caused large pieces of their flesh, particularly from the extremities, to drop away. Whether this was one of the forms of leprosy, or some other disgusting disease, I cannot tell. These two unfortunates, a man and woman, were debarred the society of the tribe, and were never permitted to descend from their aërial habitation; but were constantly supplied with food by their relations from the houses below. The loathsome diseases of the bazaars are unknown amongst the Dyaks, as far as I could ascertain; but madness is said to be not uncommon among them: this may arise in some measure from the practice almost constantly adhered to, of marrying from their own tribe, which though they avoid it as carefully as possible, amongst their immediate relations, must make the whole of the inhabitants one family in the course of

time, though the affinities and relationships are not remembered by the people themselves.   Madness is supposed amongst the Singhie Dyaks, to be the punishment
inflicted on the hardy offender against the Pamalion
deer's-flesh, and a man is now living in 'that tribe
who committed the horrid crime of parricide to save
his family from the disgrace incurred by his father
running about the woods in a state of nudity, making
the noises and imitating the habits of a deer, of the
flesh of which animal he was supposed to have eaten.

The wens, or goitres, common among the people of
the hilly countries of Sumatra and Java, are met with
here amongst the tribes inhabiting the Sangow River.
I observed them at S'Impio, and am told they are much
more common at Secong and Si-Panjang.   On account
of their great size and length, they must be very
inconvenient, though the persons afflicted with them
suffer no pain from them, nor is their general health
at all affected by them.   I have myself seen young
women with them, so long as to hang below the breasts,
and was informed that amongst other tribes they were
frequently thrown over their shoulders by the people
troubled with them.   They appeared to me to be more
frequent amongst the women than the men.   I did not
see them exceed more than two in number on one
individual.

This disease cannot be attributed to the effects
of an elevated atmosphere, as those living on
the borders of the rivers, not more than 100 feet
above the level of the sea, are troubled with them

quite as much as those, the situation of whose houses is more elevated. Nor can it be here—as it has been supposed to be in the mountains of Europe—from the effects of drinking water which has been frozen, for neither ice nor snow are known; and if it were, as Marsden supposes, from the fog prevalent in the mornings in the valleys between the mountains, how is it that amongst tribes similarly situated, it should be prevalent in some and unknown to others?

Parturition, from the more hardy and robust frames of the women, is not here attended with the danger and consequent weakness peculiar to more civilized and polite nations. Amongst the delicately-kept women of the Malayan harems, child-birth is almost as much dreaded as by the ladies in Europe, and they are quite as long in recovering their strength. I have been told that women among the Dyaks are rarely confined to the house more than two or three days, and frequently are seen at their ordinary employment within that time: their attendants, during the period of labour, are the old women of the tribe.

In the practice of medicine and surgery, we cannot look for much skill amongst so simple a people; yet they are not ignorant of a kind of phlebotomy, and practice both bleeding and cupping in particular cases. The former operation is performed very rudely, by cutting large gashes in the limb which pains them. The cupping process is curious, and, as far as I know, peculiar to the people. The wounds being made with a sharp knife, or a piece of bamboo, a small tube of this cane is placed over them, with fire on its upper end, so that the air of the tube being exhausted by the action of the fire, the blood flows readily, and the operation is successfully carried on. Wounds are always covered with a kind of paste, made of pounded turmeric roots, and other herbs, which entering the sore, keep it in an unclean state, and prevent rather than assist the cure. From the simple nature of their food, and their way of life, inflammation in wounds or sores is rare amongst them, and generally to a small extent.

Rheumatic pains are very common, and they are grateful for the relief Dr. Treacher affords them at Sarawak, with his blisters, mustard-poultices, and other appliances. For the cure of internal diseases, turmeric and spices, taken in monstrous quantities, are the favourite remedies; but for anything at all serious, recourse is had to the 'Pamali,' both in medical and surgical cases. They have great faith in the medicinal powers of the Europeans, and fancy that all of them are doctors.

In travelling through their tribes, I found great advantage in carrying a little laudanum, quinine, and castor oil with me; by the assistance of these, administered in small doses, I frequently had the satisfaction of seeing those afflicted with agues, diarrhœas, and stomachic pains, recover; but some cases brought to me, were beyond my very moderate skill, and one I think would have puzzled the first doctors of our country. It was that of a young woman who, being married to an old man, was childless, and she requested me to give her some medicine which would cause her to have children which she felt persuaded I could do.

In one case, when a man was dying of dysentery, those attending him had prescribed the frequent use of plantains as his only food. Honey enters largely into their medical practice, and to it they ascribe heating qualities. The Malay women of bad character use it with hot spices, which they swallow in great quantities, to procure abortion, a practice which, amongst the Dyaks, is never resorted to under any circumstances. They have not that antipathy to the use of castor oil so frequently observed amongst other people; but, on having taken one dose, generally hold out the glass and ask for another, saying at the same time that it is very good. European medicines have great effect upon their constitutions, so that, in all cases, smaller doses than usual must be prescribed for them. Mr. McDougall, the head of the Borneo mission, will be a great acquisition to the Dyaks; his surgical education fitting him as well to relieve their temporal ailments, as their spiritual destitution.

The domestic animals of the Land Dyaks are few, consisting of pigs, which in the time of harvest are carried to the farm, and penned up under their houses, —as by the Arafouras of Magindanau, and other places —that they may, with their owners, partake of the plenty of that joyous season. In killing a pig, which is done at all the village festivals, the length of the animal is carefully measured while it is still alive, and should, after death, he be found a little longer, as from the distension of the muscles in the dying agony is generally the case, the omen is accepted as one of prosperity to the tribe in all its undertakings for the ensuing season ; but if, on the contrary, the pains of the slaughtered animal should cause it to contract its limbs, the omen portends misfortunes to the tribe.

Goat's flesh being, as has been elsewhere observed, prohibited to the Dyaks by their customs, none of these animals are kept about their villages, as is the case amongst the Kyan and Sea Dyak tribes, where no superstition forbids the people the use of these hardy animals. Small dogs are kept occasionally, they are not so well-trained or practised as those of the Sea tribes. It is astonishing how such little curs can bring the fine stag and the wild boar to bay, but such is the case, and while the trembling deer defends himself from the snapping of the curs around him, he is speared by the Dyaks who have followed the dogs. It is said that the deer are so terrified by the dogs, that when the Dyaks come up, they find the trembling stag an easy prey, his quivering limbs almost refusing him their wonted support.

A few cats, generally in a half-starved condition, are found about the Dyaks' houses : they are of the Malayan breed, with curled tails. Fowls are plentiful, but preserved more for sale to the Malays, than the use of the families who rear them. Like the Malays and others, they are more partial to the flesh of fish, which the Malays bring to them in an almost putrid state,

particularly the large " ikan-pari," or skate   I have
seen them also carefully gather up the body of a pig
which had been overlooked in their traps, until it was
falling to pieces, so that they evidently admire a
" gamey" flavour more than the epicures of Europe.

On the Sangow, and other large rivers, the Dyaks are
very expert with the rod and line, which is constructed
with a reel and spare line, precisely like those of Europe.
Having hooked a large fish, they play him with a
dexterity which would delight old Izaak Walton, and
finally, having exhausted him, land him with a net
in the most skilful manner. Their hooks are of brass,
of which also their shining bait is manufactured. The
rod and line, are, I believe, used both for trolling and
fly-fishing, but I never saw them practise the former.
They destroy, in a great measure, the supply of fish in
the upper part of the streams by the use of the " tuba,"
the narcotic before described. The fish most common
and most esteemed resembles a perch, and is barred
with black bands across the back. With this I was
abundantly supplied during my stay at the S'Impio
village by these dexterous anglers ; at the same place,
I observed the children playing at peg-top, precisely as
do those of England; but their tops had no iron pegs,
and more resembled those which at school we used
to called whipping-tops. I looked on at the game with
delight, and saw the spinning top, the mark for the
others, receive several smart blows, but they appeared
to be of very hard wood, and though driven to some
distance, were never broken.

Besides the gongs and their varieties, the chunang and tertawak, which differ only in being smaller and more harsh sounding, and the tomtoms which they have borrowed from the Hindus, the young men and children may be frequently seen amusing themselves with a kind of pipe, which resembles a child's penny wooden whistle, and is formed precisely on the same principle, being about a foot long, and made of reeds, which have five or six holes in the lower part of the tube, on which the fingers are made to act like keys. Another instrument, of more soft and melodious sound, is sometimes seen: it is formed of a joint of bamboo, which having been dried so that it cannot shrink, is cut lengthwise sufficiently deep, but not through the cane, into narrow strips, about half an inch apart from each other: these strips of the outer skin of the bamboo are then stretched and raised above the surface of the cane by small pegs or wedges forced under them at each end, and being played upon by the fingers, as are the strings of the harp and guitar, produce very melodious sounds, and it is a pity that the Dyaks do not endeavour to improve this instrument, rather than use the deafening and disagreeable noisy gongs.

When they sing, which they rarely do, it is in a low and plaintive voice; but as I did not sufficiently understand the Dyak language, I could never learn anything respecting the composition of their songs. I never heard them but at night, when most of the inhabitants of the village were asleep. They do not practise vocal music at any of their festivals.

The weapons used by the Hill tribes in their wars, are very like those described as appertaining to the Sea Dyaks. The swords of the Hill tribes differ, however, in having no wooden handle; this part of the weapon being of iron, and a mere continuation of the blade. The handle of this weapon and its sheath are ornamented with hair, instead 'of the feathers of the argus pheasant. But this is put on sparingly, and in small tufts only at the extremities. The sheath is always stained red, and very rarely carved, and if such decoration be attempted, it amounts to nothing better than mere scratching.

The spears are formed, as to the blade, like those of the Sakarran people; but among the Land tribes, particularly those of Sadong, each family generally possesses one, the haft of which is made of balean wood, and towards the brass plate, which binds the blade into the handle, are carved rude representations of the human figure in high relief. These stand with their backs to each other, and are from three to five in number: like those on the war-boats of the Sea Dyaks, these figures generally represent indecent attitudes. Their spears are also ornamented with sheets of tin foil, with which the haft of the weapon is covered, and also with the feathers of the argus pheasant and the rhinoceros hornbill, which latter are usually stuck on three little prongs, into which the handle has been cut for that purpose

Their shields are precisely like those of the people of Sarebas, but they do no use the sumpit-an, and are without the padded jacket of the Sea tribes. It is,

perhaps, their poverty more than custom that renders
the latter article rare amongst them.

These people, expert in all their employments in
the jungle, particularly exercise their dexterity in the
search for the wax produced in their forests, and the
birds' nests of the mountain caves. The former
valuable production is found on the sheltered sides
of rocky precipices, and on the lofty Tapang. The
Dyaks ascend by ladders of bamboo. When their
nests are to be built in the former position, the bees
always select such places as are kept dry by the overhanging precipice, so that they can only be obtained
with difficulty and danger; but for the value of two
or three dollars' worth of wax, and by the assistance
of rattans and bamboo ladders, the Dyaks never fail
to overcome all obstacles, and carry off the coveted
prize in spite of the stings of the enraged architects.

The wax is more frequently found on the gigantic
Tapang-tree than in the rocks. The genus of this tree
which, from any elevated position, may be seen just throwing out its branches, when its main stem has shot past the
tops of the foliage of the surrounding jungle, I have not
been able to determine, as I never could procure either its
flowers or fruits. It appears, however, to belong to the
great genus *Ficus*, or the fig tribe, species of which
are common in the islands: it rises with a straight and
beautiful stem, to a height which would be thought
incredible, far surpassing the most lofty of its gigantic
neighbours, which frequently attain a height of a
hundred feet of clear stem. The bark is white, soft,
and very milky. The wood is white and soft, excepting

near the heart of the tree, where it is of a chocolate colour, and very hard and tough; it turns black on long exposure to the atmosphere. The branches are large, and extend high above the tree, being long as the stem itself, over which, with the small light green leaves, they form a round, regularly and beautifully formed head.

The bees generally place their nests on the underside of the larger branches, and the Dyaks ascend to these by torchlight, by means of spikes of bamboo, which are driven in a sloping direction between the bark and wood of the tree. These are about two feet apart, and project about twelve inches from the stem. They are connected by a rail of bamboo, which is placed perpendicularly along them, and attached to each by rattans, and this ladder is all the assistance to the Dyak in his perilous undertaking; which, when we consider the height from the ground, the time at which the ascent is made, and the tormenting and sharp stings of the large wasp-like bee (*Lanyeh*), must make us wonder how the temptation of a few dollars can cause the Dyaks to expose themselves to so much danger.

One ascent I witnessed: a little boy who had never been up before, accompanied his brothers, who all ascended, singing and making as much noise as possible, and with torches in their hands. The little fellow got safely to the top, but when the nests were disturbed and the bees began to sting, as their domiciles were placed in the baskets on the backs of the Dyaks, his cries were pitiful, and he had nearly fallen, but saved himself by catching hold of the leg of one of his brothers, who brought him safely down, in addition to the bees' nests and basket with which he was burdened. On reaching the bottom, the boys were swollen all over from the effects of the stings; but no cry or complaint had been uttered by them, and they, together with their father, who waited below quietly, began to separate the honey from the wax, and place the former in the bamboo.

The honey produced by the *Lanyeh* is very fine and rich, equal to the honey of Europe; but the nests contain but very little of it. A smaller bee, called *Nuang,* by the Hill Dyaks, and which is sometimes domes-ticated in hives of bamboo, or bark, about their houses, makes very little wax, but gathers abundance of honey, which is, however, of a very inferior quality. It is very plentiful along the coast, and at Hoya, Egan, and Mocha, is sold very cheap, a gantang being procurable for a shilling. In its wild state the *Nuang,* of which there are several varieties, builds its nest in the holes of decayed trees.

The edible nests of the little swallows are all of the black kind, the beautiful white ones being only found in the rocky caves on the borders of the ocean: they are built by two different and quite dissimilar kinds of birds, though both are swallows. That which produces the white nest is larger and of more lively colours: its belly is white, but as these birds are very rare in Sarawak, I could not get specimens, though, on one occasion,

I had opportunities of observing them, but as I was
without my gun, I could not secure one. Skins of
the smaller and darker bird, which inhabits the limestone mountains of the interior I have sent home. This
kind is never found on the sea-coast, nor does the
other bird ever frequent inland places.

The nest produced by the small bird is of a much
inferior kind, being, like the bird itself, of a dusky colour,
and mixed with feathers: that of the coast is white and
transparent, and resembles a net-work of isinglass.
Feathers are not mixed with this, and it is free from all
other impurities: it is this kind which sells for so high a
price in China. The nests are found in deep and dark
caves, in situations extremely difficult of access, sticking
to the sides of the rock in considerable numbers. Stages
and frames of bamboo are erected along the sides of the
precipices leading to the caves, and on these fragile
pathways the Dyaks advance to their mouths; in other
situations they are let down by rattans from the heights
above. Both means are highly dangerous, and accidents
are said frequently to occur. The black kind are sold in
Sarawak at four rupees per pound, but the price varies
according to the demand and supply.

In their agricultural operations these Dyaks differ in
no respect from the tribes already described, excepting
when they have land of an easily flooded nature,
as is the case with the two tribes of Sow and Singhie,
but with none of the others. In these places the
Padi Sawah, or wet land Padi, is cultivated: it is quite
different from that grown on the hills, its stems being

stronger, its foliage broader and of a dark green colour. The land being prepared by burning down the weeds and grasses, the small brooks which run through the valley are dammed up with stakes, which support an embankment of weeds and rubbish. The field is divided by ridges into parcels of land of different levels, and the water is so managed by attention to levels, that any of these can be flooded or drained, as the growth and appearance of the crop may render necessary. The Padi seed is not planted in the fields, but sown in another piece of land, and taken up and transplanted into the wet land of the farm.

The rice of the wet land growth is of a larger and coarser grain than that produced on the hills, and does not fetch so high a price in the market as the other kinds; it being said not to keep long either in the rice or Padi state. The crop from it is, however, larger and more certain than that from the dry farms; the prosperity of which, more than the other, depends upon the quantity of rain which falls.

They have no implements for the cultivation of wet land Padi different from those employed on the other farms; but in these situations buffaloes and ploughs of a simple construction might be introduced with advantage. I am not aware that the Dyaks possess more than one kind of wet rice, but of the upland Padi they have very many: the one most esteemed and in most general cultivation, is the Padi ber-sabong, a good kind and an abundant bearer. There are others of a whiter nature and smaller grain, but these are not so productive, and are consequently less grown. The Padi-pulut is a curious species, each family grows a little of it; it is a fine strong growing kind, but when cleaned and boiled, is of a peculiar clammy nature, and is much used by the Malays in their cooking for Juadahs and sweet-meats: the Europeans also use it for puddings. It bears a higher price than the other kinds in the market, and is never eaten by the Dyaks unless it has been cooked in a green bamboo, as they suppose that the priuk, or cooking pot, spoils the flavour, and the Malays also are of this opinion.

Land being so abundant, in proportion to the number of inhabitants, but little of it is the property of individuals; though each tribe has its limits, which have been handed down from father to son for ages, so that every old man of a tribe knows the exact extent of its district. But, as in a country where beasts of burden do not exist to assist the farmer in bringing home the produce of his lands, it is a very great advantage to the cultivator to have his field as near to the village as possible, we find that the tribes situated at a distance from the banks of the river, or where the brooks are too small to admit of the use of the canoe, the property in the vicinity of the houses divided into plots, which are the acknowledged property of certain individuals. During one of my visits to the Sennah tribe, a farm of about fifty acres was sold by one Dyak to another, the purchaser giving in exchange one large jar, said to be of the value of sixty rupees, or six pounds English.

The rich men of a tribe often possess four or five such pieces of land in the favoured situations, and are, consequently, enabled to farm one piece every year near their own villages, as well as a larger farm at a distance, and in the vicinity of others of the tribe. In choosing the place for their farms, the locality is generally settled in a council of the tribe, so that one road may lead to all, at the making of which the whole village is called upon to assist. On the death of a Dyak, his land, together with his other property, is divided equally amongst his children, without distinction of age or sex.

CHAPTER X.

OF the remaining tribes, differing from each other sufficiently to be classed under separate titles, the Kyans, as
the people most numerous and powerful, first claim our
attention. Personally, little is known of their divisions by
the English, though the Netherlands' (India) Government
has been supplied by its officers with many particulars
concerning those who inhabit the south and south-east of
the island. These people, differing however in various
customs, are found on the great rivers Banjar, Pasir, and
Coti, and probably on all the rivers of the eastern coast.
The Orang Tedong are, most likely, a tribe of the great
Kyan division of the nations of the island. On the north
and north-west parts of the island, they are found in
the interior of the Bintulu, Barram, Rejang, and other
great rivers, as far west as the country of the Sarebas
Dyaks, but they only occupy the inland parts, at a

great distance from the coast; always having between it and them other tribes, and frequently Malayan states; which latter have, by their intrigues, in a great measure prevented our acquiring that knowledge of them, which the settlement at Sarawak might otherwise have obtained.

The Kyans of the rivers Banjar, Coti, and Pasir, appear to have been always subject to the European or Malayan power, which held the mouth of their respective streams. But the Kyans of the north-west have always been feared by the inhabitants of the Malayan towns of the coast; and the chiefs of Hoya, Mocha, Egan, and Serekei, have always eagerly sought alliances with their barbarous, but powerful neighbours; and, on several occasions, such as have quarrelled with them, have found to their cost, that they were implacable foes, several coast towns having been burnt by them to the ground. The populous town of Sarebas was last year attacked by them, in conjunction with their ally, Dattu Patingi Abdulrahman, of Serekei, to whose assistance they are reported to have come, with ninety boats, under three of their Rajahs, or most powerful chiefs.

In their government, they are said to resemble the Sea Dyaks, each village being under one chief, who is, however, much more subservient to the authority of a higher chief, than either the Sarebas or Sakarran Orang Kayas. The country is divided into little states, each of which contains many villages, tributary to that in which the Rajah of the province, as he is said to term himself, resides. The principal chief of this kind is the Rajah

Nipa, on the head waters of the great Rejang river, and he is very much feared by the neighbouring tribes of Dyaks, Milanowes, &c. He is the ally of the Chief of Serekei, who, though a Mahometan, is not of the pure Malayan race, his mother having been a Kyan woman.

The country of the Kyans is reported, by all who have visited it, to be very populous ; much more so than any other parts of the island. In some parts of it, gold and diamonds are found. On the Banjar river the people are said to wash the earth for these precious commodities, as do the Dyaks of Suntang, in the interior of the western branch of the Batang Lupar river.

Bees'-wax and camphor are exported by them largely from Bintulu and Serekei, at which towns these valuable commodities are collected by the Mahometans, who ascend these rivers for the purpose, and by whom the whole of this valuable trade is carried on, in exchange for salt, cloth, beads, brass-wire, and ivory. The bees'-wax and camphor are reported to be so plentiful, that the Dyaks never collect them until the arrival of the trader from the sea; who, having delivered his cargo into the hands of the chief, and having fixed his price for the whole of it, either waits until the day stipulated for payment has arrived, or returns in time to receive his goods in exchange, which he knows are more valuable to him than money. So punctual are these people said to be in their payments, that if when the day has arrived, the Malay merchant is not there to receive his return cargo, they consider he has forfeited his right to the security of his property, and, after the time

has elapsed, the chief no longer holds himself responsible if any portion of the stipulated quantity should be
wanting.

The houses of the Kyans are built, like those of the
Sea Dyaks, in one long terrace, with the verandah front-
ing its whole length. They are said to be formed of
the most substantial materials, the posts being always of
the very hardest wood, and the roof of planks of the
same material. In the south of Borneo, where there
are tribes who live only to desolate each other, all the
villages are said to be surrounded by a high and strong
pagar; but the low country of the south of Borneo
has its effects upon the customs of the people, as
there are no paths in that flat and swampy part of the
island, as in that of the country of the Kyans of the
north; and all communication between the tribes of the
Banjar river, even far inland, is carried on by boats.

The Kyan tribes of the north are not engaged in
incessant conflicts with each other, nor do they seem to
have any foreign enemies whom they dread. They are
the hereditary foes of the Dyaks of Sarebas and Sakarran,
than whom they are more powerful; although I once
heard a chief of these rivers say, that the report
merely of two or three muskets which they possessed,
sufficed to beat the Kyans, of whom, I believe, in
reality they have great dread. They are allowed by all
their enemies, and others who have known them, to
possess in a much higher degree personal courage, than
any of the other tribes inhabiting the island. Their
bodies are beautifully tattooed, of a blue colour, in

various patterns; but images of the sun, moon, and stars, are amongst the most frequent.

It is reported that some of the tribes on the Barram and Bintulu rivers do not tattoo the persons of the males, and that the practice is there confined to the women, who thus discolour their arms and legs only. The Kenawit Dyaks, whose country borders that of the Kyans, also practice tatooing, as do the Orang Tatow, who live near the Bintulu river, and more towards the coast than the Kyans. These people also call themselves Dyaks, but the races appear to be so easily traced through the Tatows, the Kenawits and other tribes, to the Dyaks of Sarebas and Sakarran, that there is no doubt that one comprehensive term, whether it be Dyak or Kyan, is applicable to all their divisions; and the whole of the inhabitants of the island are certainly of the same race.

The Dutch authors always speak of the Kyans of south Borneo, as the "Dyah Kyan," including all the infidel natives of the island under the former term, and using the names of divisions and tribes as specific names of this generic appellation. In dress and person, the Kyans very much resemble the Dyaks; the women wearing the small bedang, and the men the chawat: this latter is said to be uniformly of greater length and width than those used by the Dyaks, and to be frequently made of European cloth, though the women are expert in the manufacture of coarse kinds, both from cotton, and it is said, also from the fibres of the pine-apple leaves, which are abundant in this country.

In south Borneo, the bedang of the women is quite narrow, and so tight at the lower ends, that in walking, they find great difficulty and inconvenience result from the practice, which has, perhaps, for its intention, the greater preservation of decency, but, as has been observed by Mr. Marsden, in speaking of the longer clothes of the coast women of Sumatra, their greater attention to appearances does not always portend really more genuine virtue and modesty, and if the statements I have heard from gentlemen who have resided in that country be correct, this opinion is strikingly illustrated; for a German missionary, who resided for some time among them, attributes to them the most offensive vices and loathsome crimes, for the gratification of which, public prostitution of females, and worse institutions, have gained a place among them; but I cannot imagine these observations to be correct, and think that such revolting practices as have been thus attributed to them, may have originated in some misunderstanding between the Missionary and his informants, more particularly as the vices attributed to them are those which have never been found in such a state of society, and the public practice of them is against all that we know of the principles of human nature; such nations as the Chinese, who are addicted to such vile habits, being the most strenuous in denying their existence.

In the south of Borneo, they are said to be carried on publicly, the wretched beings who gratify the public vices, inviting their associates by the sound of gongs and other descriptions of music. As far as I know of the Dyak character, and as far as I have been able to learn, by strict enquiry of those best acquainted with the customs of the northern Kyans, no word for prostitution exists in their language, much less can any term for more degrading vices be found among their tribes. As no such practices are mentioned by Mr. Dalton, who resided for some time amongst the Kyans of Coti, very near those of the Banjar river, I am contented at present, to hope, as I previously stated, that this conclusion has been hastily adopted, from the difficulty of conversing freely with the Kyans, who, if they are like the Dyaks in this respect, speak badly and understand with difficulty the European pronunciation of the Malayan tongue.

These observations of the German missionary are, I believe, intended not to apply to the whole of the Kyans of the Banjar river, but to one village of them, not far above the Malayan town. If such be found really to be the case, their vicinity to the Chinese of Banjar may account for it; but the same gentleman who gave me the information, assured me that the Chinese had at no time influenced them in any way.

The dress of the Kyan women of the Bintulu river, I am informed, consists of two cloths, a little longer than the bedang, which are tied on opposite sides of the person, the one covering lapping over the other; but I have seen their dresses from the Rejang, and found them made like the bedang. The jacket of the Kyan women is not loose, like that of the Dyaks, but fits closely to the person, and is longer than the cotton ones of the Hill tribes : it is also frequently made of the pine-apple fibre.

In war, the dress of the men differs much from the Dyaks of other denominations. The jackets they wear on these occasions are made of the skins of beasts; those of the panther and the bear are the most esteemed, but those of goats and dogs are sometimes substituted in a scarcity of the others. The jacket is formed by a hole being cut in the skin, at about the neck of the animal, through which the head of the warrior is thrust, the skin of the head of the animal hanging down over his breast, ornamented with little shells, placed over one another, like scales, and to the end of which a large mother-of-pearl shell is attached, which reaches to the middle. The broad part of the skin forms the back part of the jacket, the edges of which are bound with wide strips of red cloth. Bunches of feathers of the rhinoceros hornbill, which seems to be the war-bird of all their tribes, depend from little strings of beads, fastened to the skin, and dangle in the breeze as they move about. Strings, fixed in the inside of the skin, and long enough to tie round the body, protect the dress from being inconveniently blown about, as, were it loose, it would be. Their head-dresses in war are also peculiar to these people, and unknown to the other inhabitants of the island : they are of various descriptions, but the favourite ones are caps made in the fashion of a man's face caricatured, and those which represent the faces of animals.

The caps, which represent monstrous masks, or faces, are formed of a framework of rattan, covered with bears' skin, or the skin of some other animal. Two round pieces of bone are tied by a string, which runs through them, for eyes; and a triangular piece serves for the nose. The mouth is formed of very small cowrie shells, to resemble the teeth; and two of the large canine teeth of the panther, or bear, are fastened as tusks to its extremities. The top is surmounted with the tail feathers of the domestic cock on each side, and at the back by the barred tail-feathers of the great rhinoceros hornbill, or of the argus pheasant.

Another kind of cap is formed round, and surmounted by the head of the rhinoceros hornbill, with its great beak; the skin of the bird's neck being distended so as to form the covering of the framework of the cap. Other kinds are merely ornamented with feathers of the hornbill and argus pheasants, being all, however, covered with the skins of monkeys, or of some other animals. The caps are not generally made to fit to the head; but another framework, inside the outer and larger one, is generally adapted for that purpose.

The ornaments of the women are said to consist of brass and ivory armlets, the latter being purchased at Singapore, and brought to them by the Malays—the elephant not being found in their country, though the rhinoceros is not uncommon.

The weapons of the men are the sumpit-an or blow-pipe: this is a long tube of hard wood, through which small poisoned arrows, or darts, having on their end a

piece of pith, or some other light substance adapted to
the size of the bore of the tube, are blown with great
force and accuracy of aim. The sumpit-an has, at its
farthest end, an iron sight, by which they regulate their
aim. It is also at this end furnished with a large
double-bladed spear. Both the sight and the spear are
nicely bound on with rattans, which are woven over
them. The dart used is poisoned with the ipoh, which
is the same as the upas and chetik of Java, described
by Dr. Horsefield ; the darts, which are very thin and
about ten inches in length, are pointed with the sharp
teeth of fish, neatly bound on to them.

The case which contains the darts is supported by
the sword belt, and is made of a bamboo joint, the lid
of it being of the same material, and fitting nicely. It
contains many charms, consisting of stones, and bezoars,
which are abundant in their country, and which are said
to be taken from the heads of monkeys. The arrows
which are ready prepared for use, are kept separate
from the others, a sack of monkey's skin being carried
in the case for their points ; as by the friction on the
hard bamboo, these would be otherwise injured.

A Meri man, in my employ, was very expert with the
sumpit-an, and, at the distance of from fifteen to twenty
yards, could readily transfix a bird of the size of a
starling with one of the little darts. The whole
distance to which the arrow can be blown with any
thing like effect, is sixty yards ; and, at that distance
they would probably not pierce the skin. The sumpit-
an varies in length, being from seven to ten feet. It

is used also by the Mui people, the Benkatan, and the Tatows, and by all the tribes of the east coast. The Idaan or Meroots, are said, by Forrest, also to possess it. I have seen specimens from the river Essiquibo, in South America, where they were collected by my friend, Mr. Henchman, which precisely resembled those of the Dyaks in appearance and size, but were without the sight and the spear to the end. The darts used were also similar, but poisoned with the urali instead of the upas.

The swords of the Kyan tribes are of very peculiar construction. The iron from which they are formed is said to be the production of the country, and prepared by the natives themselves. This may be the case in some places, as it is well known that excellent ore exists in many parts of the interior. In the manufacture of their swords, the Kyans display considerably more ingenuity than the most improved of the Dyak or other wild tribes are masters of. The blades are convex on one side, and concave on the other; so that they can only be used in cutting from right to left; though in that manner they cut more deeply than a common weapon. They are generally about two feet long, and two inches and a half in breadth at the broadest part; towards the point they are all ornamented with patterns, cut right through the steel of the blade—by what process I am unable to learn. Towards the back of the weapon, and frequently down its whole length, are figures of the sun, moon, and stars, of brass, inlaid into the iron of the blade,

The handle is of buck's-horn, beautifully carved; and one which I have before me, and which was the property of a Kyan chief, presented to me by the Patingi Abdulrahman of Serekei, is so elaborately carved, as to put one in mind of the ivory of the Chinese, the work being executed so as to resemble the head and open mouth, in which are seen the teeth and tongue of some curious and monstrous animal.

The handles of all these weapons are ornamented abundantly with human hair, stained of a red colour. The sheath of the weapon above referred to, and which is represented in the plate, is the most beautiful I have seen amongst numbers of them. The iju, or horse-hair-like substance, beautifully plaited, is made to pass under the beautiful carved work on the sheath; this, from the thinness of the sheath itself, must have been a work of great nicety. The carving is executed with the greatest care, and far surpasses the most beautiful specimens of the South Seas; though it must be taken into consideration, that these people have iron to assist them, which, when the South Sea Islanders excelled in carving, they had not.

On the inside of the sheath of the ilang, is a smaller sheath for holding the knife used in cutting rattans, and in carving, &c. It is a clumsy blade, about three inches long, and fixed in a handle which is a foot in length; the sheath which contains it, is made generally of the scape which covers the inflores-cence of the betel-nut tree, previous to its bursting into flower; and to it, and not to the sheath, which is made of beautiful red or veined wood, the red and black hair is attached. The belt is made of fine rattans, prettily plaited: one end being formed into a loop, the other supports a large piece of mother-of-pearl, or some other substance, which, together with the tassels of various colours depending from it, are passed through the loop, which catching the mother-of-pearl, supports the sword on the person, and the ornamental little tassels, which are gathered into bunches, hang down before. The spears used by them in their wars, have all short and broad points. They are not thrown; those used as missiles being formed of hard wood, pointed. The dress and weapons above described, and the tattooed bodies of these people, must, with their fine persons, have a savage and imposing appearance: their long black hair flows over their back, but like the Dyaks, it is cut short in front in a straight line across the forehead to the ears.

I have already said that these people possess a high character for courage, and from all we can learn, the Dyaks of every tribe have given way before their superior prowess, and gradually retreated to the westward of the country they formerly occupied. They must be very numerous. The tribes on the Coti river, were reported to Mr. Dalton, who resided for the purposes of trade for fifteen months in the years 1825 to 1826 at the Dyak (Kyan) town of Tongarron, above the Bugis settlement of Semerindem, to be above 270,000 in number; and if we may judge from the tribes of the west, this number is not likely to be an exaggeration, but on the

contrary, as the Dyaks who pay tribute to Malays—
and these are said to do so—invariably state the number
of their people at much less than they actually are, in
order to evade the payment of the head-tax imposed
by the Malay rulers.   This number was given to Mr.
Dalton, by the chief of Tongarron, who was the most
powerful of the three who ruled, in different districts,
their many villages.   Mr. Dalton was adopted by this
chief as his brother, by means of a ceremony which has
been used by other nations, consisting of each drinking
a little of the blood of the other mixed in water; but this
is not practised amongst the Dyaks of the western coast.

Notwithstanding this comparatively large population,
Mr. Dalton informs us that head-hunting is practised to
a frightful extent, and that desolating wars are constantly carried on for the purpose of obtaining these
ghastly trophies.   In war they, as well as the Kyans
of the north, wear shields ornamented with the hair
of their foes—a piece of iron also runs along the
centre, for the greater security against the sword cuts
of their foes.   Generally, these shields are ornamented with small and regular tufts of the black hair,
without being dyed ; but I have seen one belonging to a
chief of Bintulu, which was covered with long hair
dyed of a bright red colour.   It is said in south
Borneo, that these shields, so ornamented, are only worn
by chiefs ; but, from their number in the north, I am
inclined to a different opinion, though I have seen some
on which were only the paintings peculiar to them all,
and the pattern of which, the Missionary before referred

to informed me, served amongst the tribes of the
Banjar river, to distinguish their tribes, as did that of
the tartan, the clans of the highlanders of Scotland.

Both sexes of the Kyans practise the custom of dis-
tending the lobes of the ears to an extraordinary extent.
Two Dyaks of Kenawit, or some of the tribes bordering
on, if not belonging to the Kyans, whom I saw at Egan,
had this part of that organ hanging nearly to the
shoulders; and I have been told that these were very
small indeed. No ornaments were worn in them, but
they had been distended by the use of heavy brass
rings while young. These two men were finely
tattooed in beautiful patterns; the shades of blue
colouring were so soft, as to resemble a well-executed
painting.

Notwithstanding the remarks on their moral character previously made, I must not neglect to mention
that the manners of the young females resemble those
of the Sea Dyaks ; but, that adultery after marriage is
punished by death to the man, who, under whatever
circumstances the criminal action takes place, is always
considered the guilty and responsible party concerned.
On the death of a person, it is said that a head must
be procured previous to his burial, and it appears
evident that, in south Borneo at least, but I believe
also in the north, human victims are massacred on
the death of a chief, and on other occasions. Those
slain on the death of a chief, are supposed to become his
attendants and slaves in a future state ; their bodies are,
with those of the chief, placed in ornamented houses

erected for the purpose, of carved hard wood, on posts of some height above the ground; or occasionally, as I have been informed, in hollowed trunks of trees.

Notwithstanding the barbarity they display on these occasions, and the bloody and ferocious tastes which lead to their wars, they are not, as they have been hastily stigmatised, cannibals; nor does any race, which, like the Battas of Sumatra, practise the horrid custom of feeding on the bodies of their own species, exist on the island. To turn to the brighter side of their character; they are said to be in the highest degree hospitable, and confiding in the honour of strangers who may have intercourse with them : they are like the Hill Dyaks, of the most scrupulous integrity, so that the Malayan trader never fears to leave his cargo in their hands, being sure that the full amount for which he has sold it will be forthcoming at the time stipulated.

On reaching the Kyan village from the sea, the Malay trader first makes known his arrival to the chief, who appoints him a house to reside in. During his stay he is at liberty to help himself to anything he may see which is outside the doors of the houses : such as, fowls, fruit, &c. ; but to take anything from the inside would be considered a robbery. The Kyan expects, on going to other villages, the same privileges; so that when they visit Serekei, which they never do in small numbers, but only in large fleets, attending their Rajahs, the inhabitants are glad to see them gone again, as their helping themselves is troublesome. They go to the trading-boats in the river, and take cocoa-nuts, and other things; but only such as they require for immediate use. On a recent occasion, being invited by the Patingi of Serekei to assist him, they had nearly come to blows about this custom with the traders at that time in the town, as they insisted upon being done to as they did to the Serekei traders who came to them, and they were too resolute and numerous to be refused.

The Malays trading to them, are not only allowed to help themselves to the fowls and goats which, as well as pigs, are said to be very numerous about their villages, but are plentifully cared for, during their stay, by the chief of the tribe; who, by his taking all the arrangements into his own hand, appears to monopolize the trade of his people. He is said (Rajah Nipah) to be attended with great state and ceremony, being covered with umbrellas, which are carried over him. These customs he has doubtless borrowed from the Malays, whose settlements he has frequently visited, and where he is treated with great respect.

Next in numbers to the Kyans, but of much more peaceful habits and practices, are the Orang Milanowes, who inhabit the mouth of the great Rejang river, and the small rivers to the eastward of Point Sirik. Their principal towns are Egan, on the river of that name, which is, however, but a mouth of the Rejang, being that most to the eastward; Hoya, on a small river twenty miles east of Egan; and Mocha, on another, fourteen miles east of the last-mentioned settlement.

The Milanowes have been more affected by the customs

z

of the Malays, than any of the wild tribes previously described. Nearly all of the inhabitants of the large tribe of Rejang, on that river, have adopted the dress, and many of them the religion of the Malays. Those of Palo Egan, and the other places at which they reside, and which are situated close to the sea, and are frequented by the Malays for the purposes of trade, have been similarly tainted by the practices of these people. But the tribes further inland, on these rivers, are said still to preserve their original customs, and to clothe themselves as the Dyaks do. Their mild and peaceful characters seem to approach those of the Land or Hill Dyaks, more than any of the other divisions of the inhabitants of the island ; and though they pursue, like them, the practice of keeping the heads of their enemies, from their peaceful dispositions it is rare that a new one is added to their store. At Hoya, where they enjoy a moderately good government, under the care of a Pañgeran, who is anxious to promote the welfare of his province, they have fine flourishing villages, or towns, in the interior ; but are much disturbed by the Dyaks of Kenawit, and others in the interior of their own, and the Rejang rivers, who make constant descents upon them.

In 1846, while we lay at the town of Hoya, in the steam-ship, ' Phlegethon,' a party of Milanowes, coming from their village to visit Mr. Brooke, was attacked by some of these marauders, who were fortunately worsted in the conflict ; and having two men killed, jumped overboard, and left their boat in possession of the

Milanowe victors. It is from the Milanowe settlement, particularly from Hoya and Mocha, that the greater part of the sago from the west coast of Borneo is exported, which is cultivated by the Milanowes, to the same extent that rice is amongst the other tribes. The traders of Sarawak, and of Serekei, and boats belonging to the place, carry this produce in its rough state to Singapore, where it is manufactured; and being purified by continued washings, is prepared for the European market, to which it has recently been sent, with profit to the cultivator and the manufacturer.

The " Meri" people, who live on the coast near the Bintulu and other rivers in that neighbourhood, appear very much to resemble the Milanowes, and like them, cultivate much sago, though they export, in addition, much camphor and bees'-wax to the capital of Borneo, where they are compelled to send it by the nobles, who annually send agents from among their unprincipled followers to collect the produce of these villages. By these Borneons, who have settled at Mocha in considerable numbers, the trade of that place has also been much injured; but the Pañgeran of Hoya, with Mr. Brooke's assistance, has been able to keep them away.

In personal appearance, the men of the Milanowes have much resemblance to the other races inhabiting the island, from whom they cannot, by their features, be distinguished. The women, however, enjoy the reputation of being far more beautiful than those of any of the other tribes, and slaves from this nation are sold for a

much higher price than girls from any other of the
many divisions of the inhabitants of the island.   I had
only opportunities of seeing those of the Rejang tribe
who live at Serekei, and cannot say that I observed
their great superiority. They were dressed in the manner
of Malayan females, and perhaps their long clothing
may have better concealed their personal defects : their
hair was kept in better order, and their faces were much
fairer than is general amongst the other tribes.

At Hoya, amongst the other people who came to
visit us, was an Albino, who was introduced to us as an
" Orang putih," or white man of the country: his skin
was white, but of a reddish or pink tinge, and rather
rough ; his hair was yellow and flaxen, his eyes greyish
blue.   He said that he enjoyed perfect health, though his
eyes were weak in the glare of the sun, and his sight
most vigorous and acute in the mornings and evenings.

Albino varieties of the human race are well known
to most of the tribes inhabiting the island, though I
never previously saw one. Some others of this man's
family were said to present the same remarkable
features of complexion.

The houses of the Rejang tribe of Milanowes at the
town of Serekei were built on very large posts of hard
wood, about fifteen to twenty feet from the ground.   A
village they possess, and which they frequent during the
fine monsoon or fishing season, has the posts of its
houses much higher; in other respects the houses
resemble those of the Sea Dyaks, and the villages are
built upon the same plan.   The posts are much more

numerous and the dwelling, individually, very much larger, though not divided into rooms, as are the larger houses of the Malays. They affirm that these high posts of hard wood are necessary for their protection against the Kenawit and Sarebas Dyaks, by whom they have been repeatedly attacked, and who recently burnt and destroyed the settlement of these people, on the Palo mouth of the Rejang river, situated a little to the eastward of Tangong Jereji, its most western mouth. The method of attack pursued by the Dyaks on this occasion, who were very numerous, was, with their large shields placed over their backs, to work steadily at the posts of the houses, notwithstanding the spears, boiling water, stones, &c., which were showered down upon them by the besieged. Two or three being employed at each post with their hatchets, the houses soon fell, and the Rejangs were murdered, or carried into captivity by the Dyaks: their houses were plundered and burnt.

The few who escaped came to Mr. Brooke for his assistance, which, as far as it was possible, was given to them, and a letter was despatched to the Patingi Abdulrahman, in whose territory the Kenawit Dyaks live, but over whom he is supposed to have but very little power, representing their conduct to him, and requesting him at his own peril, to use his best endeavours for the suppression of their piratical habits, though it is probable that the attack was made at the suggestion of this chief himself, who wished the Rejangs to leave their settlement at Palo, to swell the numbers of the inhabitants of Serekei, the town at which he resides, and where, as has been previously stated, the remainder of this tribe of Milanowes has its houses.

The Rejangs are very expert in catching fish, and their large establishment for this purpose at the mouth of their river exports large quantities, in a dried state, along the coast and to the interior of the island, to which their fine stream gives them easy access. All the tribes are said to practice slavery, but the other vices of the Malays are rare among them. Each person contents himself with one wife, and polygamy and concubinage are unknown among them. They appear to be amongst the most simple and easily governed of all the inhabitants of the island ; and if good government be secured to them, their industry will develop the resources of the country they inhabit, with but trifling assistance from without. The new settlement at Labuh-an will confer a great boon upon their towns by regulating the amount of taxation to be paid to the Borneo government, and preventing repetition of the extortions of which they have been too frequently the subjects.

The Kadyans are the native inhabitants of that part of the island in the immediate neighbourhood of Bruni, the capital. Many of their tribes are converted to the Mahometan religion ; and they have, for the most part, adopted the customs of the Malays. Like the other tribes, they preserve the skulls of their enemies, but the practice is now much disused, having given way to the Malayan influence. They are a quiet agricultural people, much oppressed : they are compelled to cultivate pepper, and search for bees'-wax and camphor for the Rajahs of Borneo, amongst whom their tribes are divided. The Idaan, or Meroots—as they are more properly called—inhabit the more hilly districts towards the north, in the vicinity of the great mountain, Kina Balou. They resemble the Kadyans, and some of their tribes, who being nearer to the capital, are, more than others, under the influence of its nobles, are, like them, compelled to plant pepper, and collect the other produce of the country for their masters. These people appear anxious for an intercourse with Europeans, and during our temporary occupation of the islands Balambangan and Labuh-an, eighty years ago, they came in numbers, in their little boats, bringing with them for sale, hogs, fruit, and other productions of their country. They are said to resemble the Kyans in the sacrifice of human victims on particular occasions.

Scanty as is our knowledge of the tribes above enumerated, the inhabitants of the east coast are still less known to us. They are said to be Dyaks, i. e. Kyans of a ferocious description. The Orang Tedong which inhabit the interior of some of the large rivers opposite the Soolu Archipelago, go to sea in fleets regularly, as do the Dyaks of Sarebas and Sakarran, but their cruises are not confined within such narrow limits as those of these people. Their boats frequent the islands of the Phillippine group, and are said occasionally to cruise as far down the western coast as the island of Labuh-an. They are settled on the Koran and other rivers, in towns, mixed with the inhabitants of the Soolu Solands, and many of these places being fortified as regular piratical establishments, fleets are annually equipped at them for the purposes of this illegal practice. The whole of the east coast, as far south as Coti, is divided amongst these people, all of whom are, more or less, under the influence of the Soolu Rajahs, though many of their chiefs arrogate to themselves the title of Sultan. They are said to treat their prisoners with much cruelty, and head-hunting is carried on amongst them to the same extent as amongst the worst of the Dyak and Kyan tribes. Their boats appear to be built on the principle of those of Sakarran and Sarebas, being easily taken to pieces and put together again as occasion may require.

The Badjus, or as they are commonly called, Sea-Gipsies, are found in considerable numbers in the sea which lies between the east coast of Borneo, and the west coast of Celebes. These curious people are said to have come originally from Johore, in the Malayan penin-sula, the inhabitants of which they much resemble in features and habits. Many of them are settled in per-manent villages on the east coast of the island, but the greater number live in their boats, which are from five ₒo ten tons' burden; during the whole year, and shift their position with the changing monsoon, so as always to keep on the lee side of the island, and, consequently, in fine weather. They all profess the Mahometan religion, and differ but little, except in their maritime habits, from the Malays, though they are said to adhere less strictly to the tenets of Islamism : the men are employed in fishing for the trepang, or sea-slug, (a dirty looking animal, which forms one of the many strange articles of luxury of the Chinese nation,) and for tortoiseshell, and the other productions of these seas. Unless they are wronged by the Malays, they also do a little, in a quiet way, in piracy, but are never reported to follow it as a profession, and as it is practised by the Soolus and others, with whom they come in contact.

During our stay at Balambangan, these people were found of great service in supplying the settlement with provisions, which they purchased from the Meroots of Borneo, and from the Tedong, Koran, and other people of the eastern coast, in exchange for a kind of bitter salt, which they manufacture from the ashes of sea-weed, nipah leaves, and other vegetables found in salt marshes. Such of them as reside in permanent habitations, have fowls about their houses, and, in all respects, resemble the other Mahometans. Their villages are built on posts, and always over the water, and close to the sea, or the mouths of large rivers, in which the eastern part of the island abounds. They are expert divers, and would be useful in this manner, if European capitalists should think proper to fish the rich banks of the pearl and mother-of-pearl oysters in Malludu Bay, and amongst the islands of the Soolu Archipelago, which, from having been so long neglected, would doubtless, be found immensely productive.

Many of the Badjus, are situated in the seas of Celebes, about the Dutch settlements, and are found very useful in carrying despatches, &c. ; they are mostly employed by Chinese merchants to fish for them, and, it is said that these cunning traders invariably contrive to keep these poor people in debt, so as to secure their continued services, and that so scrupulously honest are they, that though nothing could detain them, they are never known to leave a place to evade their creditors.

We have now mentioned the greater part of the inhabitants of the large, rich, and beautiful island of Borneo; but, from our little communication with it, this is all that can at present be done. The Kyans, those numerous and interesting people, have never yet been visited by Europeans; and though the Malay Chief of Serekei will throw every obstacle in their way, in the ascent of the Rejang river to the country of Rajah Nipah, before described, it will not be long after the new settlement shall be formed, before this powerful tribe is in communication with it; Rajah Nipah having frequently intimated his wish to visit Sarawak, or that Mr. Brooke should send some one to visit him. This information has been frequently communicated to us by natives of Serekei, who are constantly in the habit of trading with the Kyans, and who further informed us—what we very well knew—that the Patingi Abdulrahman in every way discouraged such intentions on the part of the Kyan chieftain.

Other openings for British enterprise, and which are free from Malayan influence, exist in the facilities of communication presented with the Kyan countries by the rivers Bintulu and Barram, which have hitherto been unvisited by Europeans, excepting at their mouths, and then only on one occasion. We shall not long— provided the settlement of Labuh-an flourish—remain in our present ignorance regarding this and the other inhabitants of the western and eastern coast. At present, even the outline of the latter is incorrectly laid down, and the mouths of its numerous and very large rivers are not inserted on our charts. The Government have recently done much towards our better geographical acquaintance with the island, and the yet unpublished surveys of its coasts by Sir Edward Belcher, and the continuation of them by the talented and industrious officer who has succeeded him as the surveying officer of the station (Lieut. D. Gordon, H.M. surveying ship ' Royalist,') will not suffer the coasts of the island much longer to remain the disgrace to our admiralty charts, which they have hitherto been.

Of all nations, the Dutch have, perhaps, with the exception of the English East India Company, acquired the best information regarding their colonies ; and their many expeditions into the interior of Borneo, up the Pontianak, the Banjar, and the Coti rivers, must have put them in possession of facts relative to the interior of the island, which it will be years before our own Government can obtain. The museums of Holland team with collections of all kinds from their possessions in the east ; but hitherto that Government has guarded with jealous care all the information, on whatever subject, which its servants and scientific expeditions

have collected.   But now a more liberal spirit seems to
have actuated it, and the magnificent national work on
the colonies of Netherlands India, will be such as, when
completed, no other nation can boast.   At the present
time there are two expeditions in Borneo ; one on the
west, the other, consisting of three scientific gentlemen,
on the southern parts of the island ; and the examination
and survey of the fine River Banjar Massing, must be
now nearly completed, as I judge, from the time they
have been engaged in it

Notwithstanding the exertions of the Government of
Holland, a fine field yet invites the attention of that
of Britain, and the lovers of science will be glad to
hear that the fine mountains, valleys, plains and lakes,
which render the north of Borneo, the most majestically
beautiful of any part of the island, have had appointed
for their investigation, Dr. Joseph Hooker, who has
already so distinguished himself by his researches
during the Antarctic Expedition, the account of which
has been published under the patronage of the Admiralty.   This selection of our Government is peculiarly
happy, as, in addition to the great acquirements of
Dr. Hooker in Botany, he possesses a skill in the
investigation of minerals, zoology, and other depart-
ments of science, which are rarely combined in one
individual.

The lofty mountains, hitherto untrodden by the foot
of civilized man, will doubtless be found as rich, or
more rich if possible, in minerals, than the lower
portion of the island ; and it is well known that the

rich botanical productions of the country, are comparatively unknown; so that on the arrival of Dr. Hooker, which it is to be regretted, will be deferred for two years, we may look for many mineral and vegetable products, hitherto strangers to the commerce of the island.

The absence of Dr. Hooker from the scene of his future labours, during the two years he is to spend in India, may have this advantage, that on his arrival, he may find the coast in a more settled state, and be able to travel with greater facility; but during that period, if it should be found difficult to travel on the main-land, which I do not anticipate, Labuh-an itself would, though small, present him with an ample and interesting field for mineral and botanical research.

CHAPTER XI.

THE Malayan, or Malayan and Dyak town of Serekei, having been frequently mentioned in the preceding pages, a short narrative of a visit to it, extracted from my journal, may be interesting to the reader.

The expedition left Sarawak on Wednesday the 6th of April, 1845, its object being to carry a letter to the Patingi of Serekei from Mr. Brooke, the late Mr. Williamson, then interpreter to the Rajah of Sarawak, being the Ambassador, assisted by the Dattu Bandar, and a man of high rank and ability, Serieb Hussein. Mr. Williamson, the Dattu, and myself were in the "Buaya" (Alligator) war-boat of seventy feet in length, and carrying a six pound brass gun and two swivels, with a complement of fifty men: the Tuanku, (his highness), Serieb Hussein, was in a smaller boat, also carrying a gun.

Having left the town at 2 P.M., we lay during the night off the fishing village at the Moratabas entrance

of the river. Got under weigh at noon on the 17th, and towards evening entered a small creek, where were the houses of a few fishermen :—this creek is situated to the eastward about twenty miles from Sarawak River. Here we remained for the night : early on the morning of Friday, the 18th, we again started, and having a fine breeze passed the mouths of the Sadong, Batang Lupar, and Sarebas Rivers, with several other smaller ones. Early in the afternoon, we entered the mouth of the Kalekka River, which is about sixty miles from the Sarawak; at 4 P.M. we anchored abreast of the house of the Tuan Mulana, an old Arab hypocrite, who, by fawning and flattery, has obtained this appointment from the Rajah Muda Hassim. The village, which is small, containing perhaps about six hundred people, principally slaves and followers of Mulana, is built like Borneo, on posts, upon a mud bank in the river. There are said to be other larger villages of Malays, under a Dattu Laxsamana, a little distance up the river : both the priest, and the Laxsamana are tributary to, and under the orders of the Patingi of Serekei.

The whole coast, as far as we could see inland, after having passed the Batang Lupar River was flat, low, and covered with jungle to the edge of the sea, where the waters have formed a sandy beach. The beautiful Arroore tree (*Casuarina littorea*) is always found growing in rows just above high-water mark, but where mud forms the boundaries of the waters, the mangrove is the first vegetation, and is immediately succeeded by the ordinary trees of the jungle. The country between the Sarawak river, and the Batang Lupar, including the Samarhand, Sadong and Lingah territories, appeared to be beautifully studded with mountains, not disposed in ranges, but, for the most part, solitary. The Gunong Penerissen, inland of the Sarawak river, and on the borders of the Sangon country, appeared to be the highest. (It has been since ascertained, by barometrical observation, to be about 4,700 feet in height).

Soon after we had anchored, we waited upon the old chief, Mulana, (which is not his name, but an Arabic word signifying teacher), in a tumble-down kind of audience hall. He was delighted to see Williamson, whom he had previously known at Sarawak, and the apartment was crowded with the inhabitants of the place. Several verses from the Koran, in large Arabic characters, were displayed on its decaying sides, under one of which the chief was seated, and white mats were spread for Williamson and myself, with our Tuanku by my friend's side: our Dattu sat with the other men of consideration a little lower down, but on the right-hand side of the priest.

When we were seated, tea and cigars were handed to us, the former in small china cups, without sugar or milk. The latter are made of Borneo tobacco, which is very pleasant, neatly rolled up in the young straw-coloured leaves of the Nipah palm, and bound with crimson silk. They are about nine inches long, and contain much tobacco. Williamson and the Mulana had a long conversation respecting the political relations between Kalekka and Bruni, which I but imperfectly understood.

After having remained about two hours, we took our departure, the old gentleman himself accompanying us to the ladder of his landing-place, which was intended as a mark of his most distinguished consideration. On descending to our boat, the ebbing tide having left the mud quite dry, our senses were saluted with the disagreeable stench which is prevalent also in Borneo; and which one would think must certainly render the place unhealthy; but such is not the case, the people here and in Borneo enjoying as perfect health as those of any other towns in the island. One thing which has astonished me, in all the Malay towns I have visited, is the larger number of children seen about them in proportion to the number of houses; this I find is easily accounted for, by the custom of two or three families living in the same habitation.

In the evening we were waited on by Pañgeran Alla-ed-din and Nakodah Serudin, the former nicknamed Paddy Graham, for what reason I cannot tell, and the latter Bull-dog, from his short figure, large head, and ferocious character. The Pañgeran has been sent, or professes to have been sent, by the Rajah Muda Hassim to collect revenue. The latter left Sarawak six months ago, with a large boat loaded with the property of the Rajah Mudah, which he left behind him, when conveyed by Sir E. Belcher to

Borneo. They are equally bad characters, and are here terrifying the people of the place, and extorting goods from the Dyaks of the interior.

The instructions of Mr. Williamson are to impress upon the native chiefs the necessity of resisting such demands, as the Rajah and Sultan have agreed to substitute a fixed revenue, instead of the exactions of such people as these, who, collecting property in the name of their masters, keep by far the greater share of it for themselves. The contents of Mr. Brooke's letter to the Patingi having been made known to the Mulana, he has sent a message to Mr. Williamson, to beg him to read a copy of it to these two men, in the presence of the people of Kalekka, to-morrow.

April 19*th.*—In the morning, we again visited Mulana, having previously sent on shore to inform him that we were coming, according to his request of last night. As this was expected to be an important meeting, our young Dattu took more than ordinary pains in dressing himself. His jacket was of blue cloth of very fine texture, and plentifully but neatly embroidered with gold; his seluars were of crimson silk with gold-thread worked into it in very pretty patterns. His sarong or waist-cloth, was of the finest make of Sarawak, and his Kris, which was stuck into its folds, was beautifully ornamented with gold. The dustar or head-dress, was a dark silk handherchief, with a broad edge of gold lace, and folded with great taste. He looks remarkably well in this finery, being of a pleasing countenance, and elegant and slender figure. He is the son of the old chief, the Patingi Ali, whose heroic courage is narrated in the Narrative of the Expedition of the Dido.

Pañgeran Alla-ed-din and the Nakodah had been summoned to hear a copy of the letter read, but on our arrival, the former only had come, so the proceedings went on without the other, his partner in mischief having been previously warned to convey the substance of it to him. All present—and the hall and verandahs were crowded—seemed very much pleased with it, and on its being finished, a murmur of approbation ran through the crowd. That which most delighted them, was the promise of assistance from the Rajah of Sarawak, in resisting the illegal demands of such men as those then in the town, whose people were at that moment acting in opposition to the request it contained.

Pañgeran Alla-ed-din had sent a tertawak (a musical instrument resembling a gong), two or three days before our arrival up the country to the Dyaks, for which he demanded forty dollars in money, well knowing that there was not a tenth of that amount amongst all their tribes. The real value of the tertawak was about ten dollars. On being informed by the Dyaks that they had no money, he said, that in that case he would take Padi, to the amount of one hundred dollars, in exchange, and ordered them to pay it immediately : of this we had been told by all the residents at Kalekka. Williamson accused the Pañgeran of this before the assembled people, and though the fact was so notorious, he instantly, and in a loud voice, denied it ; and challenged any one present to say to his face that he had done so.

None of the number present had courage to accuse him, so that Williamson could do nothing but warn him to leave the place as soon as possible, and return to Borneo; but this he will probably not be in a hurry to do.   Thus are these people terrified at the name and rank of Pañgeran, and dare not resist his demands, more particularly as he is backed this time by his own desperate crew, and that of Nakodah Scrudin, who has many of the Rajah's guns, and much of his ammunition on board, which he would not scruple to use, as he has formerly often done, against any one who may offend him, and whom he thinks himself sufficiently powerful to attack.

After Williamson had finished his business, I took my gun, and with a small boat, and accompanied by the Bandar, went up the river to see the country, though the natives tried to persuade me that I should very likely meet with some of the Sarebas Dyaks, with whom we were then on bad terms.   We went about six miles, five of which were through a salt marsh, apparently of immense extent, and covered with the Nipah palm, which here grows most luxuriantly. Inland, the ground was slightly undulating, and covered with fine jungle, in which the nearest springs of water to the town are to be found, so that the inhabitants have to fetch all their fresh water from a distance of five or six miles.   We passed several salt-making establishments on the banks amongst the

Nipahs, from the ashes of the leaves of which it is made.
It is much used by the Milanowes and Dyaks, but is
very bitter and of an unpleasant flavour, and very dirty
appearance.

On my arrival at the boat in the evening, I found
that Williamson had received a dinner from Mulana.
It consisted principally of rice cakes, and sweetmeats
of rice flour, and curries in small dishes. Spoons
which were also sent, were made of the young leaves
of the useful Nipah, which being folded into the proper
form, were secured in it by small pegs. In the evening,
many people visited Williamson, and some sent
presents. Mulana sent fowls and ducks with a fine
sarong—for the manufacture of which this place is
celebrated—for each of us. Pañgeran Alla-ed-din had
the impudence to send a similar cloth in the evening for
Williamson's acceptance.

April 20*th*.—Weighed anchor at three A.M., under a
salute of—I cannot tell how many—guns from the
impertinent Pañgeran and Nakodah, who were, doubtless, glad to get rid of us with the expense only of a
little powder which did not belong to them. During
the morning we coasted along to the eastward with a fine
breeze, until we opened the mouth of the western
branch of the great Rejang river. There are four
or five other larger mouths to the eastward, but none
of them so deep as this. Egan is the furthest to the
east, but is very shoaly, not having more than nine feet
on the bar at low water. The natives assured us that,
in the channel, the branch we had entered was six

fathoms in the shallowest part. On doubling the point Tanjong Lallang, we had a fear of the large fishing establishment of the Rejangs, a tribe of the Milanowe race, who have houses at which they reside during the bad monsoon at the town of Serekei. On each of the houses, or rather ranges of houses, was displayed a white flag, in token either of fear or welcome, probably the latter, as they had, doubtlessly, heard of our arrival at Kalekka, which is distant about sixteen miles from Tanjong Lallang. We passed the village and sailed about twenty miles up the river with a strong flood-tide. The banks are well wooded, the trees, as in all the other rivers, overhanging the water. Here the wind failing, the ebb tide forced us to anchor at half past six P.M. We were informed that about ten miles further up the stream, is the mouth of the small river Serekei, on which the town we intend to visit is situated.

April 21st.—Having weighed early with the morning flood, we paddled up the river, the banks of which were here a little cultivated by scattered farms, until we reached the mouth of the Serekei. The town is about five miles from its junction with the great Rejang, which itself, about six miles further up, joins the still greater Palo branch of this mighty river: the banks of the Serekei are all clear of wood, having been recently cultivated as Padi fields. We anchored at seven A.M. about half a mile below the town, and sent to inform the Patingi Abdulrahman of our arrival. He immediately sent back some of his principal men to beg us to wait for a little while, that Mr. Brooke's ambassador and letter might be properly conducted into the town. About two hours afterwards, while we, having dressed, were waiting for our breakfast, a fleet of large boats with drums (*i. e.* tomtoms), and trumpets (*i. e.* gongs), were seen coming towards the place where we lay. We supposed from the number of boats that the Dattu himself was coming, and in a few minutes ascertained that such was the case. He was in a covered boat, pulled by about twenty men, and followed by twenty other boats, some larger than that he occupied, all of which, when he came alongside of us, drew up in a line on the right-hand side of the river.

The chief inquired of us whether we were ready to enter the town, and begged us to excuse him from coming out of his boat to ours, as he had a disease in the bone of one of his legs which prevented his using it. His house, he said, had been burnt down some time since, and he had since constantly resided in this boat. As soon as we signified to the chief that we were ready to proceed up to the town, a signal was made from his boat to those on shore, on which they immediately took a hawser from each of our two boats, and towed us slowly through the town until we came opposite the Balei or Town-Hall. The town was everywhere decorated with flags of all shapes and colours; the music of the noisy gongs and tomtoms was also in high requisition, and brass guns were fired on all sides of us: during our triumphal entry nothing they could devise was neglected to give us a high idea of the estimation in which they held the honour of this first European visit from any of the Rajah of Sarawak's people. All the houses on the river side were crowded with women and children in all the gaudiness which pink and yellow dresses could display.

The Balei is situated on the right bank of the river, in nearly the centre of the town, on a small hill which is covered with fruit trees : this, with the exception of a similar one on the same side of the river, and near to the former, and on which the Dattu is now building a large and fine house, is the only rising ground within sight of the town, the remainder being flat, and occasionally inundated at spring tides. After having been some time at our anchorage, a deputation of people appointed by the Patingi came to inform us, that if convenient to Williamson, everything was now prepared for the reception of the letter; the epistle was accordingly placed on a brass waiter with a foot to it, between two cloths richly ornamented with gold embroidery, one of the persons appointed to conduct it then placed the waiter on his head, and carrying it in this manner, was followed by Williamson and myself, and by the Dattu Bandar, the Tuanku, and the people of the Dattu Patingi, and many others, to the number of three or four hundred, to the Town Hall, a distance of fifty yards, where it was to be received. The path leading to this building was decorated on each side with flags, and the moment the letter was landed, it was saluted by many guns, which seemed to me to be in dangerous proximity to us, as they not unfrequently

burst; but this time the important epistle was landed
without accident.   The bearer of the letter and its attendants soon reached the room, and the letter-carrier
seated himself, or rather knelt before a chair at the
farther end of the chamber, which was covered with
beautiful Sirhassen mats : similar ones were placed on
the right of the chair for our use, the adopted son of
the Patingi sitting with us.

We had been all thus placed about ten minutes, and
I was anxiously watching the hangings of the room,
expecting the chief immediately to make his appearance, when I heard his nephew and adopted son,
a fine-looking youth, dressed in silks and gold, ask
Williamson if the letter might now be opened.   On his
giving assent, the person who had charge of it, on his
knees, and with his head bent on the ground, placed
the salver containing it upon the chair, with many
tokens of respect, intended, I suppose, both for the
letter and the representative of the Patingi, which the
chair undoubtedly was.   Another person then shuffled
to the chair on his hands and knees, and took the letter
which was finally opened and read to an admiring
audience ; but few remarks were made upon it, as
though it had been read to the representative of the
Patingi, the chief himself had not heard its contents.

The chair, which had been so conspicuous through
these proceedings, was neither a new chair, nor a good
chair, but a very old and very bad one.   It was so
small, that it could not have contained the portly person
of the chief, though it was thought sufficiently large for

his dignity. It was made of common wood, and was very dirty, and I should have remained a stranger to the mystery of its appearance, had not a gust of wind through the crevices of the room raised one of the white and beautiful mats which covered its unsightliness. The footstool was a common deal box, as old as the chair, and like it covered with mats. The hangings of the room were crimson and white cloth. After Mr. Williamson had made some remarks to the assembled people on Mr. Brooke's intention in sending this " friendly epistle," we adjourned, by especial desire, to the boat in which the Patingi lived; which, after some trouble, on account of the difficulty of walking on the sticks which had to serve for paths through the mud, we reached.

I had fallen from one of the sticks—doubtless much to the amusement of the people, who, however, like all Malays, were much too well bred to express it visibly— into a puddle of dirty water which had reached to my knees, so that, having been dressed entirely in white, I presented myself to the chief in mottled attire. The Dattu received us very kindly; he had been anxiously waiting for our visit; and, having read the letter, told us how much he was delighted with Mr. Brooke for having sent it, more especially that he had caused Mr. Williamson to be the bearer of it, of whom, as Mr. Brooke's secretary, he had often heard from his people, by whom he was much liked. The chief is a stout man of about fifty years of age, with dark complexion and an intelligent expression of countenance; but his appearance is spoiled by his having no teeth, and by his being in the constant habit of preparing and chewing sirih-leaves and betel-nut. He has two or three long, ugly hairs growing from his neck, much below his face, which he appears to cultivate with great care. His conversation with Williamson was respecting his wish to govern the country of Serekei as Mr. Brooke did that of Sarawak.

He frequently expressed his anxiety to attempt a reformation, but said that many things at present interfered to prevent him, particularly the unsettled state of the countries bordering on his province, and the fear in which he and his people lived of the Dyaks of Sarebas; by whom, he told us, small parties were constantly cut off, both in this and his other river of Kalekka. The Dyaks are said to lie concealed in their boats in the vegetation of the banks of the rivers, until the unsuspecting Malayan boat passes their hiding-place, when they rush out, and without any parley, take the heads from their victims, which they carry up the country in triumph.

This conversation lasted during two hours, at the expiration of which time we rose to return. By some mistake the Dattu fancied I was intending to leave the boat without shaking hands with him, on which he seized me by the left, and having hauled me towards him, heartily shook my right hand. In this ceremony he was imitated by all those whose consideration entitled them to a seat in the boat. In the cabin kind of place in which the Dattu sat, was behind him a curtain drawn across: during our audience I had frequently seen large black eyes peeping from behind it, which belonged to some fair faces—I suppose those of his adopted daughters.

In the evening I got a small boat to take me to see the remainder of the town. The right-hand bank of the river contains the Malayan Kampongs; the left those of the Rejang Milanowes and the Scboo Dyaks. The houses on the left-hand side are built on posts of very hard wood, about sixteen or twenty feet from the ground. They are constructed on the principle of the Sea Dyak houses, that is to say, each row is an assemblage of domiciles, all of which open into a large common verandah, where the women were about their ordinary employments. The women here make baskets, called " umpuk," of a square form very neatly; the rattans they use are all coloured, and these are worked into very beautiful patterns.

I accidentally stopped at the house of the head man of the tribe : he was a fine-looking man, named " Galong," and when he saw me land, descended to assist me up to his aërial mansion. It was a very large house inside, and instead of the notched pole generally used by the Dyaks for steps, it had a broad and good ladder to ascend by. These houses were much better built than any Dyak habitations I have hitherto seen, and few Malay houses are so strongly put together. Galong told me that they were obliged to build their houses thus high, to prevent the Dyaks of Sarebas thrusting spears through the open flooring at night, and thus killing the people while they sleep. The women and men I saw were all dressed like the

Malays, and the chief informed me that he himself and a great many of his tribe, had embraced the Mahometan faith; but that the Milanowes, in general, held much the same notions of religion as the Dyaks.

Lower down the river are the houses of the Siboo Dyaks; they are not so large or well built as those of the Rejangs I had just left. These people still retain their Dyak dresses and customs, and many of them had stars tattooed on their persons. This, and the peculiar Parang called the Parang ilang, shows that they have been infected, in some measure, by the customs of the Kyans, whose country is in the interior of the Rejang river.

The ilang is remarkable for its convex and concave blades, (described in the preceding chapter.) The Dyaks rarely laid aside their swords and spears, even in their boats: this would seem to argue a state of insecurity incompatible with the size of the place; unless, notwithstanding the friendship they profess for us, they are in reality jealous of, and afraid of our intentions.

On the right hand of the river, are the houses of the Malays—miserable residences, built on Nibong posts, and of Atap or Nipah leaves. They appear, however, to contain very many inhabitants, and are placed thickly together along the bank on each side of the hills; on which stand the Balei, and the large new house which the chief is building. I should suppose the whole population of the place to be between four and five thousand. Though the houses are poor in appearance, a great trade is carried on by their proprietors, who must, consequently, be as rich as the generality of their class; but, perhaps, they fear to attract the avarice of the Patingi, who, as far as his power extends, would probably treat them as their Rajahs did those of Sarawak; but being himself one of the people, the same reverence is not paid to his title as to that of the noble of high descent, and, consequently, he cannot be so despotic.

We saw a great number of large prows hauled up on the beach, most of which were repairing and getting ready for sea; this being the beginning of the south-west or fine monsoon. They export rice in very large quantities; also sago, fine cloths, bees'-wax, &c. They import iron, coarse china ware, Turkey red cloths, &c. Gold is found in the country, but not worked to any extent.

In the evening, many people came off to our boats; some to see if they could do a little trade with our people, who trade wherever they go, and others to see Williamson, and talk politics and business. Many of them wished him to let them accompany us to Sarawak; but, as they cannot do this without the permission of the Patingi, and he is naturally averse to it, Mr. Williamson gives them no encouragement. At present, the numbers of persons who flock to Sarawak is perfectly astonishing—whole tribes of Dyaks, and villages of Malays. At this time, a Dyak tribe, belonging to the Sambas territory, are anxious to come in, and sent, some short time since, their chief men to beg Mr. Brooke to allot them a territory, and take them under his protection.

April 22nd.—At 10 A.M. we went to the Patingi. During this visit, the conversation was turned by the chief, on European nations, their customs and manufactures. The only two people he had ever heard of, were the English and Dutch; and he asked us many questions relating to each. He fancied that Holland was a much greater and more powerful nation than Britain; he inquired more particularly about our steam-ships, of which he had been told by his people who had seen them. It was difficult to make him understand how they could be made to go along by smoke, for he knew no word for steam; so that Williamson translated it, "Asup ayer panas," the smoke of hot water. He was filled with amazement, when told that we considered it a trifle to go ten miles an hour in a steam-ship, and that the distance between Borneo and Sarawak could be travelled, in our own country, in thirteen or fourteen hours by land. His most anxious inquiries were reserved for our cloth manufactories; and he wanted to know how we could possibly make so much cloth of different kinds, when it took his women so long to make him a sarong. We explained this and other things to him as well as we could; but his inquiries seemed as if they would never end; so great was his anxiety for knowledge of this description. He wanted to know about our wars, our armies, and our navies, and wished us to tell him the cost of a large ship of war, which—when we had given some large amount, at a venture—he said, all his country, if it were sold, would not produce. We had been with him two hours, answering such questions, when Williamson rose to go; but the old gentleman pressed us to stay. Williamson, however, said he would call again, and so we departed.

Williamson is anxious to be home; as, in Mr. Brooke's absence from Sarawak (at Singapore) he is very much wanted. I was very much pleased with this man's intelligence and anxiety for information; and think that if Mr. Brooke and he can once thoroughly understand each, the character of the other, that the present good understanding existing between them will be strengthened. On account of his leg, he cannot bear the motion of his boat at sea, or he says that he would go to Sarawak. At present, Mr. Brooke has too much to do to think of coming here.

The Patingi has no legitimate children to succeed him: those of his relatives who are with him, are either too little liked, or not possessed of sufficient energy or talent to acquire the necessary authority to become the chief of this trading community. Should his life terminate before a successor springs up amongst his nephews and adopted children, this settlement will, probably, be split by factions, and, in a great measure, broken up. If such be the case, many of the families will immediately emigrate to Sarawak, where the government is more liberal and secure.

At six P.M. we went to take leave of the Patingi, and to thank him for some fowls and goats he had sent us as presents ; dropped down with the ebb tide, and about midnight came to anchor in the Rejang, having met the flood.

April 23rd.—In the morning, with the ebb tide, we reached the Rejang fishing village, at the mouth of the river. The houses are built on the trunks of trees, from thirty to forty feet high. They were filled with inhabitants, all of whom were occupied in catching and preparing fish, great quantities of which, in a dried and salted state, are exported to the towns along the coast, and to the inhabitants of the interior. They are much molested by the Dyaks of Sarebas and Sakarran, who, during the fine season, are constantly cruising about their fishing grounds. Shrimps form an important branch of this trade; they are dried in the sun, and esteemed a delicacy : along the coast, they make excellent curries in this state.

The women of these people, who are said to be the most beautiful of the natives of Borneo, are fairer and with more decided features than any others I have seen. On the whole, neither Williamson nor myself deemed the reputation they have obtained unmerited.

These people were very much astonished at my double-barrelled gun : at first, they did not understand how the two reports were produced in immediate succession, but their astonishment was extreme, when they saw two swallows drop, which were flying over their houses. They

B B

had never seen shot before, and had no idea that birds could be killed on the wing. After having staid ashore about two hours, we returned on board, and were detained another hour in taking in dried fish, which the inhabitants brought off in abundance as presents to Williamson, who gave it to our natives who were pulling the boat. This gentleman's knowledge of their language, and kindness of disposition, have gained him a name amongst these, and many other tribes which he has never seen, that will ensure him everywhere a kind reception, whenever, in the course of his duty, he may have to visit them. At last we got under weigh, but soon brought up again in sight of thei houses on the sandy beach, at the right-hand point of the mouth of the river, as the natives could not be induced to go to sea till they had another tide. We humoured them, and I went on shore with my gun, accompanied by the Tuanku, who is an excellent shot, and very fond of sporting, particularly deer shooting. There were large flocks of sand-pipers, curlew, and plovers, on the beach, amongst which we made sad havoc—as we wished to bag enough to feast all the men, many of whom followed us for the purpose of cutting the throats of the birds, without having done which, they, being Mahometans, cannot eat them. At each double discharge, we generally knocked over two dozen birds of all descriptions. During the night, we made a fresh start, but were soon aground, as our people did not know, or pretended not to know, the channel—they said there

was too much sea outside, and that we must put into
a little inlet to the westward of Tangong Lallang, which
we accordingly did, much against our will.

April 24*th*.—Morning cloudy and threatening, but as
we had been brought here against our will, so we determined to get out of it at all risks, though the Malays
protested that we should be swamped in going over the
bar, on which the sea broke heavily. We, however,
pushed safely through it, though not without considerable difficulty, and having shipped a good deal of
water, to the injury of our stock of rice: the smaller
boat would not attempt to face the surf, and found a
passage where the water was less boisterous, close in
shore. By the favour of a fine breeze, we reached the
Batang Lupar river the same night, and anchored in
the first reach, which is about ten miles long, at á
distance of five miles from its mouth.

April 25*th*.—The morning flood took us up to
Lingah, situated five or six miles up a branch of the
Batang Lupar, which flows from the westward. I
went with Williamson to the court-house, a ruinous
building, and the whole of the small Malayan village
seemed equally miserable. It is situated at the foot of
a table-topped mountain, the sides of which are covered
with fruit-trees, the property of the Balow Dyaks, who
call their village, which is close to that of the Malays,
Banting. This tribe belong to the sea division, and
has always maintained an equal contest with the tribes
of Sakarran and Sarebas. The Indra Lelah, Lelah
Wangsa, and Lelah Palawan, are the Malayan chiefs;

but I fear the settlement does not flourish under their management. The whole of this country is under the immediate influence of the Governor of Sarawak. The exports are birds'-nests, wax, scented oil (Miniak Katiow), and large quantities of rice.

Williamson having delivered the message with which he was charged, we left with the ebb, and anchored at a creek on the left bank of the Batang Lupar for the night. Here one of our men, who had been ill all the voyage, died: we tore off part of one of our sails, and having wrapped him in it, made all haste for Sarawak, where we arrived at six o'clock on the following day, just in time for dinner, which we were glad to eat again in a civilized manner, our food having been, during the greatest part of our voyage, boiled rice and curried fish or fowls.

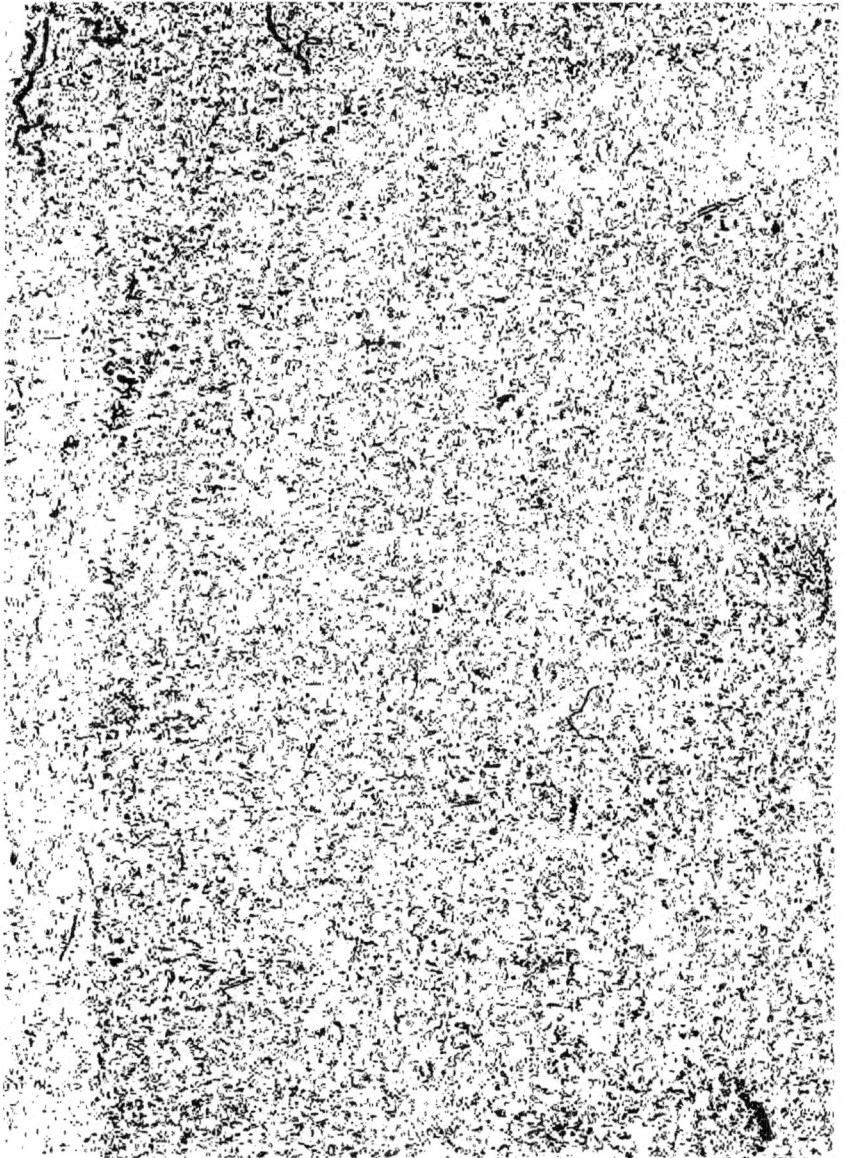

Falls at Ginjang Santubong. Sarawak

CHAPTER XII.

Extract from Journal, containing description of the cave Lubong Angin, or the Wind-hole, and of a visit to the country of the Gumbang Dyaks.

Nov. 21st. 1845—Left Sarawak with the flood-tide, in my fast boat, which is a canoe, thirty-six feet in length, and with five feet beam, to visit the cave of Lubong Angin, of which I have heard strange stories. It is situated on the western branch of the river, about forty-five to fifty miles above the Malayan town. Europeans have not, hitherto, been so far up the river. In the evening, arrived at Seniawan, the Chinese village, situated at the foot of Mount Serambo, but did not land. Dined and slept in the boat, being much troubled with musquitoes, and in some dread of alligators, from the body of one of which animals, I saw the bones of a man taken a few days since. He had been drawn out of his boat by the voracious beast.

Nov. 22nd.—Left Seniawan at 8 A.M.; and pulled against a strong current to Tundong, the next Chinese settlement. This village is occupied entirely by Chinese belonging to the Kungsi, or Company of Sambas, who have here a Juro-Tulis, or clerk, who manages their affairs in Sarawak. Part of the members work the gold at Bow, and part the antimony. In-shore of this place, those residing here are employed in the production of vegetables and other food for the miners, all sharing equally in the profits. The whole company at Sambas, and elsewhere, is said to comprise 30,000 members. In the dry season, the flood-tide reaches this place, but in heavy rains does not reach above Ledah-Tanah, the junction of the two rivers, fourteen miles above the town of Sarawak; and during freshes, it does not even extend to the town.

At half-past one P.M., we reached the landing-place of Bow, opposite to which is the Dyak village of Subah, belonging to the Sow Tribe. Two hours' more contest with the current, brought us to the Lubong Angin, where we intended to pass the night. Since leaving Subah, below which is a rapid dangerous in the dry season—but now the rocks are, for the most part, covered with water—the river has been confined by banks of limestone, in which are dispersed perpendicular veins of quartz, in some places numerous, in others not visible. The limestone is much water-worn; but the overhanging projections, so beautiful on the southern branch, are not common here. The scenery is not so beautiful from the river, as the mountains do not, like those of the other river, rise from its bed. The still river, winding its way amidst the limestone, which is shaded with over-hanging trees, is, nevertheless, very pretty; and the hill opposite to which we now lie, rises in a precipice 200 feet above our heads, its face being covered with climbing plants, and the projections of the rocks covered with ferns and other plants, among which I observed the bright flowers of the beautiful and new yellow *Rhododendron Brookeanum,* and the elegant fern-like foliage of a large-leafed, stemless palm.

The entrance to the cave is a large, curved fissure in the rock; the base of which is now a few inches below the level of the river, so that I have drawn the boat into the cave, and our fires for cooking are made on a platform of the rock to the left of the entrance. This part of the rock, as is that of all the limestone I have seen in the country, has its surface in little ridges, like that of the sand of the sea-beach, which is caused by the rippling of the retiring tide. I was anxious just to look into the cave, while my servant was preparing my dinner, but having been told by the Malays, none of whom had ever entered it, that it extended a very long way into the country, that it had no outlet, and that it was the habitation of dragons and bad spirits, I had no intention of exploring it till the morrow. Having lighted a little lamp I had with me, and requested one of my men to follow, much against his inclination, I followed the course of a little stream which was flowing out of it, in the water-worn and slippery bed of which I walked; the channel being very narrow, and the limestone rising on the left hand, and a bed of alluvial soil on the right: this has been

deposited here by the freshes of the river, which have
caused the water, at some seasons, to rise very high
in the cave. About ten yards from the entrance, the
cave turned suddenly to the right, and I could see
by the light of the lamp, that a platform above me
seemed to be the main flooring of the cave. The rocks
rising high on each side of the channel through which
the water flowed, I climbed up the bed of soil until
I found a firm footing on the broken and decayed
stalactites, which formed the flooring of a very large
apartment, the roof of which was arched and water-
worn, in the manner described of the limestone at the
entrance.

I found that the stream was occasioned by the drip-
ping of water from the highest part—about forty feet—
of the roof of this apartment, which was not decorated
by the stalactites of ordinary limestone caves ; though
some decaying ones were seen on the walls of the cavern.
While admiring the vaulted roof of this place, I heard
a noise precisely similar to that of a gale of wind, which
terrified the man who accompanied me. I was sure
that there must be an outlet at the other side of the
mountain, from the draught through the place, and which,
from being always perceived at its mouth, has given the
cave its name, and thought that the noise I now heard
must be caused by the wind in the crevices and confined passages of the cave ; and I had not advanced
fifty paces further, before I saw light through an
orifice in the rock at a little distance before me, and
myriads of large bats fluttering about the roof over

my head, and crowding to the two orifices, another being perceptible on my right, to which I advanced, as it was the nearest to me

I was followed now by my man with pleasure, who, seeing the light, lost his fear of traversing the cavern. It proceeded from a hole in a hollow projection of the rock above us, which looked, with the stalactites on all sides of it, like the inside of the steeple of a church. Here we had no difficulty in procuring specimens of the bats, which we knocked down with our caps in numbers. I then returned to the centre of the cave, and followed the direction of the greater orifice before me, which I rightly judged to be the main opening of the cavern on its southern side. This we approached with some difficulty, on account of our feet being without shoes, the slippery nature of the wet limestone at the entrance of the cavern having caused us to throw them aside for the greater safety in walking on it. This hole was a considerable height above the cavern, and could only be reached by climbing up the ridges of limestone, which had been worn by water until the edges were so sharp as much to endanger our hands and feet. I was encouraged to ascend by seeing many land shells, which had been brought into the cavern by water, and I hoped to find some live and perfect specimens of them on the outside. At last I succeeded in reaching it; but could not prevail upon my man to follow.

On the shrubs which were growing amongst the fragments of rock, I found four or five specimens of a

small shell, covered with spines, and a plant or two of a
beautiful *Anœctocheilus*, with golden veins traversing
its velvet-like leaves, as in the *Anœctocheilus setaceus*,
or ' Gauna Rajah,' King of the Jungle of Ceylon.   Two
uninteresting species of *Begonia* were also found with
it, and a species of *Justicia*, with purple and pink flowers.
In returning, we found the remains of torches which
had been used by the Dyaks in taking the birds' nests,
and on lighting them we saw the stages before us they
had used in ascending the narrow crevices in the roof
of the cave, which seemed to be very deep and dark.
We passed over large beds of " Guano," or some such
substance, produced by the many bats, and were soon
convinced that the sound of wind we had at first heard,
was caused by the flapping of the wings of these animals
which, having now disappeared, the noises were no
more perceptible.   The whole cavern may be about
200 yards in length, and twenty to thirty in breadth :
in height it varies from twenty to fifty feet.

On our reaching the outside, I found myself indebted
to my men for three plants of the yellow Rhododendron,
which they had insisted it was impossible to obtain ;
but which the offer of a dollar for each had caused
them to exert themselves to procure.   In coming here
up the river, many shrubs were in flower, particularly
the   sweet-scented   kinds   of *Anthoscephala*,   which
attracted many beautiful butterflies.   We had passed
several of the gigantic Tapang trees, and two large
shrubs of the magnificent *Clerodendron Bethuneana*
which were in full flower.   At night we slept in our

boat, and were free from the attacks of mosquitoes. Though sand-flies had been troublesome during the day they did not disturb us at night. During the evening, the man who had accompanied me through the cave, related the particulars of his wonderful adventure to an astonished audience.

Nov. 23*rd.*—Left Lubong Angin at eight A.M., intending to call again on our return to look for more Rhododendrons, and *Anœctocheilus :* those we have already, having been planted in a box, are placed under the shade of a large *Malvaceous* plant opposite the cave. In three quarters of an hour—the river still passing over its limestone bed—we passed the village of Incotong, or Passir Bruang, belonging to the Sow Dyaks. On a fine bamboo hanging·bridge were standing some of the Dyaks, who wished us to stop at their houses; but this I did not do, as I wished to get on to Gumbang while the fine weather lasted. Opposite a little gravelly islet, just above the village, I observed on a high tree a large mass of a new species of Tanda in full flower : the spikes of the flowers numbered upwards of a hundred, each being from 9 to 10 ft. long. The foliage of the plant is very fine, being 18 to 24 in length, and of a dark green colour; the chains of flower rise out from amongst the leaves : the roots, which are very large, arc all confined to the hard and woody base of the stem of the plant, and never arise from amongst the leaves, as is common to the various species of *Banda Ærides,* &c. Each flower was three inches in diameter, of a light sulphur colour, transversely barred with bands of rich cinnamon brown : the small labellum is purple in the centre, and spotted with brown towards the edges. The flowers as they get old, do not fall off, but gradually lose the rich brown colour, until blotches of it only remain, and finally, these also being lost, the flower retains a deep golden yellow, which colour it gradually acquires as the brown fades, apparently for some weeks before it finally drops off. (I have since ascertained that it remains many weeks in perfection.) The peduncle of the flower is protected by a sheath over its upper surface ; and this, with the footstalk and the flower-stem, are all densely covered with a beautiful mossy substance, like that which gives its name to the favourite of the rose tribe.

Having been delayed half an hour to secure this prize, we pushed on to Battu Bidi, at which place we arrived at half past ten A.M. Here are two or three Malayan houses, the occupants of which are employed in getting antimony ore from a rich vein in a limestone hill, half a mile inland. In another hour we passed the mouth of the Sunghie Jagusi, on a hill of the same name, near the sources of which is a large village of the Sow Dyaks. Near this place, I saw two fine horned owls of a very large size, but could not get a shot at them, though I had procured several specimens of other birds during the morning. We had also passed, above Bidi, many specimens of small fossils in the limestone on the sides of the river, but did not observe any of the very large ones, so abundant below the Rheum

Panjang, or Long Rapid, on the southern branch. At half-past two P.M., we past Sunghie Kirit, a small creek on the right bank (left going up), and soon after went under another fine bridge, (there being one also opposite Kirit), in the neighbourhood of which are situated on the left high bank, the Dyak village of Klokong, also belonging to the great tribe of Sow, whose chief village is at a place called Gunong Rât, inland of the Subah village formerly mentioned.

The country we have passed to-day, for more than half the distance, is limestone which supports a rich alluvial soil : the rock occasionally breaks through in round-topped precipitous hills, of from one to three hundred feet in height, as at Bidi; but soon after leaving the Jaguoi river, the limestone is succeeded by a soft kind of yellowish-coloured sandstone, which is seldom seen, being lower than the limestone. The banks above this rock rise higher, and the ground is much more undulating ; the soil is yellow loam of great depth, the banks are beautifully wooded, and the trees overhang the water. Early in the day we had observed some trees of the gorgeous *Lagerstrœmiœ regia,* covered with its beautiful bunches of lilac flowers, but these are not so common as about Ledah Tanah, and other places within the influence of the tides. We rested for the night on a pebbly bank, on the side of the river, a little above the village of Klokong.

November 24th.—Started again on our ascent of the river this morning soon after 7 A.M.; at 8 passed a small stream on the left bank of the river called

Serekin, and Lubok Pilin, a wide part of the river immediately after. At half-past 9 A.M. we reached the Sunghie Tubah on the left, and an hour afterwards passed on the opposite bank another stream of small size, of which I did not learn the name : here I gathered a pretty climbing plant with bunches of fragrant white flowers in the axils of the leaves. At 10 A.M. we passed a bed of large pebbles, called Karangan Kaladi, over which the now shallow river ran with great velocity. At 11, I found a small and very minute *Arum* growing on stones under the waters of the river, which were clear as crystal, with transparent colourless flowers, and leaves with very short petioles. At half-past 11, we reached Sunghie Kandong on the right, and three quarters of an hour after, passed Sunghie Kasong on the left. A little farther on I saw a plant of the very magnificent new scarlet *Æschynanthus Aucklandiæ*, which I have described. When first discovered, this plant like all the others of it I have seen, was hanging from a tuft of the beautiful bird's nest fern (*Asplenium*), which is common in the jungle. We have also passed some plants of the *Acrostichum grande,* and plenty of the *Polypodium quercifolium* is to be found on every tree.

Wild sirih leaves (*piper*) were gathered by my men, and in a tree near I found a curious and beautiful flower of the genus *Hoya*, growing in the hole of a tree, in extracting which I was bitten, till the blood flowed from the wounds in my hands, by a species of large black ant, which had also located itself in the same place as the roots of the plant. The flowers of this Hoya hang in long umbels from the axils of the leaves : the inside of the petals is of a rich brownish purple, which is beautifully relieved by the white ivory-like parts of fructification : the leaves are opposite and large, of a leathery texture; and the plant is of a climbing habit, and when wounded, plentifully emits a milky-looking sap.

We have ascended to-day between high banks of rich yellow loam, the water clear as crystal, and flowing over a sandy and pebbly bed. Many fruit trees were on the banks of the river, some of which having ripe fruit upon them, were plundered by my people. On account of the shallowness of the water, we have had much difficulty in getting the boat over, several of the karangans or gravelly places, and fallen trees having obstructed our progress. At 3 P.M. we arrived at the junction of two streams, which appeared of about equal size, that coming from the north being named Sebuloh, that from the west being the main river of Sarawak, coming from the hill of Teringush. They were both too small and too much obstructed to admit our boat more than a few yards, so that we stopped at the landing-place of the Gumbang Dyaks just inside the Sebuloh. We are now much higher than any European has hitherto penetrated into the Sarawak country, they having confined their visits to the deer-grounds of the Rât and Singhie Dyaks, the former situated on a river, a little above the Tundong Chinese village. It being too late to start for the houses, and rain falling, we stopped here for the night.

Nov. 25th.—We started early for the village, and found the road very bad. We crossed the Sebuloh several times, and were told by the Dyaks that it has its rise from springs on the Gunong Api, the mountain, at the foot of which the village of Gumbang is built. We walked about six miles from the boat, and as we approached the village, the jungle was composed entirely of fruit trees of the ordinary kinds. Mangusteens, called by the Dyaks, Scoup, are as common as the others : they were all now in fruit, and most of them nearly ripe, and the perfume which filled the air we breathed was very delightful, and fully rewarded our wretched walk, which I was just beginning to regret I had ever undertaken. Many sago trees were growing in all the swampy places, and cocoa-nut and betel-nut trees were plentiful about the houses. In our slight ascent to the houses, we passed many springs of delightful water, which running down the hill, form the Sebuloh at its base, abundantly supplying these Dyaks with excellent water. The tribe is situated on the confines of the Sarawak territory, and immediately to the westward of the mountain, begins that of Sambas, the river of which is not more than three hours' walk from the village we are now at. The chiefs were very glad to see me ; though an European, Mr. Hupé, a German missionary, having once passed through this village, on his way to Sarawak, from Sambas, I was not the first they had seen.

These people are not clever with paddles and boats, so that they rarely descend the river to Sarawak. I went over the village, which contains upwards of sixty houses, not built in one row, but in several, accompanied by one of the Orang Kayas; there are two in the village. The houses are more commodious and clean than most of those I have visited amongst the Land tribes, though not nearly so large or well built as those of the Sea Dyaks of Sebooyoh. It has two Pangahs, or head-houses, in one of which I took up my residence; but they do not contain many skulls, which, as this is an ancient tribe undisturbed by the Sakarrans, is a proof of the bloodless character of their wars. The houses look very pretty from the head-house, among the fruit-trees and boulders of porphyry which cover the face of the hill. In the evening I held a levee in the head-house, at which all the inhabitants of the village attended, each bringing a basket of fruit as a present. My servant distributed beads and tobacco amongst them, and I gave the chiefs each a Battik handkerchief, which very much delighted them. They begged of me to stay for two or three days to eat fruit with them, and that they might get up a feast; but I did not wish to do so, as I wanted to take the plants I had collected to Sarawak.

Nov. 26.—Having refused all entreaties to stay, on account of the plants in the boat, I left the village at 10 A.M. with many Dyaks following laden with fruit. One of the Orang Kayas accompanied me, the other sent his son, begging me to excuse his personal attendance, as one of his children was ill. At 1 P.M. we left the landing-place of these friendly Dyaks, and I regretted that I could not stay; but the plants I had collected were too rare and valuable to be thrown away. On our way down, we gathered two more plants of the *Œschynanthus Aucklandiæ*, the flowers of which, excluding the exserted stamens, were 4½ in. in length : the tube yellow at the base, and orange-coloured scarlet towards the limb, the throat of which was barred with black inside. The leaves were undulate and verticillate, many in a whorl; the stem 4 ft. long, woody; the seed-pods 10 in. long and terete. At half past 3 P.M. we arrived at the Klakong village, where we determined to remain for the night. On ascending to the houses, I found them to be thirty or forty, well built, in a single row, with a Pangah for the bachelors at one end. No fruit trees but plantains surrounded it, as the village has been but recently established. These people, who were then living with the tribe at Sow, were great losers by the destruction of that village by the Sakarran Dyaks, who still held many of their children in slavery. They very anxiously inquired concerning our relations with those Dyaks, and expressed regret that peace was concluded with them, expressing their conviction that the Sakarran Dyaks would never abide by the promises they had made.

Nov. 27*th.*—Started at daylight, and breakfasted at Incotong. This Sow village contains twenty houses, the tide, or rather current, flowing very strong, a slight fresh having been raised by the rains of last night. We soon reached Lubong Angin, and I succeeded, with two of my men, in reaching the top of the hill. It is of limestone, worn everywhere into sharp

ridges, with knife-like edges, and contains many caves,
in and out of which numerous bats and swallows were
flying. In its highest part it is about 250 feet, and
having cut down some trees, we obtained a beautiful
view of the white limestone-hills to the southward. We
obtained three more plants of the *Rhododendron
epiphytal* on trees, and found many of the beautiful
Anœctocheilus growing on the moss-covered rocks.
Dead land-shells are strewed about, but I could only
find, with the greatest difficulty, two or three live ones.
A large snake, called by the Europeans the hammer-
headed viper, was on a tree or bush in our path. The
reptile had drawn back its head in act to strike at
the first of us who should approach him, but was
fortunately perceived by one of my men. We did
not suffer him to live long, and as he never attempted
to escape, a sharp parang severed his head from his
body. It is the kind called Ledong *(Trigonocephalus
Waglerii)* by the natives, and is very venomous.
Having descended the hill, and packed the plants carefully in the boat, we reached Tundong at half past
four P.M., where we dined. Pulling hard after dinner, we
soon passed Seniawan, and at midnight arrived at
Sarawak.

CHAPTER XIII

As a narrative of one of my visits up the southern branch of the Sàrawak river will contain some notices, not in the preceding pages, I extract the following from my journal of 1845.

Dec. 1*st.*—Left Sarawak at 2 P.M., intending to ascend the left-hand river as far as the village of the Sennah Dyaks, the most distant of the tribes of Sarawak, excepting those of Si Panjang and Goon, on the Sangow waters, to the S.W. of the Sennah village My crew, which consists of ten stout young men, pulled well; so that, having passed the junction at Ledah Tanah at 4 P.M., we stopped at Karangan Landi, a little above the river Staat, a small stream, which comes from the westward, and on which, in a limestone hill, is a small but rather pretty cave, formerly said to have been a retreat of the Dyaks from persecution. The Karangan Landi is a large bed of gravel, amongst which are many pretty agates, and being above the ordinary height of the river, is much used as a resting-place by the Malays,

H Williams. del.

J W Cook, sc

Dyak bridge of Bambu over the river above the
Sennah Village, Sarawak.

who pass it on their trading expeditions to the Dyaks. Here the limestone formation begins: the hills below, such as Gunong Serambo, Singhie, and Suntah, are of porphyry, as I am informed by Mr. Williams, the geologist sent out by the Admiralty. Slate is found at Gunong Matang, in the Singhie country, and marble at the Santubong entrance of the river. Granite has nowhere yet been discovered on the western part of the island.

At Landi, which is overhung by the leaves of a beautiful species of palm and some large fig-trees, we cooked our dinner, and slept, unannoyed by musquitoes or sand-flies, though the former are found in numbers a little way down the river, as I have proved on many distressing nights; they do not appear to be so numerous in the river beyond the influence of the flood-tide, which at this season does not reach within four miles of this place, though in the dry season it sensibly affects the water four miles higher up. Landi is about twenty miles from Sarawak.

Dec. 2nd.—Started again at daylight, and soon reached Dampul, a temporary farm village of the Sempro Dyaks, since abandoned. A mile and a half further brought us to the mouth of the Suntah river, where we stopped; and walking about the same distance, we reached the Bungalow, in the nutmeg plantation belonging to Mr. Brooke. The nutmegs are neglected and covered with weeds, but many of them flourish notwithstanding. The house, which is now tumbling down, was erected when the diamonds, which abound in

this district, were attempted to be worked, three years
ago. It is situated eighteen or twenty feet above the
ordinary level of the river, which often overflows its banks
after heavy rains, so as to come up to it; it appears to
have done so quite recently. At present it flows in a
clear and tranquil stream over its sandy and gravelly
bed. A large trench, situated close to the house, and
which was dug at a great expense, has been neglected;
as the river, the course of which it was intended to turn
into it, broke down the dams, and insisted upon running in
its old bed, and covering from the cupidity of the miners
the valuable minerals which are found in its sands.

Some Banjar miners have recently been digging in
the trench; and I saw some small diamonds, on a
previous visit, which they had obtained; but they say
there are no large ones. These cunning fellows fear to
tell us that they find any of value, as they suppose the
working them would be immediately taxed. We knew,
however, that they have been offering good diamonds
for sale. I took a small canoe, and with two men went
up the river, in search of plants, but did not find any
which I had not previously observed. Opposite the
house, the Bunga Bungor (*Lagerstrœmia regia*) was
flowering beautifully: *Durians* and *Lansats* were ripe on
the banks of the stream, and we enjoyed, to our hearts'
content, their delicious fruits. On a point of land which
we passed, was a place, under the shade of palm-trees,
railed in, where, I was told, the Sempro Dyaks bury
the bones of their dead, after the bodies have been
burnt. It may be so in this tribe—I had not an oppor-

OF THE SARAWAK RIVER. 391

tunity of inquiring of them—but other tribes have frequently assured me that the bones of the dead are all calcined by the fire, and that they bury no part of the corpse.

Dec. 3rd.—I sent one of the men to the Dyak village, situated at the foot of the Gunong Coum, a hill, or rather limestone rock, about 600 feet high. In a straight line it does not appear more than half a mile from the house, and presents from it a white and naked precipice of unstratified stone : it is, like most of the limestone hills, of a round form, and the top is covered with jungle. It is said that it can be ascended from the opposite side, which is not so precipitous. Between it and the house, rises a lofty Tapang, high above the other jungle trees. The village at the foot of the hill, to which I sent my man for fowls and eggs, belongs to the Sempro Dyaks, who farm in this neighbourhood.

I went myself, with my butterfly net, into the jungle, in search of flowers and insects; of the latter I caught some fine specimens of a large butterfly, with semi-transparent wings, covered with black spots. This insect usually flies so high, that I had been hitherto unable to procure it, as it is not common; but here it was plentiful, and came near the ground. Its lazy flight is exceedingly beautiful, as in the sun it looks like a falling flake of snow, gilded with metallic colours. A specimen of a rare and magnificent species of Papilio was also captured; the flight of this was near the ground, and rapid as that of a swallow. I could never have captured it in the jungle, had it not, in flying past me, accidentally rushed into my net.

I followed the course of a small rill, in search of a little plant I found at its mouth, which conducted me to a great many holes, dug in the ground, at some distance from each other; they were about nine feet deep, and all connected by the gravel having been taken out of them at the bottom: these I had no difficulty in recognizing as pits for the working of the diamonds. A little further on, I came to the dams and other works which had been employed in cleansing the precious stone from the soil which contains it. These are the works of some Banjar men, who have been caused to desist, as they do not wish to pay any revenue for the jewels they obtain. They are now working successfully in the main river, which is free to them. I was not successful in finding any plants, excepting *Scitaminæ*. A scarlet flower of this order was very pretty, and a beautiful *Alpinia* was growing on the banks of the streams, with its stems drooping towards the water.

Dec. 4th.—Returned early this morning to the boat, and ascending the river, stopped, at 8 A.M., to breakfast, on the left bank, (right, going up), at a place called Bajuk, where was a Dyak farm-house, at which we cooked our rice and fowl for breakfast. Notwithstanding the lateness of the season, many men are employed in the river, washing gold. They tell me that they are very successful, though the height of the water makes it more injurious to their health, as many of them stand nearly up to their armpits in water, all day, at this employment. At noon we passed the Rheums Panjang and Besar, meaning long and great rapids; having passed over the strata of fossils at the Battu Lichin and Battu Tikus. The Battu Tikus, or rat-stones, have taken their name from the curious fossils which project from the limestone rocks which line the river. They are not arranged in any particular order, but scattered on the surface, from which they stand out in high relief, the softer limestone having been worn away by the action of the water.

On the left-hand side of the river is a hill, also of limestone, about 100 feet high, on the steep sides of which numbers of small specimens, principally shells and reptiles, are observed; but in the bed of the river are many strata of enormous fossils, like roots of trees, or the gigantic relics of the animal monsters of a former world. These are disposed in parallel strata, and cross the river in south-east and north-west directions, though in some instances, the parallel direction is departed from. These also stand out from their rocky bed; and in July, form a rheum, or rapid; and by their hard angles and edges, are formidable to canoes, which on account of the shallowness of the water, necessarily come in contact with them. It is to be regretted that these remains have not been examined by a competent person, as they were not discovered till just as the geologist, formerly mentioned, was recalled to England, so that he had not time thoroughly to examine them.

Soon after noon, we reached the village of Sebayet, situated at the foot of a mountain of limestone, the face of which, towards the river, is about 1,000 feet high, displaying a naked precipice of limestone. Opposite to

it, and on the right side of the river, where also are
some houses, is the peaked rock, called Si Gigi: this
is higher than Sebayet, and, like it, is precipitous.
Si Gigi is the end of a round-topped range of limestone
hills, which is continued along the banks of the river.
The village of Sebayet is the head-quarters of the
Sempro Dyaks, who were at this time absent at the
farms; but as I intended to stay for the night, I went
up to the houses, and took up my residence in that of
the chief.   This was situated in the middle of a long
row of finely-built houses, before which stood the
Pangah, or house for bachelors, universally found in the
villages of the Hill Dyaks.

About dark, the family of the Orang Kaya returned,
though he himself stopped at the farm, not knowing of
my arrival.   His wife and I were old friends, as it is her
unfailing custom to dun her visitors for bottles, who
by this means recollect her.   I found that bottles were
still in demand; and after having concluded a bargain
for some rice for my men, for which, to her delight,
I paid her the Sarawak price, I gave her two or three
empty bottles, in consideration of the use of her house,
of which I had so unceremoniously possessed myself.
Others of the tribe came in the evening, bringing small
presents of fruit, rice and eggs, for which they received
Javanese tobacco and beads, with which they were
delighted.   The river, which near here is very tortuous,
flows peacefully along between its steep banks over
beds of sand and gravel, though the rapids below, and
the high walls of limestone which endeavour to confine

it lower down, give it, in many places a boisterous and turbulent character.

Dec 5th.—Breakfasted a little above the village, in one of the prettiest spots imaginable, and where I delight to stay. It is a large bank of pebbles, on the left-hand side of the river, overhung with beautiful trees and graceful bamboos. Opposite me, the high mountain, Si Gigi, comes sloping down until near the water, when it takes suddenly a precipitous form, past the base of which the river peacefully glides; though a little above, where it flows over a bed of large pebbles, a rippling disturbs its surface, and causes a murmuring sound. The mountain is beautifully wooded, and graceful palms and ferns have sprung out of the crevices, and adorn the precipitous sides, which overhang the water. The mountain before us is pierced with innumerable fissures and caves, the residence of the pretty little mouse-coloured swallow *(Hirundo esculenta)*, which is now flying over our heads, catching its insect food. The nests of this bird form a source of considerable profit to the Sempro Dyaks of Sebayet and to all those tribes inhabiting the limestone districts, in which alone this species of bird builds, caves being most abundant in this formation.

Having taken our meal, and enjoyed this delightful solitude, disturbed only by the harsh notes of the hornbills from the neighbouring mountains, and a solitary species from a Tapang-tree, close to us, at which I fired without effect—shot being useless for birds on these high trees—we started, and pushed on slowly up the stream, several hornbills and pigeons being disturbed by our

approach, from their feast off the fruit of the Kayu Ara, a
species of fig.   A hornbill flying over, makes such a
rushing noise with the action of his powerful wings upon
the air, even though he be at a great height, that I have
never observed the like in any other large bird. They fly
with a steady, regular, and straight flight, like a crow.
The highest woods on the most lofty mountains are the
favourite places of their residence; but they frequently
are tempted by the fruit to the plains.   They are generally seen in small flocks of from three to six individuals.
There are many species of them in Sarawak; but the
largest and most common is that known as the rhinoceros hornbill *(Buceros Rhinocerus)*.   Of pigeons
and doves we procured many kinds, and shall have a
famous feast off them at night.   The kinds of doves, or
small pigeons, called " punei" by the natives, are very
tender and excellent eating; the large " preggam," or
wood-pigeon, though excellent when young, is generally
tough when old.   They are very large birds, and some
just shot weigh as much as a good Dyak fowl.   Nothing
smaller than No. 3 shot will bring them from their
lofty perches.

Shooting as we went, and having made a good bag, it
was noon before we reached Si Budah, a temporary
farm village of the Sempro Dyaks, situated at the foot
of the mountain of the same name, which, like the
others, is limestone, and precipitous   It appears higher
than either Sebayet or Si Gigi, peaked on the face,
towards the north, and appearing to be a narrow ridge on
the top, as, through a large hole, which pierces the lime-

stone, the sky can be seen. There is a hanging bridge at this village, but not so fine a one as that of Sempro, or any of those on the western river, in the territory of the Sow Dyaks. The river we have passed to-day is still confined within its limestone barriers; but so much has it undermined the rock, and overhangs in many places so much, that two or three larger boats than mine might lie abreast of each other protected from the weather. Rapids from rocks and fallen trees have been frequent, and karangans, or gravelly shallows, numerous. Generally, the limestone tracks, traversed by the river between two rapids, are very deep, and the water still, a current being only perceptible at the angles of the stream. Here small aligators and large fish are sometimes seen.

We collected the Dyaks, and requested them to show us the cave in the mountain Si Budah, which we had been informed existed there. After some delay, the Dyaks were got together, and we walked along the base of the mountain and bank of the river about three hundred yards, till we came to a small brook, up the course of which we turned, and were soon at the entrance of a large cave from which the stream came. Having lighted our torches, we followed the gravelly stream of pure and cold water through a lofty passage into a very large and high chamber of a tent-like form, the stream running through the centre of it.

It was a magnificent apartment, the walls being hung with stalactites, which are all in a decaying state: we passed on among limestone, through which the stream had worn a narrow passage, through a corridor about a hundred yards in length, which conducted us to the open air on the other side; so that we had passed, as through a tunnel, under the mountain. This stream does not, like that in Lubong Angin, rise from the interior of the cave, but passes through it from the side on which we now stood. In a country like Italy and Spain, what a romantic and beautiful retreat for banditti, or any similar curse of those countries! A troop of cavalry, a thousand strong, might reside here, with shelter for man and beast at hand, and the luxury of a delightful stream running through their dwelling.

Having gained the opposite side, I tried to ascend the lofty rock by a path used by the Dyaks for reaching the caves to get the birds' nests which abound in them. Having succeeded in getting half way to the top, I found it impossible to proceed without very great danger, a single stick, not thicker than my wrist, being the only ladder by which an overhanging rock was surmounted. I climbed up to the top of the rock, but looking below me at the rocky depth over which I hung, and not seeing any good hold above, I returned, much to the amusement of the Dyaks, who had told me the path was very difficult, and accessible only to Dyaks—who they truly said were like monkeys.

Descending the stick and hill, we returned through the cave, which is a regular road of the Dyaks to the village, where we intended to remain for the night. I had collected some plants of the fine Ixora, which I had discovered previously; but neither flowers nor seeds of it were procurable. At night I purchased some spears and other weapons from the Dyaks, in exchange for beads and brass wire. Slept in the boats, the houses being small and dirty.

Dec. 6th.—Left early for Sebongoh, and passed through beautiful mountains of limestone. One at the back of Sibudah, which has a reddish and stratified appearance, is in shape exactly resembling the face of a pyramid, and looks as if it had been built, so correct is its outline: it has no trees upon it. One mountain near it had had all its trees destroyed about twelve months since, by a fire which had been ignited by the intensity of the sun's rays on the rock beneath, and which had so dried the vegetation, that it spontaneously took fire, and the whole were destroyed. Nothing but a succession of very wet summers can again restore it. About three miles from the village is the Rheum Sebongoh, a large, but not dangerous rapid. The houses of this tribe are situated on both banks of the river, which here again runs through banks of sparkling sand and beautiful pebbles. Fruit trees surround the village, and, during the day, ·we have passed through immense numbers of them, the property of this tribe. The fruits are ripe, and the Dyaks brought me baskets of all kinds in the evening as presents. I did not go up to the houses, but staid in the boat, in which I was visited by the chief people. The Orang Kaya wanted medicine for cataract in the eve, which, if he does not take care, will soon blind him. I advised him to go to Sarawak, and be operated upon for it by the doctor, but he does not seem to consider it of sufficient importance.

These Dyaks seldom use paddles in this shallow stream, but propel their boats with long canes of bamboo, which they use more adroitly than any other tribes I have visited : the women are equally expert with the men. Of some pigeons we had killed, fowls, fish, yams, fern shoots, and fruit, we made an excellent dinner, and having supplied the people with tobacco, slept soundly, undisturbed by dreams, in our very comfortable boats. My bed is a hearth-rug laid on the flooring of the boat with fine mats over it. We are protected from the rain by an awning of Kajangs, or mats made of the leaves of the Nipah palm, impenetrable to all weather. These last two days we have journeyed very slowly, as I have been gathering plants and enjoying this most beautiful part of the river, through which it had been a sin to hurry.

Dec. 7th.—We left Sebongoh early, and passing the mouth of the Samban, a shallow river which comes from the Gunong Seroung to the westward, reached the landing-place of the Brang Dyaks, where is a fine sandy beach. Some Malays, who were here trading with the Dyaks, informed me that the Brang village was under the Pamali, so that I could not visit it without causing them to break through a custom which I had no desire to do. They live on a high limestone, round-topped mountain, half a mile in-shore. Having collected some fern, which is plentiful on the loamy banks where the limestone does not prevail, we cooked our breakfast on the sandy beach, and had, in addition to our usual fare, an omelet made of eggs we had obtained at Si-bungoh. Whilst waiting here, a boat, which had been sent after us by Mr. Williamson, reached us, with a letter for me, requesting me to assist the bearer in collecting a debt for the Tuan-Ku Sireib Hussin of Sarawak, from the Tumma Dyaks. I had promised to assist him, if he obtained Mr. Brooke's permission; and this was contained in Williamson's note. Accordingly, having breakfasted, we pulled up against the stream for about six miles in a heavy rain to the Rheum Ledong, a rapid formed by limestone banks, which contracts the stream, leaving a narrow passage for the water, which rushes through with great velocity and a boiling torrent-like appearance. It is rendered dangerous to boats descending the river by a large rock just under water, directly opposite to the passage, so that to avoid it, boats must turn suddenly to the left while shooting the rapid, and again to the right, to avoid the rocky bank. This requires considerable practice and dexterity; and Chinamen, who visit the Dyaks in search of pigs, have frequently lost their porkers, and sometimes themselves, by their boat splitting on the centre rock, or filling, in the strong ripple occasioned by the velocity of the current over its rocky bed. A mile above this rheum, is the Pinkallan Ampat, at a point of land where a torrent from the Tabiah country falls in from the westward.

We kept up the river leading to Sennah, which is small and shallow, and filled with boulders of a hard porphyritic rock, the limestone disappearing at the Rheum Ledong. The Padi farms of the Sennah Dyaks are on the sloping banks on each side of us. The delightful, lively green of its young foliage is a welcome relief to the eye from the more sombre tints of the jungle, the thick foliage of which admits but seldom the rays of the sun. The rain has cleared away, and the sun is now shining beautifully on the industry of these Dyaks. Their farms appear very extensive, and each has a plot of yams and other garden stuff, close to the waters of the river. The land here is beautifully undulating; in the limestone districts it is more flat, but broken by the immense mountains of that rock, which arise in all directions from it.

At five P.M. we reached the Sennah village, and remained in the boats until the return of the people from their farms, a few women and children only being present in the village. The Orang Kava Bye Ringate is in his house, but has some days since placed himself under the " pamali" hoping by this means to recover from a severe sickness a favourite child. On the arrival of the men at dark, we were escorted by the relatives of the chief to a new and very nice Pangah, where we took up our abode, being able to gather the ripe fruit of the seebow or rhambutan from the windows. Having cooked and eaten our food, we were waited upon by the people of the village as usual, bringing presents of rice, fruit, eggs and fowls. The eggs we get amongst the

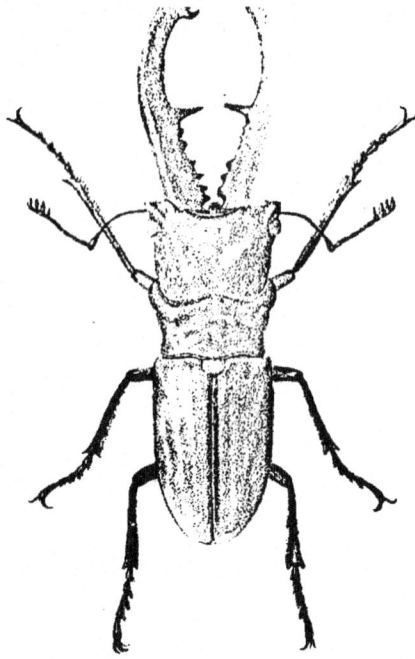

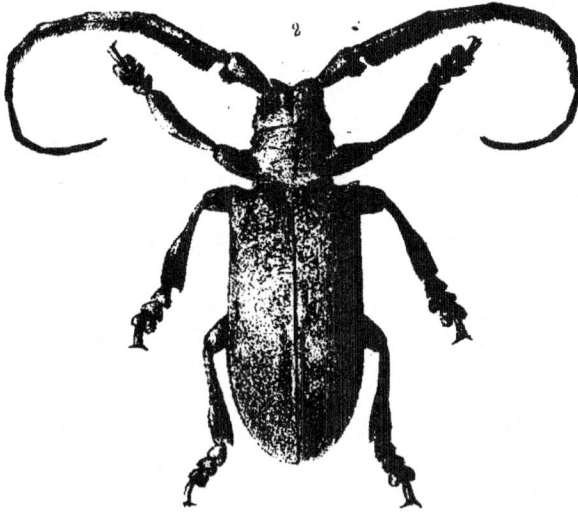

1. A Bornean Stag Beetle (CLADOGNATHUS TARANDUS (Thunb)
2. Low's Brush-horn Beetle (SAROTHROCERA LOWII (White)

Richard Bentley, London 1848

Dyaks are frequently not good, as they never remove them from the nest, and on a visitor's arrival, take them from under the hen, and bring them to him, so that they are frequently nearly hatched. In this state, they are eaten by the Dyaks themselves, as well as when fresh. In return for their presents, my servant gave them tobacco, &c. Bye Ringate, the chief, sent Pa-pata and Pa-Benang, his sons-in-law, to inquire if I had any bechara, (business conversation) for the tribe; so I told them what I had come for, and requested them to send a man to call the chiefs of Tumma early to-morrow morning.

Dec. 8th.—Pa-pata himself started early for Tumma, which is said to be half a day's journey in an easterly direction from Sennah. I amused myself by looking about the village, which consists of several rows of houses, at some distance from each other, on both sides of a beautifully quiet stream about knee-deep, flowing over a bed of yellow sand. Extensive groves of fruit-trees surround the place in every direction, amongst which are the Krakak (a small fruit resembling the lansat, but growing in terminal bunches); the Langyir, a large fruit, resembling the mangusteen in size, but of a curious sickly flavour; the Kinan (rambye); Rhambut-an Barangan (chesnut); Manggis (mangusteen); Tampuri (Durian); Blimbing (an acid fruit); Champadak; Nangka (jack); Tankallah (Parrit), and many others. All of these are now ripe, and have a beautiful appearance.

In a Rhambut-an tree was a small hut, the residence

of persons afflicted with a kind of leprosy which has been described previously. In this village, while waiting for the Tumma chiefs, I collected a good deal of information respecting the customs of the Dyaks (see chapter on Hill Dyaks). They say that after a person deceased has been burnt, his spirit haunts the house in which he lived for four days, during which period rice is spread daily on the floor, from the door across the house to the window; at the expiration of that time, a basin is broken outside the door, and the rice swept away; after which, the spirit departs to the mountains. They also said, that on a person's decease they burnt a portion of his property with his body.

Dec. 9th.—In the evening, the chiefs of Tumma and of Sinangkan, and of other neighbouring tribes who had heard of my arrival, came to visit me, and brought fowls, rice and fruit in great quantities. I gave each of the chiefs a battik handkerchief and some beads, brass wire, and tobacco, as well as similar things to their numerous attendants, none of whom had come empty-handed. I laid the business I was charged with before Bye Ringate, the chief of Sennah—who had broken through the Pamali to attend this gathering—and the Tumma men. They allowed the claim, and agreed to pay the rice, forty pasus at once, with the exception of ten, which they wished to remain till next season. This I had no doubt the Tuanku would do, so I settled the arrangements to the satisfaction of all parties concerned. The original debt was the price of a slave which belonged to the Tumma tribe, and having been

purchased by the Tuanku at Sadong, ran away to his
friends on being brought to Sarawak.

At night these people made a great feast, to which
I descended, walking on gongs and other musical instruments of brass placed for the purpose, to the
verandah. When the dancing was to take place, I was
conducted to a kind of couch, which they had made of
bamboo, and covered with their finest cloths, as my
particular seat: a canopy of scarlet cloth hung over my
head; by the seat were placed immense baskets of Padi
and rice, to which many fowls were secured, which I
found were all intended for me; but which I represented
to them that, as I was not going any further, I should
not want, and refused as well as I could. I was
obliged, however, to take some, so chose a basket of
delicious fruits. The dancing was similar to that
described in former parts of the journal; but my Malays
were requested not to come in while the girls were
present. As I have never seen this practised before,
I fancy there must be some particular reason for this
prohibition. I retired early, but the music and dancing
were continued during the night. Though a pig had
been killed, none of the people were intoxicated when I
left.

Dec. 10*th.*—At 9 A.M. left Sennah on our return.
The heavy rain last night has caused a considerable
fresh in the river, so that—the stream being very strong,
and the rocks all covered—we were carried down with
great speed, though accompanied with some danger
from the sunken rock. I collected a good many seeds of

the fine new *Ixora*, and many other plants, but did not observe any thing which I had not previously seen. I have three hives of bees, which are from the Sennah Dyaks, who keep them hanging from their houses. The bees are of two kinds; one hive of small yellow ones, and two hives of a brown-coloured one, both different from the honey-producing bee of England. These are said to yield much honey, but very little wax. Staid during the night at Sebongoh.

Dec. 11th.—Before leaving Sebongoh this morning, we were overtaken by a boat belonging to Bandery Samsu. They informed us that another boat had been lost in passing the Rheum Ledong, with a valuable cargo of brass goods, &c. We ourselves when passing it yesterday expected to have been swamped from the rippling of the water caused by the heavy rains, which have so deepened the river, that the rocks of the rapid are all covered, but with a great swell on them. Left Sebongoh at 9 A.M., and with the heavy fresh reached home at 3 P.M., feeling unwell with diarrhœa.

APPENDIX.

Borneo appears to teem with animal life, and is especially rich in kinds: as yet the country may be said to be an untrodden field.

The Dutch Naturalists have collected and sent to Leyden some of the more prominent species, which have been described by M. Temminck, Schlegel, and Dr. Müller: some of the more showy have been figured in the illustrated work of the latter author.

Amongst the few animals collected by Mr. Low, and sent to the British Museum, there appears to be several species not noticed by the Dutch authors; and as soon as these species can be prepared and examined, they will be described.

MAMMALIA.

List of Animals from Borneo, which are contained in the collection of the British Museum.

> Simia Satyrus.
> Nasalis larvatus.
> Presbytes chrysomelas.
>   ,,   frontatus.
>   ,,   rubicundus.
>   ,,   cristatus.

Tarsius spectrum.

Stenops tardigradus.

Galeopithecus variegatus.

Rhinolophus trifoliatus.

Cheiromeles torquatus.

Felis planiceps.

Viverra zibetha.

Hemigalea zebra (Viverra Boei, *Mull.*)

Paradoxurus leucomystax.

Paradoxurus musanga.

Cynogale Bennettii (Potamophilus barbatus, (*Mull.*)

Linsang gracilis.

Hylogale Javanica.

     ,,   ferruginea.

Pteromys tana.

     ,,   nitidus.

Sciurus ephippium.

     ,,   melanotis.

     ,,   exilis.

Bos Bantiger.

Sus barbatus.

Moschus Napu.

Dr. Müller (Verhandelingen, Leiden, 1845), gives the following additional species as also inhabiting Borneo :—

Hylobates concolor.

Cercopithecus cynomolgus.

Inuus nemestrinus.

Pteropus funereus.

Macroglossus minimu

Pachysoma brachyotis.

Dysopes tenuis.

Vespertilio pictus.

Vespertilio macellus.

„ tenuis.

Nycticejus Temminckii.

Hylogale murina.

Sorex Myosurus.

Aonyx Horsfieldii.

Lutra Simag.

Canis rutilans.

Felis macrocelis.

„ minuta.

Mustela nudipes.

Ursus Malayanus.

Sciurus Rafflesii.

„ nigrovittatus.

„ modestus.

„ lati-caudatus.

Mus Decumanus.

Atherura fasciculata.

Manis Javanica.

Rhinoceros ——— ?

Elephas Indicus.

Tapirus Indicus.

Cervis equinus.

„ rusa.

„ muntjac.

BIRDS.

Pontoætus ichthyætos.

Spizætus cirrhatus ?

Hierax.

Poliornis liventer.

Athene scutellata.

Ephialtes mantis.

Syrnium leptogrammicum.

Trogon flagrans.

    „   fasciatus.

    „   Diardii.

Halcyon concretus.

Nectarinia simplex.

    „   mystacalis.

    „   Hasseltii.

    „   hypogrammica.

    „   phœnicotis.

    „   lepida.

Arachnothera chrysogenys.

    „   longirostra.

Phyllornis Cochin-Chinensis.

    „   Malabaricus.

Orthotomus atrogularis.

Pitta cyanoptera.

    „ Baudii.

    „ atricapilla.

    „ granatina.

Timalia maculata.

    „   poliocephala.

    „   trichorrhis.

    „   nigricollis.

    „   atricapilla.

Muscicapa pyrrhoptera.

Rhipidura Javanica.

Pardalotus thoracicus.

    „   maculatus.

Artamus sanguinolentus.

Cracticus gymnocephalus.

Glaucopis aterrimus.

Buceros galeritus.

,,   antracicus.

,,   corrugatus.

,,   gracilis.

,,   convexus.

,,   rhinoceros, var. Borneonensis.

,,   Malabaricus.

,,   Malayanus.

,,   galeatus.

Bucco chrysopogon.

,,   mystacophanos.

       frontalis.

,,   corvinus.

,,   fuliginosus.

Indicator archipelagicus.

Calobates radiceus.

Cuculus lugubris.

,,   flavus.

Treron cinnamomeum.

,,   aromaticum.

Euplocomus ignitus.

REPTILES.

LIZARDS.

Tachydromus sex-lineatus, *Daud.*

Norbea Brookei, *Gray, List of Reptiles in British Museum, p.* 102.

Tiliqua rufescens, (*Shaw*), *Gray, l. c.* 109.

Euprepis Belcheri, *Gray, l. c.* 116.

Hemidactylus Brookii, *Gray, l. c.* 153.

,,   ,,   vittatus, *Gray, l. c.* 155.

Platyurus Schneiderianus (*Shaw*), *Gray, l. c.* 157.
Gecko monarchus, *Gray, l. c.* 161.
Tarentola Borneonensis, *Gray, l. c.* 165.
Heteronota Kendallii, *Gray, l. c.* 174.
Monitor bivittatus.

EMYDO-SAURIANS.

Mecistops Journei, (*Bory.*), *Gray.* Gavialis Schlegelii,
 Müller.
Crocodilus biporcatus.

SNAKES.

Homalopsis Schneideri.
  ,, Aer.
Naja tripudians, *var.*
Pelamis bicolor.
  ,, — n. sp. *Zool. Sulph.* t.
Hydrus.

BATRACHIANS.

Rana cancrivora.
Bufo.
Hyla.

FISH.

Echeneis.
Tetraodon argenteus.
Monoplerus Javanicus.
Conger ,,
Leuciscus cirrhipes.
Helostoma Temminckii.
Glyphysodon unimaculatum.
Trichopus trichopterus.
Rhynchobdella gigantea.
Osteoglossus formosus.

Osphromemus œfex.

Rohuta ænea.

Eleotris puella.

Silurus, *n. sp.*

Ophiocephalus.

Pleuronectes.

Blennicus.

Periopthalmus.

Balistes.

Acanthurus.

Agriopus.

Scorpæna.

II. *Descriptions of two species of Beetles brought from Borneo by* HUGH LOW, ESQ.; *by* ADAM WHITE, F.L.S., *Assistant Zool. Dep., British Museum.*

The *Fauna* of Borneo, so far as annulose animals are concerned, seems to be extraordinarily rich : insects of all orders, and spiders of numerous genera, abounding in the woods; while the *Myriapoda* found in damp forests, especially those allied to our globe millipede (*Glomeris*) are gigantic, and, compared with it and many of its allies, seem rather as if they had belonged to some primæval creation. Of these which are large species of *Zephroniæ*, there appear to be several; and of the *Polydesmi*, many of the species are as pre-eminent for their size, as they are for their beauty and curious appearance.

The seas are plentifully supplied with *Crustacea*, belonging to families (such as the *Leucosiadæ*) but feebly represented in our temperate climate; and the peculiar position of Borneo, brings to its shores the crabs of the Chinese. seas, Indian Ocean, and north-east coast of Australia. In the works of Schönherr and Dehaan, and other authors, many of the annulose animals brought to Europe by the Dutch, are described; while many more are scattered in European collections without names.

In the British Museum we have not a few, principally brought over by Hugh Low, Esq., Arthur Adams, Surg., R.N., and other officers of H.M.S. "Samarang." It would take a long time to get these together, and to describe them, and so far as *Crustacea* go, Mr. Adams and the writer of this notice are engaged in describing them, and in figuring the new species.

As a sample of the *Coleoptera* of the island, the two following fine species may be described, more especially as the accompanying figures will make these descriptions plainer.

It is only with a very limited and narrow portion of the coast that we are yet acquainted, and even of this part the productions are but very slightly known: much, however, is expected from the energy of Mr. Brooke and the Colonial Secretary; while the enterprise and curiosity of colonists will soon make us better acquainted with the animals, and add to our too limited collections.

I subjoin the descriptions of two very fine *Coleoptera*, sent by Mr. Low, with several other Borneo insects.

Family LAMIADÆ.

Genus SAROTHROCERA, White.

The antennæ in this genus have the basal joint thick, and furnished at the end on the inside with a tuft of hairs; the second joint is very small, with one or two hairs; the third to the seventh joints are fringed behind with longish hairs, those on the third and fourth joints very thickly distributed, and extending over a considerable part of the hind edge.

The Thorax is almost as long as it is wide, the sides are nearly parallel, somewhat depressed above, with a short spine on each side. The Scutellum is somewhat elongated, the sides parallel. The Legs have the femora compressed, especially above; the tibiæ are much compressed, slender at the base, getting thicker towards the middle, and from that to the end wide, with the sides parallel. The tarsi are very wide. The elytra are strongly angled, almost aculeated on the shoulders, rounded and simple at the end.

This genus comes close to *Cerosterna,* Dejean, Serville, with which and *Batocera* it has several characters in common, as well as a general resemblance.

Of this genus I have only seen one species, which in the Annals and Magazine of Natural History (Vol. XVIII), is amed in compliment to Hugh Low, Esq., the author of this work, who found it in Borneo.

Sarothrocera Lowii, White, *l. c.* 47, *t.* 1. *f.* 6. See *fig.* 2 of the plate of Insects.

Of a rich brown, slightly tinged with ochraceous; the hairs on the antennæ are of a very dark brown or black; the scutellum is of a pale yellow; the base of the elytra is finely verrucose above, the small warts not extending to the middle, but running further along the outer margin than they do towards the suture. The length of the specimen is 1 inch and 8½ lines.

Family LUCANIDÆ.

Genus CLADOGNATHUS, Burmeister.

Cladognathus Tarandus (Thunb.). *See* Fig. 1 of the Plates of Insects. Var. *Lucanus Dehaanii,* Westw. Burm. Handb. V. 375.

This fine species of Stag beetle has longer jaws than any other species of the genus I am acquainted with; the jaws are depressed, considerably curved upwards about the middle, and then depressed toward the tip, which is sharp and slightly hooked, and with a strong tooth on the inside, not far from the tip, the edge between this tooth and the tip being crenulato-denticulate; there is another strong tooth on the inner edge, considerably before the middle, and between that and the base a few slight irregular projections on the edge. The head is very wide in front, the eyes nearly globular, the front hollowed out, and forming a small part of a circle. The elytra and femora above are of a fawn colour, with a slight metallic tinge, the suture of the elytra, particularly, bronzed with metallic green; the mandibles, head, thorax, legs, and under parts, of a greenish bronze colour, on the mandibles passing into reddish. The legs are slim, and without teeth on the edges of the tibiæ, at least, in the males.

Professor Thunberg first described this species in the " Mémoires des Naturalistes de Moscou," tome I. 1806, p. 190, and gives a rough but recognizable figure (t. 12, f. 1.)`

Dr. Burmeister seems to think the *L. Dehaanii* a distinct species; but has some doubt of it. I can see no difference between our two specimens in the Museum and Thunberg's description and figure. The figure is from the larger of two specimens in the British Museum, and is of the size of nature.

On some other occasion I hope to be able to draw up a list of such Borneo species as we have in the Museum, adding references to those which have been described by Schœnherr, Dehaan, Burmeister, Erichson, and others.

END.

LONDON:
Printed by Schulze and Co., 13, Poland Street.

CPSIA information can be obtained
at www.ICGtesting.com
Printed in the USA
LVOW13s2135160117
521174LV00012B/980/P